The Straight Man

The author, aged four

NICHOLAS PARSONS

The Straight Man

My Life in Comedy

WEIDENFELD AND NICOLSON
London

First published in Great Britain in 1994 by
Weidenfeld and Nicolson

The Orion Publishing Group,
Orion House, 5 Upper St Martin's Lane, London WC2H 9EA

ISBN 0 297 81239 4

A catalogue record for this book is available from the British Library

Filmset by Selwood Systems, Midsomer Norton
Printed in Great Britain by Butler & Tanner Ltd, Frome and London

Contents

Illustrations

Vicar sketch, *The Arthur Haynes Show* (author's collection)
Dustmen outside Number 10 sketch, *The Arthur Haynes Show* (author's collection)
Russian roulette sketch, *The Arthur Haynes Show* (author's collection)
Doctor sketch, *The Arthur Haynes Show* (author's collection)
With Arthur Haynes and Aileen Cochran during *The Arthur Haynes Show* (author's collection)
Showing off my new Alvis (author's collection)
With Denise in the Martians commercial for Blue Cars Holidays (author's collection)

between pp. 178–179
Suzy (photo Nicholas Parsons, author's collection)
Suzy and Justin on the beach (photo Nicholas Parsons, author's collection)
With Justin, Suzy and Tunky the dog (author's collection)
With Denise, Suzy and Justin (author's collection)
'This Is Your Life' sketch, *The Benny Hill Show* (Thames Television)
With Benny Hill and Bob Todd in medieval costume, *The Benny Hill Show* (Thames Television)
'Bob and Carol and Ted and Alice' sketch, *The Benny Hill Show* (Thames Television)
With the girls from *Sale of the Century*, 1978 (Anglia Television)
After the final edition of *Sale of the Century* (Anglia Television)
With three of the original *Just a Minute* team: Kenneth Williams, Clement Freud and Peter Jones (BBC Archives)
With Cyd Charisse and Dora Bryan when we appeared on Denis Norden's show (author's collection)
As a vicar in *Dr Who*, with Sylvester McCoy and Sophie Aldred (BBC Archives)
As a pantomime dame (author's collection)
As a punk rocker (author's collection)
With Alice Cooper on *Night Network* (author's collection)
With Johnny Speight and members of the Dead Comics Society, putting up a plaque to Arthur Haynes (photo Nigel Sutton, author's collection)
One of the posters advertising my campaign for Rectorship of St Andrew's University (author's collection)

To

my children Suzy and Justin

and

my grandchildren Annabel and Tom

Preface

When this book was first commissioned by the publishers a few years ago, I was flattered and looked forward to writing it. It was only when I started, however, that I realised how difficult and sometimes how stressful it was to recall all the experiences both good and bad, happy and depressing. At times it felt like writing an extended personal obituary.

I delayed a long time before beginning. I tried to record on tape first, and then have someone transcribe the information and anecdotes. It failed dismally. I discovered that, as an actor, you describe humorous incidents in words quite differently from the way you express them on paper. The only way that would work for me was the painful one of writing it all down in longhand. There were many times when I wanted to give up, and there were times when I abandoned the writing altogether for a spell. At one point I began to wonder whether the whole exercise had become a personal catharsis. Who really wanted to know about my life? The task seemed more ephemeral than acting, and certainly more difficult.

It suddenly seemed worthwhile when my daughter Suzy told me that she was delighted to hear I was writing my autobiography as her children would have a record of what their grandfather had done during his life. I was encouraged to keep going by my commissioning editor Allegra Huston, and latterly by the enthusiasm for the project of my editor, Lesley Baxter, whom the publishers engaged to help me with the painstaking task of bringing the finished manuscript down to the required length. In the process, many personal associations and anecdotes sadly disappeared.

My final thanks must go to Annie, who has somehow managed to put up with my demanding way of life and has also found time in her own busy life to type 300,000 words for me, only to have the frustration of discovering that barely half of them were required for the finished book.

In writing, I have been candid, and I hope I have been fair. I also hope that I have conveyed the fun and humour which is inherent in so many of the situations, and which has sustained me throughout my life.

1

Early Years

I GAVE my first theatrical performance at the age of two and a half. Apparently, I had hardly spoken a word until then. I was taken by my nanny into my mother's bedroom to be introduced to my young sister, who had just arrived. (I had been told she had been found behind the poppies in the garden.) I took one look at the little wrinkled creature, went straight to a huge standing mirror and, pointing at myself, tried to speak my name. Presumably, the actor in me sensed he was about to be upstaged by this new arrival and was trying to establish his identity.

I think the role of 'straight man' is one that I assumed at a very early age, although my conventional, middle-class professional family had no theatrical connections. I felt that I was distinctly the odd one out. I was treated as of less than average intelligence, even foolish, by my parents, and discouraged by them at every opportunity from expressing myself at the one activity I enjoyed and for which I showed talent. I was also afflicted with a stutter, due probably to the fact that I was born left-handed and, because of the prejudice against left-handedness when I was young, was forced by my mother to use my right hand. In addition, I was also mildly dyslexic. Not the ideal start for a youngster who was determined to become an actor.

Whether this burning desire to perform arose from something in my genes, or was motivated by a need to identify myself within a family from whom I received no encouragement, I will never be sure. I was a child at a time when parents conventionally took little or no interest in their children's academic or sporting achievements. Perhaps I felt I had to play the fool to win attention from my father, who was more interested in his hobbies than his three children. Or perhaps it was to win affection from my mother, who found it difficult to relate to me, her second son. It seemed it was my destiny as a child to be 'put down' at every turn. Perhaps it was no surprise that, as an adult, my destiny was to be put down as a 'straight man'.

There are, traditionally, two kinds of straight man in show business: the conventional one, the character who does not play for laughs but becomes the foil or 'feed' for the comedian's jokes; and the character who plays for laughs at his own expense by being the butt of put-downs from more aggressive types. I played both from an early age as a means of survival.

I was born in Lincolnshire, in the small market town of Grantham, which has since become famous as the birthplace of a very well-known political figure. In fact, rumour has it that certain members of the Conservative Party have been known to say to Margaret Thatcher, 'Did you know that you were born in the same town as Nicholas Parsons?' – presumably Tories who did not vote for her in the leadership crisis of 1991. My father was one of three doctors in a partnership whose patients included Mr and Mrs Roberts, the parents of young Margaret. They ran a grocer's shop, which my family used. I have been told that it was my father who brought their daughter into this world – something of which he was probably very proud, but for which he has perhaps never been forgiven by certain people of strong political persuasions.

In the 1920s, a family doctor in a country practice lived well. The leaders of the community in those days were members of the traditional professions of medicine, law, dentistry, teaching and, of course, the Church. Leaders in industry were respected, but those in commerce were not regarded as part of the establishment, and if you were a businessman, you were often dismissed simply as being 'in trade'. My grandfather on my mother's side was an extremely successful businessman, Walter Maggs. With his brother, he built up the large Bristol store, B. Maggs and Co., to its eminence in the 1930s. My mother, a staff nurse, trained at University College Hospital in London, where she met my Cambridge-educated father. He came from a very well-connected family, whose Scottish ances-

tors were landed gentry in Dumfriesshire and whose English ancestors owned tracts of land in Oxfordshire. One in particular, Sir
Humphrey Parsons, was Lord Mayor of London in the mid-eight-
eenth century. Rumour has it that the English ancestors drank their
inheritance away, and the Calvinist Scottish ones gave it away in a
puritanical desire to help others. My grandfather on my father's
side died young, leaving my father, his brother and mother little
money, a magnificent family crest, a deeply imbued Christian faith,
and a dedication to the service of others. I sensed sometimes that
my mother felt her family were socially inferior to my father's,
when she had every reason to be proud of them.

My father was much loved by all his patients. Tall and dis-
tinguished-looking, he bore a strong resemblance, both physically
and vocally, to Harold Macmillan. He had a naturally charming and
courteous manner, and was a fine speaker, but said he could never
have been an actor since he was too self-conscious. He was a well-
read and cultured man, a great philatelist and expert on postal
history, a fine photographer, a good painter and keen gardener. He
found it difficult to give emotionally to his family, and left our
upbringing entirely to our mother. He never understood show
business; indeed, he was very nervous about it. I think he wondered
all his life when I was going to get a proper job. I remember him
saying, after seeing me in a production of *Charley's Aunt* at the
Palace Theatre in London in 1949, that the stage door through
which he had just passed to reach my dressing room was the very
one his mother had pointed to when he was quite young with the
words, 'My son, that is a stage door. Beyond there exists a den of
iniquity. If you should ever pass through those portals, you could
be exposed to a degradation which could lead you down the slippery
path to hell.' No wonder he was anxious about me becoming an
actor.

My mother, in many ways, could not have been more different:
small in stature, tense, nervous and full of psychological hang-ups
from her childhood with which she never came to terms. In fact,
the mere mention of the word 'psychology' made her flare, and
she would deliver her favourite catch phrase, 'Psychology is only
common sense made difficult.' She could be very unpredictable
and also quite sharp on occasions, and because I reminded her of
her younger brother, whom she never understood, I irritated her.

She was terrified that I would turn out to be no good. She had an indomitable spirit and was a hard taskmaster, to herself as well as to others. She was fascinated by medical matters, yet would never admit to feeling ill or off-colour. 'Mind over matter,' she would always say and press on; the pleasure of taking things easy was something her nature would never allow. I know that I have inherited some of her driving energy, and the example she set was one that I instinctively followed.

We always had a domestic staff before the Second World War. My father may have been a country GP, but at one time could afford a butler, cook, parlourmaid and, of course, a nanny. I enjoyed escaping to the domestic quarters in our large house; I found everyone there easy and natural, and also I sometimes made them laugh, which was reassuring. The great comfort in my early life was my nanny, a young country girl, Nellie Kettle, from the village of Swayfield. She came to us at the age of nineteen, shortly after I was born, and stayed until I was seven. I loved her dearly. She was gentle, kind, wise and loving, with a natural Christian understanding of right and wrong. Her faith left a lasting impression on me, and I was truly heartbroken when she left to get married. Some of the happiest memories of my young childhood are of staying with nanny's family in their cottage, feeding the chickens, walking in the fields, picking cowslips to make wine, pinching nails from the workshop of her two brothers, Percy and Ernest, the local builders, so my brother John and I could pretend to be like them, and build imaginary houses in the disused pigsty in the garden.

I was equally devoted to nanny's fiancé, Joe Cox, also from Swayfield, the son of the local publican who ran the Royal Oak. Joe worked as a masseur at the nearby RAF station. He was a man of great charm and integrity, who frequently visited us in the nursery and encouraged my play-acting and showing off. His father was a large, jolly man who, discovering that I was a natural mimic, taught me funny rhymes and little songs he had heard in the music hall. One was a Randolph Sutton ditty, 'I Want to be Alone with Mary Brown'. The lyrics I forget, probably because I never understood them. One day my grandmother, my father's widowed mother, a devout churchwoman of evangelical fervour, came to visit and called in on the nursery before bedtime. Just as she was about to leave, I announced that I had a song for her. I leapt on to a stool, all of five years of age, and recited what I knew of 'wanting to be alone with Mary Brown'. I never understood why I was not allowed to finish, why she suddenly left and I was put to bed early, why Joe was not allowed in the house for some time, and why I was stopped from reciting songs I had learnt.

There are two large schools in Grantham, serving a wide area: the King's School for Boys and Kesteven and Grantham High School for Girls. I went to the girls' school, for the simple reason that its kindergarten took both boys and girls. I was nearly six and my time there was memorable in many ways, not least because of the headmistress, Miss Pike. I remember an incident in which her wisdom and intuition saw that justice was done – something very important to a child.

Some of the older boys – and to a six-year-old, a seven-year-old is considerably older – had hatched a plan to capture a little blonde girl who had just started in the kindergarten and have their way with her. I am not sure, at seven, that they knew what 'their way' was, but it all seemed very sinister to me and thoroughly unjust. My sense of fair play, as well as the fact that I was deeply attracted to the young lady, overcame any fear I might have had of these bullies, and when they captured her near the rose garden, I leapt like Sir Galahad into their midst, punched the ring leader on the nose, grabbed the young maiden by the hand, and before the others could recover from the surprise attack, said to her, 'Quick, follow me.' I ran with her through the rose garden, behind the school building and into the vegetable garden, where we crouched down behind some tall gooseberry bushes. The sheer bravado of it . . . the success of my first romantic encounter. I had been too shy to talk to girls before; they seemed a world apart. This adorable creature, with her soft blonde curls and deep blue eyes, gazed at me and said, 'Nicholas, I don't know why you're doing this for me.' I was too young to know why, either, except that I no longer felt that I was the supporting actor in the straight man role; I was playing the lead.

Later, I was called before Miss Pike because the other boys had 'sneaked' to her, giving a garbled version of what had happened. Miss Pike heard what I had to say and completely exonerated me. In fact, I remember her saying, 'Nicholas, you were right to do what you did. You behaved very well.' My admiration for her was reinforced. Justice had triumphed. I never knew the name of that blonde-haired little girl. For a long time, I lived with the romantic notion that my boyhood act of chivalry might indirectly have contributed to a famous era in the political life of this country; it was many years before I discovered that Margaret Roberts had started at a different school and only later went to Kesteven and Grantham High School.

One of the most exciting experiences in a child's life is when he or she sees live entertainment for the first time. To a young, impressionable mind there is something magical about the atmosphere of a show in a large theatre, with real people performing, as opposed to the images seen on a television screen. My first experience of this was the circus, and I have never forgotten it.

We lived in a large house overlooking a small green in the centre of the town, Number 1 Castlegate. In those prewar days, with no television and little radio, a visiting entertainment was the cause of great excitement. I remember watching from our nursery window as the circus lorries and trailers arrived, and was fascinated by the elephants plodding along in file, each holding the tail of the one in front with its trunk.

The day eventually arrived when my brother John, sister Patricia and I were taken by our parents to the show. I was captivated by the animals, awestruck by the trapeze artists, loved the clowns and was thrilled by the acrobats, particularly when two of them jumped on and off a horse that slowly cantered round the ring, performing tricks while balancing on the animal's back. As someone who was agile and a natural tumbler, I think that is something I most wanted to do. In fact, if someone had whisked me away to work with that circus group at the tender age of five, I think I would have been blissfully happy. I have never worked in a circus, although there was one memorable occasion when Arthur Haynes and I, at the height of our success, appeared in a comedy sketch for a television Christmas special transmitted from Billy Smart's Circus. In the show, Arthur persuaded me, as an apparent spectator in the audience, to come forward and be fired from a cannon.

When we returned home I immediately started taking off the clowns and trying to emulate the tumblers. Later, John and I put together our own circus show in the nursery and invited our parents and other relations to watch. John was the ringmaster, Patricia, who was only three, and I appeared as the show horses, scampering around on our hands and knees in response to our brother's orders. I did a tumbling act on a mattress and Patricia was then instructed to be a trapeze artist, which, in a flood of tears, she quite rightly said was not possible. We compromised and let her go on as a solo horse. John and I then came out as the two clowns we had seen, who called themselves Cuckoo and Sparrow. We tried to reproduce their routine, which mostly consisted of me, as Cuckoo, the put-upon clown or straighter of the two, appealing to Sparrow in a cooing voice, 'Cuckoo . . . Sparrow'. For weeks, the house echoed to the sound of me calling out, 'Cuckoo . . . Sparrow', until my parents, bored with the repetition, told me to stop being such a clown and to keep my antics for the nursery.

I left the kindergarten when I was seven and a half and went to the King's School. I was only there a term before my parents decided that I should join my brother at Tenterden Hall, a boarding prep school in north London. This decision was obviously made by them in my best interests, but how wrong they were. We even moved to London and, at a time when a doctor bought his medical practice from another doctor, my father purchased one on the edge of Clapham Common at the top of Battersea Rise, at 1 Leathewaite Road. Clapham was by no means considered smart in those days, and Battersea was definitely down-market. We shopped in Battersea, but lived in Clapham. Such social niceties, however, did not mean much to someone who was barely eight years old. Because Tenterden Hall was a long way from Clapham, and because parents who could afford it traditionally sent their young sons away from home to be educated, I became a boarder. I was only seven years and eleven months old.

The conditions at this small school could only be described as Dickensian. It was run by a Mr and Mrs Bacon, two of the smallest people I have ever seen – they were not much taller than most of the boys. The masters were mostly injured survivors from the First World War. There was Mr Edwards, with a horrendous bayonet wound on his head, which made me feel ill every time he looked down to speak to a boy in his class. There was Mr Stavitsky, who limped horribly due, we were told, to unremoved bullets in his legs; and Mr Smurthwaite, who slinked about like a Cheshire cat and taught music in his spare time. I was terrified of them all, especially as being slippered or caned was a regular punishment for even minor offences. The real horror of the place, however, was the matron, Mrs Blanche – 'Ma Blanche' or 'Blancmange', as we called her. Dressed in the full regalia of a hospital matron from the turn of the century, with starched cuffs and a huge starched head-dress, she was a forbidding character with no sensitivity towards, or understanding of, children, and she ruled the dormitory with a rod of iron. Worst of all, however, were her weird and fixed ideas about what kept a child healthy.

It was very cold in winter in the rambling Victorian building which housed the whole school. There was no running water in the dormitory, and at 7 a.m. we were awakened by Ma Blanche arriving with a huge jug of water, which she tipped into basins lined up on a bench. It was considered healthy for us to start the day by washing our faces in this water, which was often too cold. Needless to say, some of us did not. We were then lined up to be marched in to breakfast. My recollections are that the food was reasonable, but plain and insufficient. After breakfast, we were marched back upstairs and lined up on the landing. Ma Blanche then walked down the row with her assistant and asked each boy in turn about the state of his bowels. If your bowels had not opened for a day, you were given some syrup of figs; if it was two days, you were given castor oil. (It was a time when regular bowel movements were considered essential to healthy living. At home, we had been rigorously potty trained – we were forbidden to leave them until we had done something. We would often scoot round the landing, in and out of the bedroom, playing 'puffer trains' until something happened.)

At these formal and embarrassing rituals at the school, when intimate descriptions of your bowels became public knowledge, it was also usual during the winter months to be fed, every other day, Friar's Balsam on a lump of sugar, which was thought to ward off colds and flu. You had to be really ill, however, before you would admit to it, since the treatment for any fever or infection was to be put in the darkened sanatorium and fed only bread and milk. Even the thought of bread and milk made my stomach turn, so when I was unwell I refused it and was given nothing, not even comfort.

I suffered more than most at the hands of Ma Blanche because I was subject to migraine attacks. My mother was forever practising her medical knowledge on me – I think most of what she knew came from my father's *British Medical Journal*. It was then thought – and is still held by some today – that migraine was aggravated by certain foods, especially chocolate, apples and eggs. My mother kept me off all of these, and when I had a particularly bad attack in the night, would follow another theory that it was all connected with the stomach and make me drink a solution of salt and water until I threw up. I do remember feeling better afterwards, although it may just have been exhaustion from the forced vomiting that helped me sleep off the pain. Once I had left home I began eating all the 'forbidden' foods and found they had no effect on the migraine. The attacks were, and still are, always brought on by stress.

My mother's ideas about not taking certain foods were passed as instructions to Mrs Blanche. This was like a red rag to a bull. How dare anyone dictate policy and request a different diet for a mere child, even if they were paying the fees? My mother's instructions had to be obeyed, but her good intentions rebounded on me, as Ma Blanche thought that I was being indulged and was determined that I should have the nonsense knocked out of me. When the forbidden foods were served, I received no substitute. When I had an attack, and went in the early hours and knocked on matron's door, I was told that it was my imagination, and while my mother might be soft with me, she was not. I was sharply ordered to return to bed, where I groaned in agony until morning.

There were some strange boys at that school. I remember one in our dormitory, Bowles, who was slightly bigger than the rest of us, and not as bright or quick. To gain recognition with the other boys, he boasted that I had made him my slave by peeing over him in the bushes in the school grounds. It was all completely untrue, but the other boys in the dormitory were very impressed. Unfortunately, Matron's little favourite, Hartley II, sneaked the story to her and I was caned for being disgusting. In fact, Hartley II discovered he only had to tell matron that I had done something of which she disapproved, whether I had or not, for it to be reported to the housemaster for another slippering.

I was miserable at Tenterden Hall, and desperate at the end of each holiday when the day arrived to go back for a new term. I survived because I found that I could make the other boys laugh, either by playing the fool, or by mimicking the masters. On one occasion, Mr Stavitsky was late to take our class, so I left my desk, took his gown off the back of the door and put it on. With the gown trailing round my ankles, I then proceeded to try to impersonate his very military way of speaking, and limped about, aping his walk. I was going magnificently. I had the audience in the palm of my hand. I loved it. Then suddenly it went quiet. Like a true professional, I tried harder. Why had I lost my audience? A second later, I discovered. Standing just behind me was Mr Stavitsky, looking distinctly displeased. I tried a nine-year-old's joke: 'You were late, Sir, so I thought I would help by talking to the class.' Mr Stavitsky's voice was even more military: 'Parsons II, you have mocked me; you have mocked my infirmities. You have made an exhibition of yourself, and I shall now make an exhibition of you in front of the whole class. Take off my gown and bend over.' I can still feel the pain of that caning, and the indignity of it, and the unfairness. My triumph was turned to ashes. I think in some ways it simply made me more determined to become a performer.

The other reason that I was able to survive in this scholastic concentration camp with only nominal scars was that I was good at games, and this wins you great respect among your peers. My brother John coped much better than I did because he was more forceful and confident. I had always looked up to him and admired his independent spirit. He was only one year ahead of me at the school, however, which made it difficult for him to give the support and encouragement an older brother normally extends to a younger one, for to do so would have earned him the scorn of his peers.

Eventually, my parents realised that I was very unhappy at Tenterden Hall. I do not think that they ever grasped the true reasons, but fortunately they took both of us away and managed to get us placed at Colet Court, the preparatory school for St Paul's.

Colet Court is an elegant, red-brick, late-Victorian building, with a good-sized playing field at the rear. I enjoyed my time there, particularly the games, and won caps for first XI soccer and cricket. It was also a boxing school because of its association with St Paul's, which had a great tradition of boxing and fine instructors, including relations of the champion boxer Jim Driscoll. The master in charge

of the sport at St Paul's, Mr Langham, would come to Colet Court
to help supervise with the master there, Mr Read – Buster Read,
as we called him – who had boxed as a leading amateur at the Albert
Hall.

I seemed an unlikely candidate for boxing success and I do not
remember how I became involved. Certainly, it was not due to my
parents' encouragement: till the day they died, they never knew
that I had won cups and medals at the sport. My greatest triumph
came in my last year, when I reached the final of the boxing
competition. I was thirteen years old and weighed nearly ten stone.
I was up against Dailey, the captain of boxing and cricket and a fine
sportsman who looked the part. My friends suggested that I should
run for cover before the final, as the event and result could be
painful for me. This did not help build my confidence. I did
remarkably well, however, and even had him groggy in the second
round. I think I was surprised, like many of those watching; but in
boxing parlance, I let him off the hook. He won by a small margin.

We were always known at school by our surnames, and were
very secretive about our Christian names. I had been christened
Christopher Nicholas, but had always been called by my second
name. I was particularly sensitive about it, because Nicholas was
very unusual then and I was afraid of being teased. One day, John
Treacher, who was, and still is, a good friend, asked me what my
first name was. I did not want to tell him, so he said, 'You look like
a Jimmy, and that's what I'll call you.' I liked the nickname, and
soon all my friends were using it. Then one day John asked me
what I was going to do when I left school. I said that I wanted to be
an actor. This was a strange ambition for someone in a conventional
school at a time when, by tradition, boys entered established professions. The only acting John knew about was the cinema, and at
the time Shirley Temple was a big star, so he re-nicknamed me
Shirley. I was rather flattered; it helped me identify with a world
that I wanted to join. Soon my friends switched to the new nickname and everything was fine until, one day, my mother said she
would collect me from school in the car, as she was passing. As this
was a rare event, I forgot. She came into the playground and asked
a boy where I was. He pointed me out, and shouted across the
sports field, 'Shirley, your mother's here.' My mother was horrified.
Her worst fears had been confirmed. In the car, she asked me why

I had been given a girl's name. I proudly told her that I had been nicknamed after Shirley Temple, as I wanted to be an actor. She could not see the connection and instructed me to stop the boys using the name immediately.

The masters at Colet Court were much more pleasant than those at Tenterden Hall. In fact, with few exceptions they were intelligent and sympathetic teachers. One of those exceptions was a French master by the name of Downs, who had been warned about excessive use of the cane. He was not my usual French teacher; that was a delightful caricature of a man called Menise. He was French, had a strong accent, and was teased unmercifully by most of the boys. I do not think he realised it half the time. I could be pretty outrageous in poor old Menise's class. He had a habit of calling us to attention by saying, 'Personnes, personnes . . .' As the word with a French accent sounded remarkably like my name, I would leap up, asking what he wanted. He would look puzzled and I would say, usually in a French accent, 'My name is Parsons, and you said, "Parsons, Parsons".' He said, 'I was calling for attention.' To which I would respond, 'Oh, attention', and stand to attention until the poor man became desperate to make himself heard above the laughter in the class. I realise now that Mr Menise was a very gentle little man, but because he could not command attention he was unable to communicate, so I learnt very little French.

The opposite of Menise was the terrifying Mr Downs, whose class I had mercifully avoided. He tried to control his pupils by fear, which is also no way to communicate, and when he took our class in Menise's absence, I learnt even less. On one occasion, he asked me to read something out loud, and because I was nervous in his presence, my stutter increased. He called me to the front of the class and said, 'I don't believe you have a stutter. I think it's part of your play-acting. Continue to read the passage, and every time you pause or stutter, I'm going to flick you with this cane', which he proceeded to do. The stutter got worse.

There were some very good teachers at the school, and one such was Mr Langford, who later became headmaster. He was my form master for a year, and as he taught classics, I did well at Latin and Greek. The same happened at St Paul's where, in my second year, I had the good fortune to be in the class of T.L. Martin, or Tommy Martin as he was affectionately known. He was a man with a true gift for teaching and could tell the most wonderful stories of the classical past, which breathed life into the dead languages we were studying. In the year I spent in his class, I think I learnt more from him than most of the other masters put together.

My year in Tommy Martin's class was 1939. The international news was very disturbing, but most people believed, either genuinely or because they could not face the consequences, that everything would be all right. My father even bought a new medical practice, as well as an expensive house in Hampstead, and we moved home. I was barely fifteen, aware of what was going on, but never dreamed the worst could happen. It was a great year for me. I won caps at rugby and cricket for the under-sixteen colts side and, academically, I was top of my form. Added to this, through one of my father's patients, Lila Henderson, I was given my first acting job with an amateur company, The Stock Exchange Players, appearing as a schoolboy in *The Housemaster* by Ian Hay. We played at two venues outside London, and then performed for three nights at the Little Cripplegate Theatre, near the Barbican in London (the theatre is now a public library). I was truly happy. I remember John Treacher coming to see the play with his parents, and next day at school saying, 'I was right to call you Shirley. You really can act.' I was also cast in a school play, and was promised a leading role the following year.

That summer I went on a holiday camp with the Student Christian Movement from school. It was there, one Sunday morning, that we heard the broadcast that so many people feared but hoped would never happen, in which Neville Chamberlain told the nation, '. . . and so this country is now at war with Germany.' Nothing would ever be the same again, and yet everything felt the same, since in the country nothing was happening. There was feverish activity in the towns, as arrangements were made to evacuate the children.

I knew that my world had come to a full stop. All the promise and joy of the last year at school was shattered. Yet it need not have been so. My parents could have sent me away with the school, which had been evacuated to Crowthorne in Berkshire. Instead, they decided that I was a non-achiever, and took me away. John, who was about to leave school, had already been offered a training course by Rolls Royce and soon he went to Derby, where he worked very hard and later became a successful businessman. Patricia, being younger, went with her school to Berkhampstead. What to do with me? My parents explained their parlous financial situation, which was due to my father's wealthy patients in Hampstead disappearing overnight. I was too upset to reason with them and accepted everything with depressed resignation.

The only school still active in North London at the beginning of the War was Clark's College in Finchley, a co-educational estab-lishment run by a Mr Savage, an aggressive man with a severe limp. There was one master, an engaging character who looked exactly like the film actor Thomas Mitchell, who took our class for nearly every subject. My father had been told that this man was conversant with Greek, which was one of the subjects that I was taking in my school certificate exams, the equivalent to present-day GCSEs. If you had five passes, you had matriculated, after which you did your higher certificates, equivalent to A Levels. If you obtained three distinctions in the school certificates with your five passes, you were eligible for university. I sat my 'school cert' that autumn term, nearly a year early. It turned out that I knew more Greek than the master, so I studied on my own, with the help of the public library. It says a lot for the grounding I had received previously that I got a distinction in the subject in one term.

There were no games at the school, but the girls were an agreeable distraction. One, in particular, was stunning. She was two years older than I was, blonde, and very self-assured. I longed to speak to her, but did not know how to begin. It was a very lonely time, as all my friends were out of London. It was the period known as the 'phoney war', with no fighting, no bombing, just eerie foreboding of what was to come. I simply studied, and passed my exams with three distinctions and five passes. I do not know why my parents were not more impressed. My father asked me what I wanted to do with my life. I said, 'Dad, you know there's only one thing I've ever wanted to do. I want to be an actor.' His reply was succinct: 'We know all about that, but let's be serious.'

2

Growing Up in Glasgow

FATE was to play an unexpected part in my future now in the shape of my Uncle Hugh, my father's brother, to whom I felt very close. He asked me what I was going to do and, as I had no ideas other than acting, he made some practical suggestions. He pointed out how capable I was with my hands, always making things. (I had a beautiful set of carpentry tools, given to me by my mother after a hernia operation when I was eight.) I also repaired old clocks – by the time I was fourteen, I had reassembled two grandfather clocks, one bracket and one mantel clock, which I still own. I always saw this, however, as simply a hobby, not a career. Uncle Hugh was a positive man, who took a personal interest. In no time, he had contacted close friends in Glasgow, who spoke on his behalf to their relations who ran a pump and turbine firm on Clydebank, Drysdale's. The next thing I knew I had been accepted for an apprenticeship by the company and was on a train to Scotland to begin a new life on my own.

During the War, travelling by train was no pleasure. There were no refreshments and strict blackout rules – dimmed lights in the carriages and blinds tightly drawn. Nor were there signs at any stations. Every signpost in the country, as well as station names, had been removed so that if the Germans landed they would have no idea where they were. I do not think the authorities had worked out that our own forces would be equally confused. Rail travel entailed shouting to anyone standing on a platform when a train stopped to establish where you were. Sometimes people refused to answer for fear you were a spy, following the slogan printed everywhere, 'Idle Talk Costs Lives'. Once the bombing started, travelling by rail became even more hazardous, as lines would be hit, and trains would be diverted or forced to a standstill if approaching a town during an air raid.

I eventually arrived in Glasgow, was met by the family friends, the McClaurens, stayed with them for the weekend in Bearsden, a very smart part of Glasgow, then was introduced to the YMCA in Sauchiehall Street, a very unsmart part of Glasgow. I found lodgings there for three guineas a week full board. The rooms were like huge, rambling dormitories, all partitioned off, with enough space for a bed and a small chest. The washing facilities were communal.

The rooms at the YMCA were at the top of a very large building which also housed the Lyric Theatre. This was let out to amateur and semiprofessional companies; during the War it was also used to mount shows for HM Forces. We ate in the canteen on the ground floor, as did servicemen and women, and it could be pretty rough on occasions, especially on a Saturday night, when soldiers on leave had been drinking.

My greatest challenge came when I started work on Clydebank. Here I was, barely sixteen years old, from a well-off, professional family, suddenly thrown into the rough, crude and demanding world of a Clydeside engineering yard. At first I thought everyone was speaking a different language. Their gutteral and idiosyncratic use of English, with an accent broader than the standard Glaswegian, aggressively expressed with poor diction and liberally peppered with words that I had only previously seen written on lavatory walls, took some getting used to. As I walked down Ferry Road in Yoker, wearing my newly acquired boilersuit for the first time, in the blackout one crisp January morning, I wondered if I had strayed into a foreign land. I was certainly not prepared for the work or conditions in this excellent but typical engineering yard. It was still run by the Drysdale family, even though it had recently been taken over by Weir's of Cathcart, a much bigger firm specialising in the production of pumps and turbines. What was I doing learning about these heavy machines? I was not interested in pumps. I did not even know what a turbine was until I arrived.

The firm was very kind, taking me on immediately and offering a comprehensive apprenticeship. I was to spend six months in each department, starting with the tool room, where the machine tools were forged and ground. The foreman, or gaffer, was Alec Woods, a gentle man who treated me with great tolerance. I found the hours extraordinarily demanding. I had never before stood for nearly nine hours with only one break, and my back ached. Sitting down was forbidden, except in the lunch break, and to begin with I found it so difficult that I would sneak off for a little rest where I could not be seen, sometimes to the lavatories.

We clocked on before 8 a.m. and your pay was docked for every minute you were late after 8.02. There was no such thing as a tea break. Forty-five minutes for lunch, and at 5.30 the hooter would sound to let us know that we were released, whereupon those not on overtime would stream out to catch the tram or train, or walk to their homes nearby. Eight and three-quarter hours a day, Monday to Friday, and four and a quarter hours on Saturday mornings. A forty-eight hour working week for which, as an apprentice, I received 9s.7d. a week for the first months I was there – not quite 50 pence in present money.

I was a complete oddity in this environment, but if I found everything very strange, equally I must have appeared very strange to everyone there, with my English public-school accent and what they called 'my right proper manners'. It is perhaps one of the few things in my life of which I am proud that I was soon accepted by the other apprentices, as well as by the men. Within a short while I was known as 'Big Nick', because I was much taller than most of the apprentices, some of whom presumably had grown up undernourished during the Depression of the 1930s. I soon discovered that swear words were sometimes used as terms of endearment, and that it was generally a compliment when I was referred to as 'Big Nick, that English bastard'. Once again, I was being cast in the straight man role, because I could make my workmates laugh and did not take myself too seriously.

Quite early on, one of the older apprentices approached me in the direct way they spoke on any subject and enquired if I was 'a boss's man'. I asked him what he meant. He pointed out that Parsons was a famous name in turbines (which I did not know) and they all wanted to know if I was related in any way and had been sent to Drysdale's to learn my trade. I told him that there was no connection. Pleased, he said, 'That's great, because if you were a boss's man, we couldn'a talk to you. You'd be oot. But as you're not, that's fine, you're one of us.' I did not realise how flattering that was. In a working-class, passionately left-wing area that was intensely proud of its Scottish roots, I was 'one of them'. I never received any special treatment from any of the men, and certainly not the foremen. In fact, some of the foremen I had during my long apprenticeship found me difficult to handle and were probably more strict with me as a result. Most of them ruled with a fairly benevolent rod of iron. They were the boss in their own area; their word was law, and it was nothing to see one of them bawl out a young apprentice with some very choice language. If apprentices nowadays were spoken to like that, they would probably go on strike.

Something else I had to adjust to was the noise generated by the engines. It stopped only at lunchtime, and the relief was indescribable. We would hungrily devour our sandwiches (or 'pieces' as they are called, presumably because they are two pieces of bread with something in the middle) with the grimy hands that had worked the machines. Only the offices had washing facilities. They also had the canteen, which was used more by the office staff than the shop-floor workers. There was a marked division between those who wore jackets and a collar and tie and those who wore a boilersuit. The two rarely mixed. In those days, headgear was fairly traditional: nothing in the offices, peaked caps for the workers, usually a bowler hat for the foreman, and always a bowler hat for the works manager. I wore a beret, which I still have.

I soon fell into the ways of my fellow apprentices. When the hooter went at 5.30, we would run down to the main Dumbarton Road, where the trams stopped at the junction with Ferry Road. To save money, the more agile ones would jump on the back of any empty lorry travelling into central Glasgow. The technique was fairly simple: as soon as the lorry slowed at the junction, you leapt to grab a crossbar on the lorry's side or rear, swung yourself up onto the top of the panel, then slipped down on the other side. First arrivals would help latecomers as the lorry gathered speed. Sometimes there would be up to a dozen youths in the lorry, and one of them would take his cap round to collect a few coppers from the others to give to the driver.

On one occasion, I was a little later than usual in leaving. As I approached the junction I saw a lorry slowing to a halt. I ran in front of it and round to the nearside and quickly grabbed a crossbar. As I swung myself up and over, out of the corner of my eye I saw a number of the lads who normally jumped the lorries. They were standing on the curbside and I wondered fleetingly why they were not jumping. A second later, I knew. I landed in a huge load of cement powder. I was covered from head to foot. I did not dare to reveal my presence to the driver, as I was now carrying some of his potential profit. At a convenient stop at some traffic lights in central Glasgow I leapt off and, looking like some ghostly apparition that had stepped out of a horror film, walked back to my lodgings, leaving pools of dust as I went.

There were, as I have said, no washing facilities on the shop floor at Drysdale's. As for the toilets, all that could be said in their favour was that they served their basic purpose. In fact, they had been very practically designed to this end, but with no thought for privacy. There was one central building in the middle of the works, which was used by everyone on the shop floor. The entrance was through a swing door, and straight ahead was a wall for urination – no cubicles. On either side was a row of lavatories in white china with no wooden seats, each separated by a low partition. At the entrance was an elderly man in a little wooden cubicle with a shelf in front of him, who gave you a metal counter which entitled you to a seven-minute session. The man's name was Sam, he had the obvious nickname, and he smoked a combination of thick black and old shag, which slightly relieved the other pungent odours. Once you received your metal disc, you knew that there was a vacant seat. You had to remember to take a newspaper – toilet paper was unheard of. You went to the empty pan and joined the other nine men squatting in a row with their boilersuits round their ankles, arms on knees holding copies of the *Daily Mirror* or *Daily Record*. Hygiene was maintained by an automatic flushing system, which was activated every two minutes. As the system began at one end and flushed down the line, it generated a fair amount of power, so if you did not rise at the crucial moment, you could get very wet. The system, though effective, was pretty antiquated, and every flush would be heralded by a rumbling in the pipes. It was customary, therefore, for the man nearest the start of the flush, on hearing the warning rumble, to shout down the line, 'It's on its way, lads. Arses up.' Ten naked bottoms of different shapes and sizes would then rise in unison to avoid a soaking. It may have been basic, but you can get used to anything if there is no alternative. My only real embarrassment was when I escaped into this room, more to relieve my aching back muscles than anything else. My foreman at the time was Jimmy Brown, whose eagle eye had spotted me leaving my bench. Estimating that I had overstayed my seven minutes, and while I was still studying the sports pages of my newspaper, he burst in and dragged me away, announcing at the top of his voice that my time was up, and that it was also my second visit that day. It is difficult to maintain any poise with your trousers and boilersuit round your ankles. Any difficult moments I have encountered in show business since have been nothing to the embarrassment that I felt then in front of this unusual, captive audience.

I grew up very quickly and learnt some surprising things at Drysdale's. For instance, one day Jimmy, a fellow workmate, asked me if I was a Billy or a Pape. Never having heard either word before, I played for time and asked him what he was. He explained that he was a Billy, and proud of it, an Orangeman who put on the sash and marched with his Protestant colleagues to celebrate the Battle of the Boyne. A Pape, or papist, was a Roman Catholic. When I asked him why he wanted to know what I was, he replied that he had seen me chatting to Willie, a papist. I said I thought that he and Willie were quite good friends. He replied that, while inside they were workmates, outside it was different, and on 16 June, the anniversary of the battle, he was the enemy. At least this showed a certain acceptance, and certainly more tolerance than is shown in parts of the United Kingdom today.

I learnt about the two Glasgow football teams, Rangers and Celtic, and the passion engendered when they met. Their supporters and, it seems, their players, were drawn from the two religions, which were fairly evenly represented in Glasgow. In fact, it was around this time that the then Lord Provost, Patrick Dollan, had forbidden them to meet because of an outbreak of hooliganism after one particular game. The incident was far milder than those today, but the authorities at the time exercised their power with greater will and determination, which meant the streets were, with rare exceptions, safe for anyone to walk alone, even late at night. There was one exception: the Gorbals, which had a reputation as a very rough area. Strangers did not stray there at night, and the police always went about in pairs.

When I lived in Glasgow, there were more amateur theatrical companies than in any other city in Britain. It was one of these, the Transport Players, who gave me my first opportunity to play an adult character. The play was *Paddy the Next Best Thing* – a strange title, which is probably why it has stuck in my mind. So many young men had been called up that the company was no doubt delighted to find someone who looked presentable and could speak lines. The play was performed at the Lyric Theatre in the YMCA building. I think I played a doctor, who had a romantic scene with a young girl, and it must have looked very incongruous, as she was thirty and I was all of sixteen. I was never intended to be a romantic actor, even as an adult, and my performance must have been embarrassing. As I hoped at the time to be a serious actor, I used my first initial as well as my more usual name, and called myself C. Nicholas Parsons. It had a ring to it when spoken, but looked very pompous in print. The habit did not last long.

In the early days of the War, I had chances to perform that would not have come my way had I been at home or evacuated with my school. A man called McCletchie was putting on an amateur show for the Forces at the Lyric and since I had been doing impersonations of cinema and radio stars for several years, I put together an act for him. I appeared using the name Nick Parsons. The act went down well and, encouraged, I set about developing both my comic and serious sides. When appearing as an actor, I was told that I was working in the legitimate theatre; the same, however, was not said about any of my music-hall appearances. By implication, the serious thespians looked upon variety as illegitimate theatre, though it was never referred to as such. With the advent of television, where a vast audience was exposed to entertainment that they had never seen before, this prejudice has to some extent disappeared. I myself have never seen any fundamental difference between the two; they just require different disciplines. I have always believed this, and I think it was always accepted in Glasgow, where there is a great respect for talent – and if your talent is diverse, they have even greater respect. In general, however, and especially down south amongst employers, it seems that you are not trusted if you can do more than one thing in show business. It is probably part of the very British, or rather English, attitude whereby people feel more secure if they can label or categorise you. Whenever the press mention anyone in the media by name, they always add a descriptive label.

During my time in Glasgow, there were nine active theatres providing live entertainment of all kinds. There was a thriving artistic community centred around the Arts Club, a great feeling for music, and also a very definite, and individual, humour. In those days, very few Scots comedians worked south of the border. It has taken television to bridge the gap. Fifty years ago, a comedian like Billy Connolly could never have worked in the South; audiences would never have understood him, or his particular style of comedy.

Drysdale's were very good to me. After I had been there a short while, Charlie Drysdale asked me to his office for a talk. He took a fatherly interest, and suggested that if I was going to be an engineer, I should really go to the university to study for a degree and become fully qualified. As I was trying to become an engineer to please my family, I wondered why they had not shown the same interest. I was given time off to apply to the university, but was informed that, with the subjects I had studied for my matriculation exams, I could enter any faculty except engineering and science. The only way I could be admitted to the engineering faculty would be if I obtained a Higher mathematics in the Scottish Prelims, which meant taking a correspondence course with Glasgow Polytechnic, studying at night, and passing the exam in six not twelve months. This was a lot to ask, since I was becoming increasingly interested in theatre work in my spare time.

I had seen an advertisement asking for performers of all kinds who would be prepared to give their time voluntarily to entertain the troops on the anti-aircraft sites and at small barracks in the west of Scotland. The shows were being organised by Scottish Command Troop Entertainments, run by Archie McCulloch, a serving officer who understood show business. It was great fun, and good experience. We were formed into small concert parties and taken by army transport to outlying camps, where we always had a warm reception. The girls naturally received the best of it, irrespective of their performing talent. I usually compered the show, did some impersonations and then a comedy routine, which consisted of jokes I had heard on the radio and elsewhere. I had no experience of writing comedy, just an instinct of how to put it over, even if the style was immature. Working on the assumption that you had to look funny to be funny, I wore large baggy trousers, a garish waistcoat and a comical hat. I must have looked ridiculous. The concert parties went out about once a week, but since I was called only occasionally, I still had evenings free for study.

In the spring of 1940, the fighting in Europe started and by the end of June, Hitler had overrun France and the Low Countries. The bulk of the British Forces in Europe had miraculously been rescued from the beaches of Dunkirk, but all their equipment had been left behind. Many thought that it was only a matter of time before Britain capitulated to the vastly superior might of Germany, now just across the Channel. One man, it seemed, stood between us and ignominious defeat: Winston Churchill. I am convinced that it was his great, oratorical speeches that inspired a nation on its knees to struggle defiantly against the odds, and not only survive but triumph.

Shortly after Dunkirk, Anthony Eden, then Foreign Secretary, came on the wireless and appealed to every able-bodied man in the country who had not been called up to sign on as a Local Defence Volunteer, or LDV. This later became the Home Guard, which was actually well organised, however humorously it was re-created in the comedy series *Dad's Army*. A friend and I at the YMCA heard Anthony Eden's broadcast and immediately went to sign up. We arrived within thirty minutes of the broadcast, and were told that we were the first to register. In fact, they did not even have the correct forms ready, so we signed a piece of paper and were asked to report the following evening. This we did, along with some very elderly men, and were told that there were no uniforms available yet. There was also a shortage of equipment, and the young ones – my friend and I – were issued with pikes. What we could have done with this fifteenth-century implement I do not know. Gone down fighting, I suppose, shouting, 'God for Winnie, England and St George.' I have often wondered whether the youth, played by Ian Lavender in *Dad's Army*, was called Private Pike because of this early issue of LDV equipment.

In spite of all the distractions, and the strenuous work at Drysdale's, I passed my maths exams in the summer and proudly registered to start at Glasgow University in the autumn. I was still only sixteen, and as I was not sure if you could be admitted to university so young, I added a year to my age.

The engineering course at Glasgow was four years long, with each year having two not three terms, leaving six months in the summer when you were expected to gain practical experience by working for an engineering firm. While I was already fulfilling this requirement by working at Drysdale's, I was unprepared for the academic side of the course. Having just passed my Higher maths, that subject was not too bad; but I had never opened a physics or chemistry book in my life. Classics and history had been my subjects at school and I was a fish out of water in this technical environment. Any aptitude I had for engineering was purely practical and even then, my heart was not in it. I was really floundering that first year, and felt very foolish. Instinctively, I became the comic of my class – or the straight man to the better-informed and more confident students.

I became very involved in the social life of the university, which centred around the university union. I took part in political debates. I joined the Liberal Club, and have remained faithful to their policies ever since. There was the Dramatic Club, where I appeared in a revue and also in J.B. Priestley's *Time and the Conways*. I also made the First XV rugby team. I had always been a second row forward at school, but now found a better position as loose head in the front row of the scrum, where I worked well with the hooker and could break quickly to catch up with the three-quarters.

Of all the friends that I made at university, there were two that I valued very much. They were both final-year students in the engineering faculty, both studying naval architecture, and both were three years older than I was. One was Alex Silverleaf, whom I met through the Dramatic Club, a brilliant intellectual with a natural understanding and appreciation of theatre and the arts in general. He directed the university plays in which I appeared, and could undoubtedly have been a great success in the theatre had he wanted. However, he preferred the world of ship design.

My other friend was Ross Belch, whom I met through the university debates. We also played rugby together; in fact, he was the hooker to my loose head. When I later stayed in the university hostel, Maclay Hall in Park Terrace, above Kelvingrove Park, Ross and I shared a small room. We had arguments, as we were different in many ways, but they nearly always ended in laughter.

During the War, a male student could only study engineering, medicine or divinity. Engineering was a reserved occupation essential to the war effort; doctors were needed everywhere and, I suppose, the same applied to clergymen. A student, however, had to pass his exams each year to continue. One failure, and he was called up. Not surprisingly, I took two years to pass all my first-year exams, but as I was still only seventeen by the time I reached my second year (I had now revealed my true age), I was allowed to resit the exams I had failed.

I persuaded my parents to let me move out of the YMCA and find lodgings nearer the university. This was a little difficult, as the lodgings were more expensive and there was then no grant system to help parents with university fees. I convinced them, however, that the YMCA was getting rougher, and studying was difficult in such congested dormitories. I found accommodation with the Misses Taylor, at 15 Roxburgh Street, off Byers Road, a very smart part of Glasgow near the Botanical Gardens and within walking distance of the university. What I remember most about the digs was the mice. They were everywhere, and I could not understand why the two ladies did not have a cat. You could hear the creatures every night, scampering round the room behind the skirting boards. They would wake me and I would put on the light, only to see them darting round the room, playing games. I even saw them mating. They got into everything – my drawers, amongst my clothes, into the wardrobe – and when I put things on top of the wardrobe, I found the little vermin could even climb up there – how, I still do not know. Once, I found them in my bed. I tried traps, but they ate the food from the wrong side – they knew all the tricks. I think it was the mice that eventually drove me away. It was only afterwards that it occurred to me that perhaps the Misses Taylor *liked* mice. There could be no other explanation.

The main BBC studios in Scotland were not far from Roxburgh Street, in Queen Margaret Drive, and some excellent productions came from there. I ventured up to the studios, asked if I could have an audition, and was invited back to read some scripts; I also did some impersonations. Perhaps to confirm the Scots' appreciation of versatility, my impersonations went down well, but I was cast in a small part as a straight actor.

I loved the quiet, relaxed atmosphere of the studios and nonchalant professionalism of the experienced broadcasters. It was another world, a world to which I most wanted to belong, and I suspect that my enthusiasm was a little overwhelming. The producer was a very able man called Moultrie R. Kelsall, from whom I learnt a great deal. Many years later, I met Moultrie in the foyer of Broadcasting House in London. I was by now well known, and pleased to be able to tell him how I remembered my first professional job in a play, and how much I owed him. He was delighted, but somewhat taken aback. Actors are not noted for giving credit for their early achievements to anyone else.

Being at the university meant that I had a break at Christmas, so I went home to London, where the bombing had now started in earnest. There was one particular evening when the sirens had gone as usual – a dreaded noise that never failed to send a chill right through you, even though you had heard it many times before. Soon a distant drone of planes was heard, then the reassuring ack-ack barrage started up. Then would come the 'crunch' as somewhere in the distance that frightening onslaught from the skies rained down. It used to be said that it was the aeroplane that you could not hear that carried the bomb which was going to drop on or near you. On this particular evening, however, there seemed to be none of those dreaded crunch noises. It did not seem like a normal raid. In the darkness, because of the blackout, I pulled back the curtain to look out. The sky had a kind of red glow in the distance, and there was more light than there had been at dusk. I told my father and we decided to investigate. We walked up to Hampstead Heath, which was only about half a mile from our house, for a better view. As we walked in silence, I swear the sky grew even lighter. At the Whitestone Pond, from where on a very clear day you can just make out the outline of the City of London, there was already a small group of people. We stared in disbelief towards the City. It was lit up by innumerable fires, the intensity of which was turning night back into day for miles around. The City looked as if it was all ablaze, a vast red and yellow fireball. Right in the centre was St Paul's, illuminated as no floodlighting could possibly achieve. There were no explosions, only fire bombs. Only later were we told that it was the famous fire blitz, intended to destroy the heart of London not by explosion but by incendiaries.

My father and I stood in silence, too shocked to speak. Eventually, I said, 'Dad, what does it mean?' My father, normally a matter-of-fact man of few words, paused, then replied with emotion, 'I don't know. Whatever it is, it's serious. Let's go, before we see St Paul's crumble before our eyes.' We walked back in silence.

Next morning, we went down to the City to see what help we could give, and with many others handed out hot drinks to the weary firemen who were still fighting the remains of many blazes. Neither before nor since have I ever seen such devastation. And alone, surrounded by gutted buildings, ruined churches and rubble-strewn streets, stood St Paul's, majestic and almost unscathed. I shall never forget it.

After months of catching trains at early hours, hard work in tough conditions, and late-night study, often over the weekend, any break was a holiday; but to take that holiday in London during the Blitz must seem bizarre to anyone who has never been through a war. In those days, however, if you had leave, you stayed where you were or went home, wherever home was. There was no place safe from bombing; it was just that London was the most dangerous. There was nowhere else to go; no one was catering for holidays. Even in summer, beaches, particularly in the South, were covered by rolls of barbed wire and guarded by soldiers. A holiday was having a little extra food or extra sleep.

You admired the stoicism of Londoners, who endured months of continuous bombing. Those who took to the underground as a safe haven at night evolved a troglodyte existence, keeping their spirits up by the comradeship they found there. On some platforms there was a communal atmosphere and groups would organise sing-songs or play guessing games, while others would be reading, trying to sleep, playing draughts or ludo. It was a strange experience. It seemed as if the trains were invading a very intimate part of a lot of people's lives. I often wondered how these troglodyte dwellers coped with calls of nature – the escalators did not run at night and it was a long walk up all those stairs to the lavatories at the surface.

Every station platform was lined with crudely erected bunkbeds, and those who had not managed to find one brought their sleeping bags or rolled-up mattresses. Some descended to their temporary home as soon as darkness fell, and if you were travelling by tube in the winter, when the bombing started earlier, it was quite natural to pick your way through prone or reclining bodies. On reaching the surface, you hurriedly groped your way through streets where no lights shone, not even from a chink in a window. Once home, you would quickly prepare yourself for hours of fitful rest in a corrugated shelter in the garden, or, as with our family, under the specially designed, Government-issued steel table, known as a Morrison table after the then Home Secretary Herbert Morrison. This served as the kitchen table by day and, when the evening meal was finished, the hoped-for protection from the bombs by night.

When I went back to Glasgow after Christmas, I continued both to study and to look for theatre work. In the 1940s, there was a very successful showman called Carroll Levis. His great claim to fame was his stage show presenting his 'discoveries', unknown and aspiring performers whom he had found and introduced as the great new talent of the future. I am sure finding new talent was nothing original: it must have been going on since the first auditoria were built. I can imagine Aristophanes introducing his latest dis-covery in one of his plays in an out-of-town try-out at Delphi. Carroll Levis, however, was probably the first to make a successful business out of it with his show that toured the top music halls. All his discoveries had talent, but some were performers who could not quite make it on their own; others were genuinely new to the profession. It did not matter; it worked, and the public flocked to his shows.

When Carroll Levis came to the Empire Theatre in Glasgow, I plucked up courage, went backstage one evening, and nervously asked if I could audition. Carroll's manager was very pleasant, put me at my ease, asked what I did as an act, and invited me to an audition session later in the week.

The actual audition was not nearly as stressful. I had some material that had gone well in the concert party shows, and I discovered that I did not stutter on stage but only in conversation and when under pressure. I did two of my best impersonations: James Stewart and Charles Boyer. Carroll liked them and asked who else I could do.

Encouraged, I gave him Max Miller, W.C. Fields, Tommy Trinder and a radio star of the time, Oliver Wakefield. He was impressed. I could not believe it. To be granted an audition had been the height of my ambition, and now he was offering me work. Could I travel to London in six weeks' time and be the discovery in an edition of his new radio series? 'C-c-c-could I? Of c-c-c-course I c-c-c-could.' Stutter notwithstanding, I had my first professional engagement.

I was due some leave from Drysdale's, so I took it to coincide with the broadcast. All radio transmissions were live then, and the broadcast came from the Paris Cinema in Lower Regent Street, which the BBC had converted into a radio studio. (Since it was at basement level in a large building, it was safer than places above ground if there was any bombing.) Light entertainment shows in the 1940s, and even in the 1950s, could afford a full orchestra, as well as a singer and a number of well-known artists. This broadcast was one in a series called *Carroll Levis Carries On*. The show had a guest star, a resident singer and orchestra, as well as special items including, as it was wartime, a patriotic one entitled 'Worker of the Week'. The whole programme, which was devised and compered by Carroll himself, was described in the *Radio Times* as 'dedicated to the workers and Forces of Great Britain'. I was introduced as his latest discovery and given about four minutes, during which I did three impersonations. The transmission time was 12.30 p.m., a popular time during the War for comedy shows, and our audience consisted of any members of the Forces who were passing through London, and civilians who were working nearby. My parents did not come. Uncle Hugh, though, whose office was not far away (he ran a business that designed and made ties) did and, when he took me out to lunch afterwards, told me he was impressed.

Carroll had talked of some more broadcasts in his next series, and he was as good as his word. The following winter I was asked to appear in three broadcasts for his new series *Happy-Go-Lucky Hour*. He had an item in each programme called 'The Radio Deceivers', in which two of his discoveries, Diane Darling and myself, did an impression. The BBC had decided that it was too dangerous in London to continue evening broadcasts with an audience, so they moved their light entertainment operation to a place as far as possible from London and the bombs, yet which was still accessible by train. This turned out to be Bangor in northwest Wales, which was a long way to travel from Glasgow, particularly during wartime, just to do a two-minute impersonation. I was so excited at the prospect of the job, however, and of staying in a hotel for the first time, that all the problems paled into insignificance. I did two broadcasts. It was another small step in the direction I wanted to go.

3

·· · · · · · ·

Engineering and Acting

URING my second year at university, my academic work
started to suffer as I became more involved in political
debates, rugby every Saturday, and acting. I also enjoyed
taking a girl out occasionally. This always required more
money than I had, so when a chance to earn a little extra presented
itself, I accepted it immediately.

Ross had secured an arrangement, through his father, to fire-
watch at the large building owned by the Institute of Engineers and
Shipbuilders in Elmbank Road, near Glasgow's Charing Cross. We
were each to receive ten shillings a night, two nights a week, and
our duties were very simple: when we arrived at 6 p.m. we were to
inspect the building, after which we could do as we wished – we
could even sleep, and were supplied with two camp beds and
blankets in the building's conference room. We had to stay until 7
a.m. and our real responsibility only came in the event of an air
raid. When the warning sirens went we had to put on our tin hats,
take up positions on the roof to be on hand to deal with any
incendiary bombs, and generally try to prevent the building from
going up in flames. A direct hit would, of course, have finished us
off, but we thought only of the ten shillings.

Ross and I would sometimes practise our debating techniques
on each other; I would also rehearse my impersonations, or try to
catch up on neglected study. We were rarely disturbed, and since
we were both working very hard, were pleased to have an early
night.

One morning, when we emerged at about 7.30 a.m. to take the tram back to our lodgings, we thought the streets were busier than usual, and the people waiting at the tram stop looked rather bleary-eyed. We realised something was amiss when the tram made a detour, and we saw fallen masonry. Then we heard the passengers comparing notes, discussing the times of the loudest bangs, which areas had been badly hit, and which people had suffered direct hits or been injured. We were deeply embarrassed. We had failed in our responsibilities. Tired and inured to the noise of the bombing, we had slept through an air raid. Fortunately, nothing had landed near the building we were guarding in our sleep, or we would have heard – or perhaps not, and we would have gone with the bomb.

When we arrived at Maclay Hall, we discovered from the radio that the main force of the raid had been directed against Clydeside. Up till then, air raids on Glasgow had been spasmodic because of the distance that the Germans would have had to over-fly Britain. As the Clyde, however, was so important industrially and as a port, the Germans had decided to mount a huge exercise to cripple the area. This particular raid became known as the Clydeside Blitz – and we had slept through it. We did what we could to ease our consciences. Volunteers were needed and we hurried down to the worst-hit areas to help the emergency services. It was grim. The Glasgow tenements might have been built as very solid, practical housing, but when subjected to heavy bombardment they caused more damage and injuries than less solid buildings. Some of them had only partially collapsed, crushing people inside. The injuries were ghastly, and the death toll high. We spent all day in the worst areas, trying to clear a way for the ambulance and first-aid services to reach the injured and dying. The Germans lost a number of planes venturing so far, particularly on the return journey, and they never attempted a major blitz on Glasgow or Clydebank again.

I failed two of my university exams in my second year, but was still young enough to be allowed to resit. I wondered, however, whether it would be better to volunteer, join the Merchant Navy, and start a full, professional career in show business after the War. I then discovered you had to be a qualified skilled engineer to be accepted as a junior engineering officer in the Merchant Service, so there seemed every reason to continue with my apprenticeship, and I went back to Drysdale's in the summer. I was now moved to the drawing office, where the work was not so strenuous and we began at 9 a.m. instead of 8.

Around this time, I had my first chance as a professional stage actor. There was then an excellent repertory company in Glasgow, run by Wilson Barrett, which performed a weekly repertory of plays at the lovely Alhambra Theatre. This was an ornate building, with huge pillars outside and swirling plasterwork inside, which was pulled down in the 1960s when provincial theatre was struggling against the impact of television. The smaller Theatre Royal and the King's Theatre were saved, but the loss of the Alhambra was a tragedy for Glasgow, because today it is the large theatres in the big cities that are in demand for lavish touring productions that cannot be seen on the small screen.

I visited Wilson Barrett at the Alhambra and asked if he would see me. He agreed, and was delighted to find a presentable young man who had not been called up and who had a little acting experience. I was immediately offered a job. He was about to revive *Mr Wu*, an early 1920s play with a Chinese setting, and I was given a tiny role as an English officer on a Chinese ship. It required minimal rehearsal, so I could fit it in round my work at Drysdale's. I was greatly excited at being in a professional company, on a huge stage, before a packed audience every night, and once more discovered that my stutter completely disappeared when performing. The other excitement was the prospect of meeting a young Scottish actress who had joined the company and had been playing supporting roles, as well as being stage manager. Her name was Elizabeth Sellers, and she later became a very successful West End and television actress. I had seen her in one or two productions in the repertory season, and was deeply struck by her stunning good looks. She was dark, petite, with a lovely speaking voice, and now I was not only going to meet her, but be on the same stage. She was playing Mr Wu's daughter, Nang Ping, and with a Chinese make-up she looked even more attractive. As a shy seventeen-year-old with hardly any experience of the opposite sex, however, I could only stare in wonder from afar and just hope she might notice I was in the same play. At the end of the week she actually spoke to me and said goodbye, and kissed me on the cheek. I felt quite weak.

Her dark good looks, with a full sensuous mouth, were the kind I found irresistible. My first serious love affair, over a year later, was with a most attractive girl called Sheena, who had similar hair and features. I met her at the university union and although she was with another young man at the time, I was so struck by her that I had to make immediate enquiries, and persevered until I eventually discovered her name and phone number. Though I was now in my teens, I was still an innocent in many ways where girls were concerned, conditioned by my upbringing and the prevailing attitudes of the time. Perhaps it was my lack of self-confidence that held me back, but nor was it usual then for young people to have a sexual relationship as soon as they became friendly. My romance with Sheena, though brief, is something I will never forget. It is said that the memories of your first real love affair stay with you for the rest of your life, and that is certainly true with me. Sheena was only sixteen, and I was not much older. We were both innocents. In fact, at one point she actually had to explain to me how her anatomy worked.

At that young age, with no settled career ahead of me, there was no future for us together. Sheena already knew a young officer in the army, who had a job to return to, so when later she joined the WRENs, the two of them became engaged. She is probably now a mother and grandmother.

Wilson Barrett offered me parts in the last two productions of his season at the Alhambra, but because of my apprenticeship, I could not take on both of them. Since the rehearsals for the first play coincided with the summer holiday break, this was the one I accepted. It was *The Silver King*, a well-known play from the turn of the century by Henry Arthur Jones and Henry Herman. I was very disappointed at having to refuse the other role, which was in a Scottish play called *Marigold*, and Elizabeth Sellers was cast in the lead. Perhaps it was as well: my stutter might have returned when I had to speak to her, and that would have been embarrassing.

The Silver King had been written at a time when asides to the audience were still employed and the revival was performed in the true spirit of the original. As a consequence, I learnt a theatrical lesson that I tried to take to heart when working as a serious straight man many years later. I had a very small part as a clerk, who had done something dubious and was now inspired, by the advice of the character played by Wilson Barrett, to mend his ways. At the end of the short scene with him, I turned to the audience and spoke a very old-fashioned, corny line, which I delivered with great passion: 'He is wonderful. From this day on, I will lead a new life.' The timing must have been right, as it not only got a big laugh, but received a round of applause. Small-part guest actors, who in this instance are not even professionals, do not steal the limelight from the leading actor. I also received a mention in the brief review that appeared in the newspaper. I might have endeared myself to the audience, but not to the star actor on the stage at the time, who also happened to be my employer. He gave me a very stern look and later gently suggested that I should not dwell on the line and should leave the stage more quickly.

There existed on the outskirts of Glasgow, in Rutherglen, a tiny theatre run by an exceptional woman, Mary S. Urquhart, who later became known nationally as Molly Urquhart. She was a distinguished Scottish actress, married to an inspector of police, a marvellous man called William MacIntosh. Molly had taken a disused church hall, turned it into a theatre, and used her initials for the name. The MSU became very successful in Rutherglen, and also well known in Glasgow, where there had always been a great many talented amateur and semi-professional actors. Molly had a wealth of talent on which to call for those prepared to accept the money. She rehearsed every evening one week, and played every evening the next, so you could hold your day job and still accept an engagement. She presented about ten shows a year, and paid two pounds for each play in which you appeared.

I first came to her attention when she persuaded a friend of hers, Paul Vincent Carroll, a distinguished Irish author living in Glasgow, who had won international success with his plays *Shadow and Substance* and *The White Steed*, to allow her to present his new play about the Clydeside Blitz, *The Strings, My Lord, Are False*. Molly rang me, asking if I could learn lines quickly. She must have been desperate, as she had difficulty tracking me down, and then I discovered that the play was opening the following Monday, and this was Thursday. I accepted happily, assuring her that I was a quick study, and assuming the character must be someone young, as actors for such parts were impossible to find during the War, and this was winter 1942. I arrived in Rutherglen the following evening to discover that I had been cast as a middle-aged, mid-European Jewish refugee, Louis Liebens, who had settled in Glasgow and was shell-shocked and traumatised by the Blitz. Not exactly type-casting. I thought my career as an actor could only move upwards from here; or perhaps it would finish the following Monday night. I learnt the part, and while I am sure I over-acted, I remembered my lines and impressed Molly, who seemed keen to employ me again. She gave me the chance to play some very good parts; she also took me under her wing and almost made me a member of her family. In many ways she became a surrogate mother, and I owe her and her husband Willie a great deal.

I met some wonderful characters at the MSU, like Guy Muir, who kept a sweet shop; Bert Ross, who worked on the railways; Rosina McCulloch, who had a reputation for chasing anything presentable in trousers. There was also a marvellous woman, Mrs McGuinness, who cleaned the theatre. An Irish-Glaswegian, with a broad accent and a gift for colourful language, she received a new lease of life through the MSU, and she worshipped Molly. In 1943 Molly became pregnant, much to everyone's surprise as she was well past normal childbearing age. She told everyone with endearing naivety that it was a miracle, since she and Willie had not been intimate for ages. We all took this with a pinch of salt, but Mrs McGuinness believed every word Molly told her without question. When the baby was on its way, Mrs McGuinness rang the hospital to enquire after Molly and told the nursing staff to take special care, as only one other child in Christendom had been conceived this way. Willie took it all in his stride, and their son James was treated like any normal child.

Working with Molly, I also met a schoolmaster called John Macrae, who was a fine actor and performed regularly at the MSU. I learnt a great deal from him about acting. He talked about economy of gesture, demonstrated the use of the dramatic pause, and said it was essential to be aware of the contours of your face, which helped greatly when making yourself up for a character role. Above all, he was a man of great integrity, who possessed high standards which he would never compromise, but who was nevertheless very tolerant of others. He later gave up teaching and became a full-time professional actor when the Glasgow Citizens' Theatre opened in 1943. He changed his name to Duncan Macrae, joined

the company and never looked back. He gave some fine performances and eventually moved to London, where his ability to
play unusual or eccentric characters brought him solid work. I
particularly remember him in Joe Orton's *Loot,* though he is probably best remembered by the public for his part in the film *Whisky
Galore.* Tired of the pressures and the insincerity he found in
London, he returned to his beloved Scotland, where he formed his
own company and toured, taking quality theatre to places that
might not normally see good plays.

Molly, too, enjoyed presenting quality plays, as well as the more
commercial ones. I was given parts in two James Bridie plays, *The
Anatomist* and *A Sleeping Clergyman*, playing alongside both John
Macrae and Molly who, because she enjoyed taking romantic parts,
cast herself as the young female lead. This she was entitled to do,
since she ran the theatre, but it must have seemed a little confusing
to the audience to find the young medical genius in *A Sleeping
Clergyman,* who looked all of seventeen, having a romantic entangle-
ment with someone who was obviously twice his age.

Molly was able to persuade the most unlikely people to appear
on stage and try their hand at acting. Someone whom she persuaded
to take a small part in *A Sleeping Clergyman* was a character with a
pointed beard called Robert Wilkie, known to everyone as Rab.
He was the most passionate Scottish Nationalist I had met outside
the university and he promoted his cause with lucid arguments
and humour in the one large dressing room all the men shared.
Unfortunately, he did not find soap useful. You had the impression
that it had rarely, if ever, come close to his body. I was used to some
powerful smells working on Clydebank, but in the confined space
of that dressing room, the unwashed body and clothes of poor Rab
became so unbearable that, one by one, we went upstairs to ask the
girls if we could share with them. Rab was so likeable that no one
had the face to ask him to wash; besides, how do you tell anyone
they smell? John Macrae, being the kindest of men, was the last to
join us in the girls' dressing room, leaving Rab alone downstairs.
Eventually Molly felt that something had to be done, if only to
relieve the congestion in the girls' room, which the men were
beginning to enjoy. She went downstairs to speak to Rab. He did
not seem concerned that he was on his own, or suspect anything
was wrong. Molly returned after a little while to say that she had

talked with him and, using great tact, had suggested that if he was surprised to find himself alone, he had to remember that 'cleanliness was next to godliness'. Rab had replied that he completely understood. When we all returned, he said he realised why he had been left alone: we were all godly people and had decided to leave the room to wash before the show. It seems that there are some personal messages that can never be conveyed without being bluntly rude. If only 'fresh air' sprays had been available then.

The fine Scots actor Gordon Jackson was a Glaswegian. He was a little older than I was, and had achieved some fame at a very young age by starring with Tommy Trinder in the 1940 film *The Foreman Goes to France*. When he was back in Glasgow for a spell, Molly persuaded him to appear in *Marigold*. He played the young officer, Archie Forsythe, who was courting Marigold, and I was his friend, Bobbie Townsend.

In MSU shows, performed after very little rehearsal, things could always go wrong, but they gave you great opportunities to learn your craft as you ad-libbed your way out of unexpected situations. Most of these were due to forgotten lines and, sometimes, unrehearsed moves. Once, however, it was the set. Gordon was on stage, talking with Marigold and her chaperone; I, as his brother officer, called to collect him. The door was stuck. I could not get on stage. Gordon shouted to me to come in. I shouted back through the door, ad-libbing something about it being locked. The two of us continued to ad-lib through the shut door, trying to sound as natural as possible. The audience by this time were laughing delightedly at our embarrassment as we tried to force the door and shook the whole set in the process. The door, however, was never going to give, and while I could not get on stage, equally those already in the scene could not get off as there was no other exit.

At the rear of the set was a fireplace, with a piece of backing scenery behind it, painted to resemble a stone hearth. Saying something about getting my batman to work on the door with a wrench, which was what the stage manager was then doing, I walked round the back of the set, climbed over the fireplace backing and emerged through the chimney. The audience gave me a round of applause. Gordon said something about it not being Christmas and asked why I had come in that way. I replied that he knew very well why I had come down the chimney, adding, 'The problem was climbing on the roof. And wasn't I clever to slide down without getting dirty?' Just as we started to pick up the scene, there was a loud noise at the door, and a tremendous creaking as it opened. Onto this period set strode the burly stage manager in modern clothes, who said in a broad Glasgow accent, 'It's all right. It's shifted. You can come off when you want.' He got the biggest round of applause, and he never knew why.

Gordon was always fun to work with and we remained good friends. When he appeared as a guest when I was a subject of *This is Your Life*, he told that very story.

I was pursuing my apprenticeship with as much energy as I could. In 1943 I had been moved to the pattern shop, where wooden patterns of the pumps are made, which are then sent to the foundry to be cast. Pattern-making is highly skilled, and one of the best-paid jobs in the industry. It was also interesting and creative work, which I enjoyed; but most of all, I loved working with wood. If I had not possessed such a strong desire to perform, I think I might have been quite content as a cabinetmaker or furniture designer.

The foreman of the pattern shop was an unforgettable character called Jock Cunningham. He had a small, raised office with glass all round at one end of the large working area, which consisted of a long workbench down either side, and various machines in the centre. Most of these were highly dangerous, particularly the sawing and planing machines. More than one worker had a finger or half a finger missing. In fact, when I was being instructed by the assistant foreman on the use of the bigger planing machine, to prove how important it was to use a piece of scrap wood, not your fingers, to push the material to be planed over the blades, he told me a story of a colleague who had forgotten to do just this. The power of the machine was such that the man did not realise he had lost two fingers until he saw blood and, looking down, two severed fingers on the floor among the shavings. He then saw two bleeding stumps and fainted. I am not surprised. I nearly passed out at the thought of it.

Jock Cunningham could survey the whole of his domain from his office and keep an eye on each worker at his apportioned section of the bench. He decided I was a troublemaker, principally because he could not make me out, and put me at the end of the bench nearest his office so that he could watch me more closely. He was a tough character, with a temper on a short fuse, but he was not really frightening; he was mostly bluster. I was more nervous of him than anything else. The reason he did not command complete respect was due, I think, to his dentures. Like many Scots of his generation, he had false teeth, which the Glaswegians blamed on their very soft water. Jock's teeth did not fit properly and he never bothered to have them fixed. You could see them sliding across his mouth as he spoke, and it made his speech sound rather slurred, as if he was struggling to get his words out. In fact, when he became very angry, he was unable to get his words out and he had been known to spit his dentures into his hand so that he could swear more freely. On one occasion a fellow apprentice gave me a warning nudge and said, 'Look out, Jock's on the warpath. He's got his teeth out.' It was difficult to take a man like that too seriously, even though he was a good foreman. Whether he was particularly strict with me because he discovered that I used to do an impersonation of him with his loose dentures, I do not know.

While I was working in the pattern shop, Carroll Levis brought his show to the Glasgow Empire. He had written to me asking if I would like to be included as one of his discoveries for that week. I was delighted, but concerned that, as I was now officially called up and working in a reserved occupation, I might be contravening some official rule if I accepted. I was also very worried that Drysdale's might think that I was not taking my work seriously, and stop my apprenticeship, with all the embarrassment that would create. To ease my worries, I accepted the engagement, but changed my name to Nick Marlowe. I have no idea why I chose such an unoriginal name – perhaps I had read too many Raymond Chandler novels.

It was a memorable week, appearing on the stage of the famous Glasgow Empire, playing to a huge, packed audience. I was billed as 'Glasgow's BBC Impressionist' and was given a marvellous reception, helped I am sure by the fact that Carroll introduced me as a local lad. There was one memorable night, the second house Friday, when a party of workmates from Drysdale's came to support me. In spite of my efforts not to advertise my appearance at the theatre, it seemed to be common knowledge around the firm. I was very touched when one of the men in the pattern shop said, 'Hey, Nick, I see yer at the Empire this week.' I said, 'Yes, but I'm trying to keep quiet about it.' He replied, 'Come aff it. We're yer workmates. We wanna come and support yer. Yer know, get a party together. Come and gie yer the big hand.' I thanked him very much, and he disappeared. He tracked me down after lunch and said, 'I've done a wee canvass roond the works. Get us forty-five seats for a start, upper circle, second hoose Friday.'

I have forgotten the final number who turned up at the theatre. It only came back to me that they were all there when my performance at second house Friday seemed to be going exceptionally well, with ecstatic reactions from the upper circle. In fact, I was in danger of overrunning my time, which was not permitted under any circumstances in the strictly run Moss Empire theatres. I could not, however, ignore my friends, so before I started my final item, Winston Churchill, I said, 'I would like to dedicate my final impersonation to my friends on Clydebank.' This sparked off a reaction that I had not expected. A voice from the upper circle suddenly shouted, 'Hey, Nick, gie us Jock Cunningham.' Another yelled, 'No, do Willy Russell.' A third took it up, 'We want Jimmy Brown.' A fourth chimed in, 'Aye, with his pipe.' A veritable chorus now started to yell various names of those at Drysdale's. I could see the people in the stalls looking up; more important, I could see an angry stage manager in the wings, indicating that my time was almost up. I was just about to launch into my Winston Churchill impersonation when a lone voice suddenly shouted, 'We don't want Winnie, we want Willie McGinty.' Immediately, a high-pitched, passionate voice from the other side of the upper circle came back, 'Hey, Nick, yer no going to impersonate me, no on that stage. If yer do, I'll come roond and put yer one in yer teeth.' This broke up the whole audience, and they roared with laughter. They now seemed to realise what was going on, which was more than the stage manager did. Carroll walked on stage and brought my act abruptly to a close. 'Ladies and gentlemen, a round of applause for Nick Marlowe.' A really rough voice came back, 'He hasna finished, yer big Jessie. Let the kid do his last number.' 'All right,' said a rather shaken Carroll – you do not argue with a Glasgow Empire audience. 'Winston Churchill in thirty seconds.' I launched into the impersonation, Carroll started the applause, the orchestra struck up very loudly, and I walked off, still doing my Churchill routine.

In the pattern shop, smoking was strictly forbidden because of the wood all around. There were two small outside lavatories at the rear of the building, which were often used by one or two apprentices sneaking off to have a smoke, or what they called 'a wee drag'. On one occasion, when I went out to the loos I opened the door of the first one to find three of my fellow apprentices, puffing away. I said, 'Oh, I'll go next door.' They replied, 'No, no, come in Nick. Quick, shut the door. D'yer wanna a fag?' I said, 'No, I want a pee.' They said, 'Well, go ahead. Don't mind us. Next door's busy.' It is difficult enough to relieve yourself comfortably with three people closely watching, but it was made worse by one of them suddenly saying, 'Hey, Nick, gie us one of yer impersonations. Gie us Charles Boyer.' It was an incongruous situation. I was standing there with my boilersuit open and fly buttons undone, putting on the deep voice and French accent of the great cinema heartthrob, speaking the words he delivered in an emotional farewell scene with Bette Davis in the film *All This and Heaven Too*: 'No, no, my darling. Don't move. As I see you standing there, with the light on your hair, and your image in the mirror behind. This is how I want to remember you . . .' I finished, did up my fly buttons and made to go. 'Hey, Nick, that was great. Come on now, gie us yer Jimmy Stewart.' They would not let me go. Squashed between the three of them, I did a passage from *Mr Smith Goes to Washington*. I then had to give them their favourite, W.C. Fields. It did not compare with the Glasgow Empire, but they were a very appreciative audience. I gave them William Bendix, Max Miller, and had just launched into an impromptu script in Winston Churchill's voice about being closeted in an outside loo with three young characters discussing the war effort when there was an almighty banging on the door. It was forced open and there was an irate Jock Cunningham, minus teeth, purple with rage at this unforgiveable waste of the firm's time. He rounded off an almost continuous string of expletives with, 'Get back to yer bench, yer big impersonator. Yer here to make patterns, no make yon buggers laugh.'

Twenty-four years later, in 1967, I was starring with Prunella Scales in the play *Say Who You Are*, a farcical comedy by Keith

Waterhouse and Willis Hall. We had finished a run at the Vaudeville Theatre in London and were on tour. It was the spring, and we had arrived in Glasgow.

I visited Drysdale's and saw as many of my old workmates as possible, and many of whom had been apprentices with me were now skilled engineers. I was very flattered when the senior management, some of whom had been in humbler positions when I was serving my time, laid on a special lunch in their boardroom. By the time I returned to the theatre after a whole day in the works, talking endlessly and reminiscing, I was on a high, keyed up by the warmth and nostalgia of the occasion. I was first to speak in the play, and just before he gave the cue for the curtain to rise, the stage manager said to me, 'Nicholas, d'you know you're talking with a broad Glasgow accent?' I did not, and was grateful to him. It would certainly have thrown the other three members of the cast if I had suddenly changed from a very English character into a Scot.

It was a great week. On the Friday, after the show had finished, I was told by the stage doorkeeper that I had a visitor, a Mr Cunningham. Puzzled, I asked the doorkeeper to find out if the man knew me. Apparently, he knew me well, so I asked that he be shown to my dressing room. A few minutes later, there was a knock on my door and there entered an elderly man with white hair. I did not recognise him, but as soon as he started to speak I knew the voice immediately. His moving dentures took me back twenty-four years. He sat down, accepted the whisky I gave him, and told me that he was nearly eighty, retired, and living with his sister on the west coast near Largs. He went on to say how he had followed my career with interest and, with a typically Scots understatement, added, 'And I've got to say, you've done no bad, no bad at all.' I was deeply touched that this eighty-year-old man had taken the trouble to travel all the way into Glasgow, at night, just to see one of his ex-apprentices, and one who had given him so much trouble. He reminisced for a little, then said, 'I've followed your career with interest. D'you know, when I'm at home and we have company, and you come on the television, I point to the screen and say, "D'you see him? He was one of my apprentices. I trained him." I'm real proud of you.' I was overwhelmed. This lovely old man, whom I had respected in my youth but found very forbidding, had actually liked me all the time, and had taken a fatherly interest in my career. I took him back to the station, gave him a huge hug, and said goodbye. I knew that I would probably never see him again, but I hope he realised how much his gesture meant to me.

4

. . . .

Struggling Against the Odds

I N the summer of 1943, after I'd left university, I was back at
Drysdale's. I was moved to the 'outside squad', a group of
highly skilled engineers whose job it was to fit the new
pumps in the ships being built in various shipyards, mostly on
Clydebank, as well as to carry out repairs to pumps which might
be needed now that a ship was in port. I was seconded to work
with any fitter who needed an assistant, or just to accompany one
and learn more about my trade. In other words, I was to be 'the
boy on the job'.

Charlie Drysdale ran the outside squad, and we would report to
his small office, where information on the firm's pumps was kept
and instructions handed out. Some jobs would last a few days,
sometimes more, others might be a quick repair job that could be
completed in a few hours. I enjoyed the travel, and visiting different
shipyards; during my time in the squad, I must have worked in
nearly every yard on the Clyde. I had a long spell at Fairfields as the
aircraft carrier *Implacable* was being built there, and many of the
pumps on board were from Drysdale's.

As a ship is constructed from the keel upwards, heavy equipment
is installed on the relevant deck and secured before the deck above
is laid. A large ship can take up to two years to build and a few
months before the launch the pumps, which could have been
delivered over a year previously, have to be checked and started.
One of the hazards in doing this can be rats, which are endemic to
shipyards. As the boy on the job, it was my responsibility to clear

each pump of any nesting rats before we started work on it. I only had one accident, when I foolishly put my hand down the exit pipe from a pump to clear away some straw without looking first or poking about with a crowbar. A nesting rat took a nip at my forefinger, which, although not serious, taught me to be careful in future. No one could understand why the rat population in this yard never went down, until it was discovered that their rat catcher was only killing the male animals; the females were left to breed, so that he would have a job for life.

One of the most incredible sights in a shipyard in those days occurred a few days before a ship was launched for its trials. It was completely evacuated of all personnel, every hatch was battened down, with only the openings through which the mooring ropes were secured left open. The ship was then fumigated, and all the rats rushed to the remaining exits and ran nose to tail down the ropes to the shore. Their numbers were quite amazing, especially if it was a large ship. Groups of workers stood at the shore end of the ropes with shovels and similar implements and tried to kill as many as they could. The shoreline was quickly littered with the corpses of the vermin, but it was only a fraction of those that had escaped the gas-filled ship.

It was while working in the outside squad that I came to understand more fully the people on Clydeside, as I was frequently travelling with one or other of the fitters, and working very closely with them. One of these men was a drinker. Not that he drank too much; he just enjoyed it, and not being married, his spare cash went on booze. The first time I was working with him, he introduced me to the traditional Scottish 'half an' a half' – a measure of whisky taken neat in a very small glass, followed by a half-pint of good, strong Scottish bitter as a chaser.

We had arrived to start on a repair job just as the pubs were opening. He swore me to secrecy, explaining that he worked better with a few drams inside him, but did not want the bosses to know. I had never drunk much until then; my spare cash only allowed me an occasional beer. Scottish pubs in the 1940s, certainly in the towns, were dull and very uninviting. They were really just drinking parlours, frequented only by men. You rarely saw a woman inside one, and if a woman entered, even accompanied, it was usually assumed that she was of easy virtue, or worse.

The pub we went into on the Dumbarton Road was so forbidding that you immediately wanted a drink to cheer yourself up. Jim set up the first round. Realising my ignorance, he showed me how you downed the dram of whisky in a gulp, tipped the dregs into your beer, then gently chased the golden liquid until the two met up and gave you a warm glow inside. My stomach and throat were completely unprepared for this potent liquid coming at them in a huge gulp, and I was coughing and spluttering before I could get the beer to my lips. Jim thumped me on the back, and said, 'Take the beer, lad. Wash it doon. Yer'll soon get the hang o' it.' He ordered the same again. I took the second one more gingerly; I was not even sure that I liked whisky. By the time I had finished my third 'half an' a half' on an empty stomach, my head was spinning. By the time we reached the engine room of the ship to begin work, I was having great difficulty focusing, especially when it came to finding the right spanner for various nuts. At one point, Jim told me to lie flat and reach down between the gap in the metal deck plates where we were standing, and loosen some nuts on the lower part of the pump. Putting my head and shoulders down through the gap was nearly the end of me. I lost my grip, slipped further down, and Jim and another engineer had to grab me before I went any further. As I was dragged up through the narrow opening, my wallet, containing all my important documents and what little money I possessed, slipped out of my pocket and landed in the bilge water. I was advised to let them go, but I was not going to lose such precious items so easily, especially the hard-earned money. To hell with the state of my head, I asked the two men to hold my ankles as I eased my whole body down through the gap. Hanging at full stretch, I could just reach the bilge water and managed to scoop up my valuables before they sank or floated away. It was some time before they dried out, and some time before I drank so much again, especially on an empty stomach.

In October 1943 the Glasgow Citizens' Theatre opened, after much publicity, at the seldom-used Athenaeum Theatre in the centre of the city. (It was only later that it moved to the Gorbals.) Rehearsals for the first production were in the evenings, so it was possible to engage me for two small parts, since I could persuade whoever I was working with in the outside squad not to keep me on overtime.

It was marvellous being in a play on a professional stage, and exciting being in at the beginning of a great new theatrical venture, which soon established itself and is now one of the country's most respected civic theatres.

In retrospect, I wonder where I found the energy to pursue two jobs. In addition, I was still playing rugby every Saturday for the university, and it was about this time that I was picked by the Scottish selectors to represent the West of Scotland against the East in a game to be played at Murrayfield, where I had turned out on a number of occasions for the university.

It was not the best game I had ever played: either I was too tired, or simply over-awed. I achieved an unfortunate distinction: I dropped a pass – something I rarely did, and I dropped it right under the main stand. The influence of my Clydeside training asserted itself and in my frustration and anger I exploded with a four-letter expletive. The word 'shit' had never been heard coherently on a rugby field in prim Edinburgh before, and I endeared myself neither to the selectors nor to the majority of the crowd. One journalist, with a sense of humour, did have the kindness to write that, 'N. Parsons backed the three-quarters with an admirable turn of speed, and his one unfortunate error produced an incredible comment from himself, which would undoubtedly have been echoed in the crowd, could they have descended to use such language.'

While I was appearing in a three-week run of *Holy Isle* at the new Citizens' Theatre, I went into Drysdale's one morning to be briefed and was told that I was going on a submarine trial. I had not been warned in advance, as in wartime such testing had to be secret. Normally, this would have been an exciting experience, but I had to be on stage at the Athenaeum by 7.30 p.m. and I would not be able to phone from under water if I was delayed. It would be pretty odd for the management to have to announce before the curtain rose, 'At this performance the parts of "Ba" and the Bishop of Orkney will be played by X, as Nicholas Parsons is unavoidably detained in a submarine.'

When the senior fitter on the job informed Charlie Drysdale that I was committed to being in a play that night, Charlie reminded me curtly that there was a war on and essential work came first. I was not even allowed to phone the theatre and warn them. I was in a state of extreme agitation all day. Nevertheless, I vividly remember the claustrophobic feeling of being confined in a vessel deep under the ocean, with no knowledge of exactly where you are. My admiration for the sailors who join this branch of the Royal Navy is beyond words. Fortunately, there were no problems on the trials, the pumps behaved perfectly, and we were ashore by 6 p.m. No bizarre announcements were necessary at the theatre.

By the autumn of 1943, I had saved enough money to buy a second-hand motorbike. It was a 500cc Norton, a pretty lethal machine, even for an experienced motorcyclist. I was a raw beginner, and as the driving test had been dropped during the war, I was allowed onto the roads with the minimum of instruction and no L plates. The machine cost me a fiver, and gave me trouble from day one.

The petrol ration was very meagre during this period of the war. For those not on essential business, it was about eight gallons a month for a car – hardly worth taking it out of the garage for – and about three gallons for a motorbike. That was less than a gallon a week, but it was enough to get me to work and back for most of the time. My plans, however, never materialised. After much labour and mechanical instruction from friends at Drysdale's, I had the machine in reasonable running order. The fateful moment occurred as I was going to the university up Woodside Terrace. The trams, which ran on parallel tracks down the centre of the road, turn at the top of the terrace into a single-track terminus at the base of University Hill. There was one tram in front of me, preparing, it seemed, to go onto the single track. What I had failed to notice was that there was already a tram on the single track and as I turned right and started to cross the double tram lines to go up University Hill, this second tram moved off at speed to begin its return journey. I did the only possible thing, and jammed on my brakes. My rear wheel skidded, both wheels locked into one of the rails, and I careered towards the trams. The one coming towards me slammed on its brakes; to avoid the other, I managed to wrest the front wheel of the bike out of the rail and aim it at the narrow gap between the two trams. There was no way it would fit, but at least I might lessen the impact. I pulled the handlebars and front wheel sideways to prevent myself from being catapulted over the top. Somehow, I managed to prevent my legs from being mangled, somersaulted off the bike and landed on my back between the trams.

Unfortunately, the driver of the arriving tram had not seen me, and started to move his car slowly forward. The driver who *had* seen me and stopped, shouted as loudly as he could. The second driver stopped and both jumped down to survey the scene: one mangled bike and a severely shaken and bruised young man on the ground. It was the end of my motorcycling adventures. After that, I returned to my trusted bicycle. Besides, I had no money to buy another motorbike and although I am sure I could have regained my confidence, I realised just how dangerous they are, and never wanted to own one again. I had been very lucky. The fact that I could tumble, as much as anything, had contributed to my survival. Perhaps I had a future in the circus after all; or perhaps I should have been a stuntman. Certainly, when I was working in films in the 1950s and my character needed a stunt, I nearly always did it myself.

In 1944 I applied to join the Merchant Navy as a junior engineer. I was young for such a position, but had almost the full qualifications from my apprenticeship work, and there was a great shortage of personnel. The losses in this branch of the services were higher than in any other, because so many of our merchant ships had been sunk by German U-boats.

I had experienced the atmosphere of a large merchant ship from working on one during sea trials, and thought that I would find this service preferable to the vigorous discipline of the Royal Navy. I was very keen to join the Canadian Pacific Company, which had some magnificent ships in its fleet. I could have stayed on as a qualified engineer with Drysdale's when my apprenticeship finished, but I felt that this was wrong. My heart was in show business, and I had proved to myself, if not my family, that I could succeed in the theatre. In family letters exchanged around this time, I was still being persuaded to follow a proper career and to 'forget the play-acting nonsense'. I knew that I could not start an acting career in 1944. I was already registered for National Service, and perhaps there was a certain aggression in my wish to join a service where, statistically, the risks were highest and the chances of survival lowest. My Uncle Hugh approved, which was some consolation. He and my Aunt Gladys had lost their only son, Basil, at the battle of El

Alamein, and they were pleased to see a relation taking such a positive step in the War.

My Merchant Navy service did not last long. In fact, I probably hold the record for the shortest stay – no more than a few days. I am not even sure whether I was officially in the service. The Canadian Pacific had told me to continue working until a vacancy came up, which could be in a week or two, so I was accepted, but had no ship. In the meantime, the pressures of work and other activities took their toll. The wartime lack of nourishing food probably contributed. In fact, my principal memories of wartime are not of bombs and danger, but of always being hungry. Perhaps the unconscious influence of my mother's uncompromising attitude to illness did not help. I remember feeling unwell, but refused to give in or acknowledge it. I kept working, thinking I simply had a bout of flu that I could shake off. Eventually, I collapsed, staggered back alone to Maclay Hall and took to my bed. There was a mature student there, Dr Munro, who was qualified and doing research. He examined me, said it was my lungs, and told me that I should go straight to hospital.

I had signed a contract for the best part I had so far been offered at the BBC and was looking forward to doing it the following week, before I went into the Merchant Navy. It was to play the student, Augustus Raby, in James Bridie's *The Anatomist*, with Alastair Sim playing the lead. I pleaded that I would surely be all right after a few days in bed. Dr Munro explained that pleurisy was serious, and without proper treatment it could develop into something worse. I spoke to my father, who insisted that I do exactly as Dr Munro had advised. With great sadness, I cancelled my appearance in the radio play. An ambulance was called, and the next thing I knew, I was in the Victoria Infirmary.

My condition deteriorated rapidly. In 1944 the necessary antibiotics did not exist to fight pleurisy. My left lung was worst, and fluid had to be drawn off, which was very painful. There was also always the risk of tuberculosis. I had not had a proper rest or any holiday since 1939 and just wanted to sleep, which I did continuously for about three weeks. The condition was aggravated by a deep depression, a result, no doubt, of letting go after working too hard for too long.

I was in the side room of a large men's ward with two other

young men of my age. After three weeks, I was the only one still alive. One had leukaemia; the other, Henry, had been a student at Glasgow with me, studying medicine. I remember him reading the chart at the foot of his bed one day when the nurses were not around, and understanding that his days were numbered. I do not know what he died of; I was too ill to ask.

Losing two friends so dramatically only increased my depression and after the fourth week it was decided to move me to a branch of the infirmary, Phillipshill, which was based at East Kilbride, outside Glasgow. My parents never came to see me. Travelling was very difficult, and my mother felt that she had to stay with my father who, as a doctor, was kept very busy with all the extra work that resulted from the continuous bombing of London. My brother, John, who was in Glasgow on company business for Rolls Royce, was able to visit me while I was in the Victoria Infirmary, and tried to cheer me up. I had played down my illness to my parents so as not to worry them, but I need not have bothered, for apparently John told them that, in his opinion, I had only a fifty-fifty chance of survival.

Phillipshill was primarily an orthopaedic hospital, but the move was the tonic I required. Surrounded by a mixed group of men of all ages, who were on the whole very cheerful – not so much ill as confined with injured limbs – my spirits soon lifted and I started on the slow road to recovery.

I have always found nurses irresistible. There is something about the trim, starched uniform and that dedication to helping others that pulls at my heartstrings, and they were a particularly attractive team on our ward, under the charming and able Sister Bruce. I am sure those pretty creatures also helped my recovery, as I flirted outrageously with them all.

I was in the hospital for five months, then spent two weeks at the hospital's convalescent home in Largs. During my stay, D-Day came and went. The end of the War in Europe seemed in sight, though it took another year, and even longer in the Far East. In late October I was finally discharged, and was free to return to London and my parents, whom I had not seen for nearly a year. Before I did so, I visited Drysdale's to say goodbye. I collected my apprenticeship 'lines', which detailed my work experience, and it was good to feel that I had some qualifications for all the long hours and hard work.

I said goodbye to as many of the men as I could; I then returned to Charlie Drysdale's office for my final farewells and he asked if I had paid my respects to Matthew Russell, the works manager, a dour martinet of a man who ran the whole shop floor with aggressive efficiency. I was truly scared of him – it was principally because of him that I had changed my name when appearing at the Glasgow Empire.

I told Charlie that I had not said goodbye, as I had hardly had any dealings with Mr Russell. Charlie suggested that it would be courteous. I went to his office, knocked on the door, and received a brusque 'Come in.' I explained why I had come, adding tactfully that I was not sure what I was going to do next. He was his usual taciturn self, but pleasant and surprisingly complimentary about my work for the firm. He wished me luck, we shook hands, and I started to leave. I reached the door and he suddenly said, 'By the way, if you ever come back to the Empire, you will let us know. I certainly enjoyed your act the last time.' I was completely lost for words. I felt an utter fool. To think that for over four years I had lived in fear of this man discovering that I was spending my spare time trying to become an actor and entertainer.

I spent my last night at Maclay Hall. The next day, Alec and Ross helped me pack and the accumulation of four years was pushed into a suitcase and huge cardboard boxes. My beloved bike was sold – at least what remained of it, as someone had stolen the front wheel while I was in hospital. I could never work out why they did not steal the whole machine. I was helped to Central Station and loaded, with my boxes, on to the London train to return to my family and the V2 rockets, or doodle-bugs, which were starting to descend on the capital. I felt very sad. I had made many good friends in Glasgow and had grown to love the city and its people. Most importantly, I had been given the chance to work as an actor and solo performer. I was saying goodbye to it. It was the end of a chapter, probably the most important chapter in my life and, I now realise, the one that left the deepest impression.

5

......

Fully Professional At Last

THE next three months were extremely difficult. I was still convalescing, visiting a chest specialist once a month and forbidden to go anywhere that people congregated for fear of infection, principally tuberculosis. This meant theatre and cinema going was out. I was told that I would never be allowed to sunbathe the upper part of my body again, as ultraviolet rays could induce TB in a weak chest. I was also told that, as my right lung was partially collapsed at the base, I would probably have to take life easily and not engage in work that was too physically demanding. So much for considered medical advice. If I had followed it, I certainly would not be writing this book.

As soon as I was told that I could begin work, I forgot what the specialist had said, and when I think of the pressures and intense demands of weekly repertory, physical as well as mental, to which I subsequently committed myself, by rights I should have collapsed years ago. I suppose I am blessed with very healthy genes, for which I must thank my parents and ancestors. I still work at intense pressure both inside and outside the profession. I can relax on holiday, but a lot of that time is spent in being physically active as I enjoy all sport and find playing any game the best way to unwind. Even on a day off, I find that the physical activity of a few hours' gardening is the most relaxing thing I know. I have been described as a workaholic because of the amount I undertake. I resent the word, since it conveys that I work hard because it acts as a drug. I work because I enjoy it, and some of it is therapeutic. Feeling driven – which I have on occasion, because of my upbringing and because I had to struggle very hard to establish myself as an actor – is not a help professionally.

Being forbidden to visit crowded areas was bad enough, but what was worse was that all my friends were in Glasgow. I barely knew anyone in London. It was also difficult learning to live again with my family. Except for brief visits, I had not been home since I was sixteen. I was now an adult who had grown up in a quite different environment from that of my parents, and I am sure they also found it very difficult to relate to me. I accepted that they had been through a great deal and were war-weary, and now the arrival of the V.1s, or doodlebugs, was particularly stressful. Up till now, sirens would announce that a raid was imminent, and when it was calculated that no more enemy aircraft were around, the 'all clear' siren would sound. Now there was often no siren warning. Once you became familiar with the doodlebugs, there was a distinctive noise made by the engine, which was detectable as it approached. If it stopped, you knew it was on the way down and you ran for cover. Later, rockets were sent over, which made no noise at all. You would be walking down the street and suddenly there was an almighty explosion. It was a ghastly way to live, but you develop a fatalistic attitude to danger that becomes quite natural, and I was never inhibited from going about my business.

My days were spent taking fresh air and exercise, on doctor's orders, every morning on Hampstead Heath, usually accompanied by the family dog, a Bedlington terrier named Polly, who was completely inured to the bombing. I rested a lot, visited the library, and wrote letters to the BBC requesting auditions for radio plays. The specialist had agreed that I could work in a studio if an engagement was offered.

I was called before a medical board to see if I might be fit to return to the Merchant Navy. Anyone with a dodgy lung was too great a risk, however, and I was discharged from all further national service. This was fine, but I had no work, no prospects, no theatrical contacts in London and no desire to return to engineering. My parents were still working hard to persuade me to consider a 'proper job'. My mother's neurotic dread of a dissolute thespian life coloured every discussion. This was completely at variance with her love of visiting the theatre. When I pointed out that I could not imagine that people like Sybil Thorndike or Edith Evans fitted her description of the thespian world, she always replied, 'Perhaps not, but isn't it sad that they have to mix with those types.' Matters were not helped when it was discovered that one of the books I had taken out of the library was the famous book on a subject about which I had been given little information: *The Psychology of Sex* by Havelock Ellis. When my mother found me reading it, she decided that I was fascinated by sex, and for that reason drawn towards show business.

It is amazing how prudish the majority of people were in those days. Attitudes were reinforced by BBC Radio, whose producers were under strict instructions to see that the rules forbidding offensive words were rigorously imposed. These rules were applied up until the 1960s. For instance, when I was a schoolboy, even 'sex' was a taboo word.

Most of my knowledge of the subject was picked up from friends at school. It was woefully inadequate, and often inaccurate, as I discovered later to my embarrassment. There was one memorable occasion, which happened when I was about fourteen. We were returning from a family Christmas outing to see Cicely Courtneidge and Jack Hulbert in the musical *Under Your Hat*. We were discussing the show in the car, and I suddenly piped up, 'I thought the chorus were a nice-looking lot of tarts.' There was silence, broken by my mother, who turned to my father and said, 'Paul, deal with the boy.' My father asked me to repeat what I had said, which I did. I was told that I would be punished for my disgusting language. I was confused. I had heard the word at school and had thought it harmless, so I said, 'What's wrong with being a tart?' My brother tried to help. 'I don't think Nicholas knows what a tart is.' My mother replied, 'Of course he does. What do you think a tart is, Nicholas?' 'Well,' I said, 'it's a girl who dyes her hair blonde, like a lot of them in the chorus.' 'Really,' said my mother sceptically. 'My friend Gwen Lewis has dyed blonde hair. Do you think she is a tart?' 'I don't know,' I said. 'Is she?' My response was born of genuine ignorance, but I still went to bed without any supper. It was a harsh way to learn the meaning of words.

1945 arrived. I had written to nearly every producer in the BBC. One of them, a charming Irishman called Fred O'Donovan, invited me to read for a part in Paul Vincent Carroll's play *The White Steed*.

He cast me in the leading role of the young man, my Irish accent being entirely acceptable. The rest of the cast, however, was made up of distinguished Irish actors, some of whom had been Abbey Theatre Players from the famous theatre in Dublin. Fred suddenly took fright at having a non-Irish member of the cast, particularly in such an important role. I was demoted to a bit-part, and an indifferent Irish actor was given the leading role promised to me.

My parents now made one final attempt to convince me that I should have nothing to do with the acting profession. My father had a patient at the time called Joan Ling. She was a literary agent and my parents knew her quite well, as my mother had helped her in the office she ran for Curtis Brown, doing secretarial work when staff were scarce during the War. Without telling me, my parents asked Joan if she would talk to me, as she knew so much about the entertainment business, and do her best to dissuade me from becoming further involved with a profession which was so insecure and fraught with dangers. A false pretext for visiting Joan was arranged, and I called on her one evening in the flat where she lived with her elderly mother. Joan asked me what I had been doing in Glasgow, and I told her of my adventures up there, and of the work I had done in the theatre and with the BBC. Then, in response to her request, I did all my impersonations, which greatly amused both her and her mother. They were very complimentary, and I left. Apparently, Joan then phoned my parents and said, 'I'm not going to dissuade this boy from becoming an actor; I am going to encourage him. He has a lot of talent.'

She was as good as her word, immediately arranging an interview with the Firth Shepherd Management, who had produced some very successful West End shows. They saw me and I was invited to audition for *Chicken Every Sunday*, which they were presenting in the spring at the Savoy Theatre. After the audition, I was asked to understudy the two young men in the play. It was my first West End job. I had no agent, so asked Joan to negotiate the contract and paid her commission. I was to receive £15 a week, which seemed a fortune at the time. Joan became a very good friend, we always kept in touch, and would meet from time to time. She became almost an adoptive aunt, and her advice on occasions has been invaluable.

Angela Baddeley and Frank Leighton starred in *Chicken Every*

Sunday, which was very American in style and content. It had been successful on Broadway and I think Firth Shepherd saw echoes in it of another American play, *The Man Who Came to Dinner,* which, with Robert Morley, had been a big hit at the Savoy. It was not to be. The reviews were terrible and we were soon all taking cuts in salary to keep the play running.

Robert Morley, at the time, was appearing in another play, *The First Gentleman,* at the New Theatre – now the Albery – and patronised a little Italian restaurant in Southampton Street quite close to the Savoy, which a number of our cast used. I was fascinated by his larger-than-life personality and the supreme confidence he exuded as he walked into the restaurant and greeted his friends in a voice that all present could hear. He seemed the epitome of how the public expected a theatre star to behave.

Most actors are very shy, and usually appear subdued in public; it is on stage that their energies are released and their inhibitions disappear. Robert Morley was the antithesis of this, and yet entirely natural, a man of great charm, a fine intellect and a wonderful conversationalist. He was, in many ways, of the old school, and in nineteenth-century theatre he would have been hailed as a great or classic actor. The public adored him, but he was a star at a time when more interpretive acting was becoming the vogue. When one thinks of his contemporaries who were knighted for their services to the theatre, it always seemed to me a shame that this hugely talented man, who contributed so much and gave pleasure to so many, never received the same accolade.

I used to sit in that little café, hoping he might make his usual theatrical entrance. Once, he squeezed his ample frame onto one of the small chairs at the table where I was sitting, and struck up a conversation. I told him how wonderful I thought he had been in *The Man Who Came To Dinner.* He simply said, 'It was a wonderful part. I just enjoyed myself. The public like to see that.' It is something I have never forgotten. The more a performer can enjoy the role he or she is playing without being indulgent, the more the audience will respond. I then had the temerity to ask for his advice to a young actor. 'It's very simple,' he said. 'Get on with it, speak up, don't bump into the furniture, and let the audience hear the words.' I think some of this was borrowed from Noël Coward, but still it was good advice, which I have never forgotten.

While I was at the Savoy, VE Day arrived, 8 May 1945. I was determined to enjoy myself on this day of national celebration, with the church bells ringing out for the first time since the war started, and bonnets being thrown over the proverbial windmill. After the show finished, an Irish friend who was in the play, Dermot MacDowell, and I made our way to Trafalgar Square. It was already packed with people. There was some singing and jollity, but where was the abandon? Where were all the pretty girls willing to kiss any attractive man in sight? It was terribly flat and dreary. Perhaps everyone was too tired after nearly six years of war. Also, there was still fighting in the Far East, and perhaps that had a sobering effect. My hopes of finding lots of girls who wanted to be kissed, of perhaps finishing up in bed with some pretty creature, of enjoying a night of abandoned lovemaking as we looked forward to a new life now the horrors of war were over, were just fantasy inspired by too many Hollywood films. Dermot and I were soon bored, very tired, completely unkissed and somewhat subdued. I decided to catch the last tube home, and wondered what I would say if I had children one day who asked, 'Daddy, what did you do on the day the war stopped?' I would have to say, 'Nothing. I went home.'

About this time, I discovered that Firth Shepherd was going to present *The Hasty Heart* by John Patrick, which had been a huge success on Broadway. I had read about the play in the American *Theatre Arts* magazine. It was set in a hospital ward behind the lines in Burma, and the cast consisted of eight men of different nationalities and one woman, a nursing sister. I felt that there must be a part I could play, so I did something that required considerable determination and cheeky persistence. In retrospect, I am amazed that I saw it through.

I went to Firth Shepherd's offices in Charing Cross Road, entered the outer reception area on the second floor which was connected by a door to an inner office that had one of those old-fashioned sliding panels, behind which sat a receptionist. The panel was drawn back and, through the small aperture, I asked if I could see Mr Laurence Green, the assistant production manager. She asked my business and, trying to control my stutter, I said that I wanted to read for the new play, *The Hasty Heart*. The sliding panel was closed. I could hear mutterings on the internal phone, then the panel was drawn back and the part of the face that was visible informed me that Mr Green was busy. I said that I would wait until he was free, and took a seat in the reception area.

After about an hour, I tapped on the sliding panel, it was drawn back, and I asked if Mr Green was free yet. The panel was closed, there were more internal mutterings, the panel was pulled back again. She said that Mr Green asked her to say that he was going to be busy all morning, and anyway, there was no point in reading for the new play, since I was already working at the Savoy Theatre. I was determined not to be put off. I said that I would still like to see Mr Green, and would return in the afternoon. This I duly did. We went through the sliding panel routine and I made the same request. A very resigned young lady said that she would ask him, but did not hold out much hope. There were more mutterings on the internal phone, then back came the sliding panel. 'Mr Green says he is too busy to see you this afternoon, and he has asked me to repeat what he said this morning.' Before she could finish, I said, 'All right, I'll wait until he is free. I've nothing else to do.' I sat down. The sliding panel was closed again, and I picked up my newspaper. After an hour, I tried again. Mr Green was still busy. After two hours, the panel was drawn back again and the half-face – I never did see more – informed me that Mr Green had left the office on business. I did not believe her, since he would have had to pass the door to the reception area. I told her that I would come back the next day.

Next morning, ten o'clock, up the stairs, into the reception area, knock on the panel, it was slid back, the same mouth and nose on the other side. The same request from me: 'Could I see Mr Green, please.' Back went the panel, phone mutterings, much briefer this time, same message back, much more forcibly expressed. I said that I would wait. After an hour, a gentle knock on the panel. It was slid back. 'Excuse me, is Mr Green free yet?' No response this time, just the panel returned, and silence. After a few seconds, the panel opened again and I was informed that Mr Green would be busy all day. I said that I would try again in the afternoon in the hope that he might be free. I had started something now that I had to see through. I just felt that if I could be given the chance to read at an audition, it would be a step forward. Getting another job now seemed entirely secondary.

I came back that afternoon, and went through the routine again, except that the half-face was now becoming very bored. I kept this up for two more days and by the Thursday the reaction behind the panel had grown very resigned. 'Oh, it's you. Yes, I know. You want to see Mr Green. You know he is busy but you'll wait.' Words had now become unnecessary on my part. I sat down and hoped, and did begin to wonder if I was making a complete fool of myself.

On Friday morning, I made one last attempt. I thought that the half-face was now a little sorry for me. I said that I would leave; I had failed. I walked towards the exit. She must have been watching me through the sliding panel, and when I was out of sight presumably told Mr Green that I had given up and left. I reached the stairs and paused. Something made me go back for one last try. I did not approach the sliding panel, but just sat in the reception area. Within a few minutes, Laurie Green walked through reception. I could not believe it. I leapt up. The stutter returned: 'M-m-mister G-g-green, can I c-c-come and r-r-read for the Hay-hay-hay . . .' I never got the title out. He interrupted, 'Oh, for goodness sake. Come to the Aldwych Theatre at three o'clock this afternoon. We're auditioning.'

Auditions are daunting occasions and in those days they were far more impersonal than they are now. Today, the artist being auditioned is usually sent the script in advance. In those days, you walked on to an empty stage, which was fully lit, and there would be one man standing in the centre with two scripts. On this occasion, it was Laurie Green. You looked out to a darkened auditorium and while you could see nothing, you knew that sitting somewhere were representatives of the management and the director of the play. You were asked to announce yourself, then handed a script and told to open at a certain page. As I did this on that memorable Friday, Laurie Green said to me, 'Will you please read the part of Digger, the Australian.' I could do most accents then, but not an Australian one. It was slipping away. All my efforts had been for nothing. I stuttered that I could not do an Australian accent, and asked if I could read it as a Cockney. This was acceptable, and it must have been reasonable, because the director then asked me what I had been doing.

At this point a voice from the back of the stalls interrupted. It was Firth Shepherd's production manager, Danny O'Neil, a very experienced theatre man, a real character with a high-pitched voice and cockney accent. He shouted, 'What's that young man doing up on the stage, Laurie? He's working along at the Savoy.' Laurie Green replied, 'He's pestered the life out of me all week; this is the only way I could get rid of him. He says he's a Scot, and would like to read the Scot's part.' I did not know at the time that the Scot in the play was the leading role. Danny O'Neil's voice came back from the empty darkness, 'All right, while he's up there, let him have his fun, ready the ruddy Scot's part.' As the Glasgow dialect was second nature to me, and it is easier to read a character part unseen than it is a straight role, I did much better at this second reading. The director thanked me, and asked where I could be contacted, at which point Danny O'Neil's voice came back, 'It's all right, we know where to find him.' I left the stage feeling content. I had been given my audition, and I think I had impressed them. It would be a good investment for the future. I thought no more about it.

That night, I was called to the stage door at the Savoy Theatre, where I was greeted by Laurie Green. He said, 'They liked your reading. They want you to play the New Zealander.' I could not believe it. I did not add that I could not do a New Zealand accent. There was time to acquire one. I was sworn to secrecy, as rehearsals were to start soon and they did not want to undermine the confidence of the cast at the Savoy by letting them think their play was finishing prematurely.

First I had to learn how to do a New Zealand accent. Using the pretext that I was planning to emigrate to New Zealand and wanted to find out as much as I could about the islands, I went to the Anzac Club, which catered for service personnel from down under. People will always talk about their home town and country, and I just sat and listened, absorbing the intonation and accent, noticing the subtle but definite difference between the New Zealand and Australian accents. This was important, as I had heard that Frank Leighton, an Australian, was to be cast as Digger in the play. It was essential that I did not sound like him.

The play was well cast. Margaretta Scott played the leading part of the nursing sister. She was always a beautiful and radiant actress, but in nursing uniform she was enchanting. I was, however, far too young and shy ever to talk to her. I was more confident with the men, except Emrys Jones, who played the leading part of Lachie, the Scotsman. He was very unsure of himself. He was extremely good-looking and had a great deal of charm, but had no idea how to cope with the star status he had achieved. The part he played was 'actor proof', that is, it was so well written and drew such sympathy from the audience that one would have had to be a very bad actor to fail in it. Emrys was Welsh, and his Scottish accent was not bad, but it never sounded quite authentic since the inflections and cadences were those of a Welshman.

There was a young actor there, about the same age as myself, who had his first West End job, as an understudy. He covered the part of Yank, which was the major role after Lachie, and my character, Kiwi. He was extremely good, and when he stepped in to play the part of Yank, with a fine American accent, he made a deep impression. His name was Joss Ackland. I never wanted to miss a performance, as I knew that I had a brilliant understudy. I contracted jaundice during the run at the Aldwych Theatre and was off for over a week, but could not wait to return, and probably went back sooner than was wise.

The Hasty Heart was launched in Glasgow. It seemed like an omen, returning so quickly to the city where I had first struggled to become an actor. The play was very well received when it opened in London, and had universally good reviews, except from James Agate, that doyen of drama critics who was then writing for the *Sunday Times*. The West End was still very different from Broadway, where a bad review from a leading critic could kill a show overnight. Mr Agate was widely read and respected, but his opinions did not destroy plays that the public liked, and they enjoyed *The Hasty Heart*. We ran for over a year, and then had a successful thirteen-week tour. This early success, however, and the unusual security of a long run, blinded me to the fact that I still had a lot to learn. I was more concerned with enjoying having a little money for the first time, as well as the chance to spend it. Part of me was making up for the freedom I had missed as a teenager.

While the play was running, I met a very attractive young woman with the most seductive voice. I have always been deeply affected by attractive voices. She was small, blonde and a few years older than I was, and I was deeply smitten. She was married, however, and though she and her husband were estranged, she also had two young children. It was a relationship with no future, but I was completely bewitched. Meeting was difficult. By day she was with her children, and I was working at night. I would call after the show; it was all very romantic. Occasionally, her mother would babysit, and we could go out together.

Everything worked fine until one evening her husband called unexpectedly. The last thing she wanted was to be caught with another man. She left him in the living room, came to the bedroom, explained the problem, bundled me and my clothes into the bathroom, and told me to get dressed quickly and leave by the downstairs exit. I had never been downstairs, and did not want to disturb her mother, who had a flat there. I might also have disturbed her husband as I searched for the back door. I thought it best to escape by the most accessible route – the bathroom window. Climbing down a drainpipe to the ground floor was something I had never tried before. I had almost reached the ground and thought that I was safe when some passers-by spotted me, assumed the worst and shouted for the police. I jumped the last few feet, hit a stone in the dark, ripped my trousers and fell into a flowerbed. Bruised, and covered with soil and dahlia blooms, I ran as quickly as I could before I was arrested for attempted breaking and entering. This would have been bad enough, but to prove my innocence would have been even more embarrassing.

It was while romancing this lovely girl that I was stricken with jaundice. I could not let her know directly, but she found out and very sweetly sent me a huge bunch of yellow tulips. When you have jaundice, you not only look yellow, you feel yellow, everything you eat tastes yellow, and the last thing you want to *look* at is anything yellow. I had to ask my mother to take the flowers away; but could never tell her who had been so thoughtful as to send them. It was sad that I could not talk with my parents about anything personal. It made me realise that, as soon as I could afford it, I must try to find my own flat.

The British film industry had made some fine films during the War, and it was now poised to take off. A feature film was being cast, *The Master of Bankdam,* adapted from a novel by Thomas Armstrong. Set in the nineteenth century, it centred around three generations of Yorkshire woollen-mill owners and was the classic 'trouble at t'mill' story. The principal part was played by Tom Walls, who had given up playing farce and was now an accepted character actor. It also starred Anne Crawford, Dennis Price and a young Jimmy Hanley.

The casting director came to see me in *The Hasty Heart* and I was invited to do a screen test for a leading role, the young man who was the son of the wealthy family. I was offered the part, but since the character appeared throughout the picture, the film company asked that I should be released from the midweek matinée, should they wish to call me. Firth Shepherd refused, which was pretty mean seeing as I had an excellent understudy, and would not even be required every Wednesday. In those days theatre managements were not only powerful, but dictatorial, and considering the career of a young actor would never have occurred to them. Nowadays, a theatre management is much more understanding. If an artist is going to be seen in the cinema or television, it helps the play and they try to accommodate accordingly.

I lost that part and was offered instead a smaller role, which would not take me away from the matinée. The part I was originally offered was given to a young actor who had just come out of the services. His name was David Tomlinson. It was an excellent role and David did well in it, going on to appear in a succession of films. Our professional paths crossed again nearly thirty years later, when I took over the leading role in *Boeing-Boeing* in the West End, a part which he had originally created.

When *The Hasty Heart* finished its tour, and the repertory companies began to present it as one of their weekly productions, I was invited to play the role of Yank, the American, at the Intimate Theatre, Palmers Green. The week-long engagement was significant because the resident producer was a man called Ronald Kerr, who later greatly influenced my career and development as an actor. He was not only a supremely gifted director, especially in weekly rep; he also had a good memory. Nearly two years later, when he was running the repertory theatre in Bromley and was casting the Terence Rattigan play *While the Sun Shines,* he was looking for a young actor to play the American. He remembered my performance in *The Hasty Heart* and tracked me down. It was the start of one of the most interesting phases of my professional life.

Before that, Stanley French, who had taken over the Firth

Shepherd Management when Firth unexpectedly died, sent out what must have been the last tour of *Arsenic and Old Lace,* the comedy that had run for a record period at the Strand Theatre in London. The music halls were not doing well; variety was in decline. Perhaps they had stuck for too long to a rigid format. To lure audiences back, Moss Empires tried something different: a very successful West End comedy adapted to a twice-nightly length of two hours. It did not quite work, because the variety audiences were not ready for plays and the 'legit' actors in the show were not conditioned to pace themselves for this kind of audience. Also, even if we had a lot of laughs in the first house, we had to keep moving to be sure the curtain came down on time. Two minutes over the allotted time and the stage manager was shouting at us, since there was only fifteen minutes in which to get the first audience out to allow the second house in. It was an interesting experience, and wonderful to have the chance to play such a marvellous comedy role as Mortimer Brewster, the leading character, created in the West End by the incomparable Naunton Wayne. I was not very good in the part: it was too much too soon. That tour did not close Moss Empires, but it probably did not help their survival.

One of the most memorable things about *Arsenic and Old Lace* was the lovely blonde actress, Sheila Latimer, who played my fiancée. It is very helpful, and enjoyable, to be attracted to the person playing opposite you. If you both happen to be unattached and the attraction is very strong, it is a joy and a bonus. It is said that some actors always fall in love with their leading ladies, and it is true that when the adrenalin is pumping and emotions are highly charged, anything can happen. Things usually calm down, however, when the curtain falls, and if those involved are happily committed to someone else, everything soon falls back into proportion. It is something that people outside show business do not understand, and it often leads to accusations of insincerity and shallowness, not helped by the type of remark I once heard in the Green Room Club, when a fairly distinguished elderly actor said, 'You need to have an affair with your leading lady when you're on tour. It's the only thing that relieves the boredom.'

The worst thing that can happen is that you cannot stand the person playing opposite you. Then it does require skill to convey any warmth, let alone passion. It has only happened to me once, and then for the saddest reason – the girl had no sense of personal hygiene. Quite simply, she smelt. All the cast, except her, were aware of it, but nobody could find a way to tell her. Even the wardrobe mistress, who had to wash all the clothes, complained to the company manager, but he did nothing. I had the worst of it as I had to play love scenes with her every night. She was a very beautiful girl who later married happily, so she must have got rid of her problem somehow. Or perhaps her husband didn't mind.

The tour of *Arsenic and Old Lace* finished and another producer with a good memory gave me an exciting opportunity. Fred O'Donovan had moved from radio to the new, developing world of BBC television. Everything was transmitted live from the tiny studios in Alexandra Palace in north London. The cameras were static for the most part and the heat from the lights was intense, so you sweated all the time you were on the set. The play was Noël Coward's *Hay Fever*. Frequently revived, it would now be seen on television for the first time. I played the juvenile lead, Sandy.

The skill of the technicians and producers in those early days helped lay the foundations for the quality television the BBC pioneered, which later gave Britain an enviable reputation in this area of entertainment. The Auntie BBC attitude, however, persisted and even the announcers at the time appeared in evening clothes. It seems that the BBC was not able to exploit their early successes and, once again, something the British had invented was taken over and exploited by a more commercially minded nation, in this instance America. At least the BBC tried to preserve the quality, while America was saying, never mind the quality, feel the length – and count the money.

6

· · · · · · · ·

Constant Change of Character

IN the summer of 1947, the theatrical impresario Emile Littler
decided to revive the classic farce *Charley's Aunt*. It had not
been seen for many years, and the great attraction of this
revival was to be the set and the costumes, which were of the
period when it was first performed in 1896. The rights of the play,
written by Brandon Thomas, had passed to his family, and Jevan
Brandon Thomas was to direct. There were no well-known names
in the cast; the management hoped that the public would be drawn
by the name of the play, and by Cecil Beaton's set and costumes,
which were magnificent.

We rehearsed in the hottest summer I can remember, and I soon
realised that Jevan was one of those directors who liked to have a
whipping boy in his cast, and that I was the one he had picked. It
could have been because he had played the part of Jack Chesney,
the role in which I had been cast, and thought no one could do it
as well as he, or he may simply have had no confidence as a director,
and had to shout and scream to make himself feel important. I had
never experienced anything like it, and tried to do as he asked, or
ordered. A director today would never behave like he did, and
certainly no cast today would stand for it, but the cast then was too
inexperienced and unsure of themselves to stand up to him.

In many ways, the part of Jack is the straight-man role. He is the
organiser of the elaborate plot to dress up Lord Fancourt-Babberley
as Charley's Aunt. It should have been a very easy role for me to
play, but I was slowly going to pieces as Jevan sapped my self-

confidence. He would suddenly stride across the rehearsal room, come right up close, and in front of the whole cast shout, 'What's the matter with you? Why can't you get it right? What d'you think you're doing? Where's the pace? Where's the energy? Don't you listen to what I say? Can't you learn to act?' Then I would over-act and become unnatural. He would say nothing for a day or two, and even be reasonable and pleasant. Then, just as I was gaining a little confidence, he would suddenly explode again and start to shout at me. I was beginning to think that I was in the wrong profession, or at least in the wrong part, and I went to Emile Littler to ask if I could be released from my contract. He was very pleasant, and gave me the confidence to continue. I never felt at ease in the role, however, and was always on edge whenever Jevan visited us on tour.

Before the tour began, I had spent most of my savings on a car. It was my pride and joy. There were very few second-hand cars around at the time, since no new ones had been built during the War. The one I found had been renovated by a mechanic who ran a small mews garage in Kensington. It was one of the very early box-shaped Fords, built in the 1930s, an open car with a very dilapidated roof. I paid £164, which was not only a lot of money then, but also all my savings; but I had what I had always dreamed of owning – my own car.

In those days, you had to obtain permission to travel by car on tour, rather than join the Sunday train call. I remember the remarks of Emile's production manager when he first saw my car. He said to the company manager, 'What have we done? It's held together with string and sealing wax. Will he ever arrive?' I did arrive, but the car became increasingly unreliable and I was later forced to abandon it for the train.

Everything for a touring production went by train in those days. The scenery travelled in pantechnicons, and we travelled at a reduced rate, third class, in reserved compartments. On a Sunday, innumerable theatre companies would be criss-crossing Britain, often with elaborate changes of train at Crewe, Nuneaton or Doncaster, where you met other groups going the other way. Today, the scenery goes by road, and the cast get there as best they can.

During the tour, I learnt about theatrical digs. All over the country, there were a host of people called theatrical landladies.

Some were good, some were embarrassing, and others were terrible. Actors would swap addresses. Nowadays, Equity has a 'digs list'; then, you obtained addresses from the local theatre manager. Actors who had toured a lot kept their own jealously guarded list, and it was wise to write well in advance to be sure of the best accommodation.

Some digs were first class, like those of dear old Mrs McKay in Edinburgh, who had been a landlady for years. She was over eighty when I stayed with her, had one breast missing due to a mastectomy, but was very sprightly and full of yarns about the 'theatricals', as we were called, who had stayed with her. She had books of photographs and appreciative messages from satisfied lodgers. She was not cheap: she asked the top rate in 1948, four guineas a week, for which you had your breakfast, lunch and meal after the show. You could not have been more comfortable in an hotel.

I think, without exception, that all landladies thought the sexual morals of theatre people very low, and if they had more than one room to let, they took it for granted that you would be jumping in and out of each other's beds. Some were sanguine; others informed you on arrival what they expected. There was one forbidding-looking lady with broad shoulders and solid build, who told me in stentorian Yorkshire tones when I arrived at her house in Sheffield, 'Before I show you your room, let me say I've been taking theatricals for years and we keep a clean house here. No hanky-panky. If you bring anyone back, she is out by 11.30. If I find anyone in your room, you'll be out before you can say bread and butter.' I believed her every word, and she had the muscles to back them up. The digs, in fact, turned out to be quite good.

One day I asked if she had ever had trouble with her lodgers. She told me how she had heard noises in one of her single rooms during the night. She apparently marched in to discover a variety comic, who was renting the room, in bed with what she described as 'some little tart from the chorus'. Then she went on to say that they had no clothes on, which horrified her even more, and added, 'It's one thing to behave like that, but to do it without clothes on, it's right indecent.' I asked her what happened next. 'I threw him out, of course. And the tart. I picked up all their things and threw them out of the window, and they followed.' I had visions of this little comedian and his girlfriend stark naked in the street, trying to retrieve their clothes and get dressed, while the remainder of their possessions rained down on them from an upstairs window.

The lady intrigued me. I asked her one day if she had any family. She replied, 'Three. They've all flown the nest.' I thought, I am not surprised; could not get away quickly enough. I tactfully enquired how she had managed to have a family if she felt it was wrong to take her clothes off in bed. Pulling herself up to her full height, she replied, 'My husband had his full married rights, but he never had sight of where it all happens. That would be disgusting.'

Other landladies were openly flirtatious. On the tour of *Charley's Aunt,* the actor who played my father, John Huson, had great difficulty with his landlady in Cardiff. He was a very good-looking man and she pursued him all week. Johnny could not stand the sight of her. By Friday she was getting desperate, and when we returned after the show for our supper, she greeted us wearing a negligée. 'Mr Huson,' she said, 'I've been making myself available all week and you've done nothing. I know you theatricals, you take these things in your stride. Why don't you make me one of your conquests? Or are you one of those pouffosexuals?' Johnny was deeply offended and could be very pompous when he wanted. 'Madam,' he said, 'I am not interested in your overtures. I am not interested in my own sex. I am interested at present only in my inner man. Kindly take your overheated body to your overheated kitchen, and bring some of your overheated food as rapidly as possible.' We did not see her again until we paid before leaving.

There are people in our profession who might have accepted the invitation, like the actor who is reported, in an almost apocryphal story, to have been going through his bill at the end of his stay when he came across an item at the bottom, 'Use of cruet, £2.' He asked what it meant. The landlady replied, 'I understand from my daughter Gracie that you've been having your way with her this week and that's in there to cover those extras you've enjoyed.'

When *Charley's Aunt* reached Reading, I stayed in a very pleasant house. The other lodger was a Swede called Gilbert Houke, whose family's circus was visiting the town. Gilbert was young with a fine physique, and had done nearly everything in the circus. He now had the most dangerous job of all, working with tigers, having taken on the task when the previous trainer had been killed by one of the animals. It had happened in Paris during the War, and Gilbert showed me a huge scrapbook full of press pictures of the tragedy.

In the middle of a performance one of the tigers unexpectedly leapt on the trainer and mauled him. There were German officers in the audience with pistols, who tried to shoot the animal, but some of their bullets ricocheted off the bars of the cage, wounding people and, I believe, killing one or two. It was an horrific scene. The tiger was eventually killed, while circus officials tried to cajole and prod the others back through the tunnel to their cages. The photographs told it all, and my French was just good enough for me to understand the newspaper clippings, which described it as a night of hideous murder and mayhem.

I was lost in admiration for Gilbert as he explained how to handle tigers. He told me that they are far more dangerous than lions. Drop your guard with them for one minute and they might attack. Consequently, you always had to dominate them, let them know you were in control. He kept me up most nights with circus tales, and I was enthralled. He then took me down to the circus encampment and I met the clowns, the jugglers and the acrobats and inhaled that distinctive smell of animals and sawdust. One evening, he asked me if I would like to join him next day in the cage with his tigers. I was a little frightened, but I readily agreed. I could not disappoint him. He said he would be feeding them, so the danger was minimal, but instructed me to stay close to him and try to let the animals feel I was in control.

I was in the cage quite a few minutes while Gilbert spoke sternly but with obvious affection to his tigers. He made them walk about, always making sure that I was close to him, and then backed out with me. When I was telling a friend this story recently, she said, 'That must have been invaluable experience for when you became chairman of *Just a Minute*.' I had never seen it quite like that before. I said, 'Well, at least I don't need a whip and horsemeat to exercise some control.'

Years later, I met some performers from Billy Smart's Circus. They had recently returned from Sweden and I asked if they knew of the Houke family. They did, to my delight, but they also told me that Gilbert was dead, killed by one of his beloved tigers.

The tour of *Charley's Aunt* seemed endless. Business was always good and dates were constantly being added. We had been out for sixteen weeks, and then came the incredible news: we were going to the West End, to be the Christmas attraction at the Palace Theatre. We had a few extra rehearsals, and more screamings from Jevan, but on this occasion I had some support. Ruth Gower, who played the real Charley's Aunt, Donna Lucia D'Alvardorez, spoke up for the rest of the cast and asked that Jevan stop picking on me, and control himself at rehearsals. He certainly calmed down, but I was never at ease with him, or as confident in performance as I should have been.

The season at the Palace Theatre was very successful. We were even honoured by a visit from Queen Mary, resplendent in her famous toque, sitting in the royal box. The cast were presented in the second interval, and as I had not been briefed about royal protocol and told not to speak unless I had been addressed, I made a terrible gaffe. I thought at one point she was struggling for something to say and tried to help out. She seemed unperturbed, and took it in her stride, but the cast fully expected to see me taken off to the Tower after the final curtain.

In the spring we were off on tour again – more train calls, more digs, more theatre gossip about who was doing what with whom. Then, in early summer, it was all over.

I was completely exhausted both physically and emotionally and could hardly move. The stress of the last year had taken its toll. I was not ill, but had no energy for anything. The therapy of work in our profession, however, is amazing. I made a rapid recovery following a phone call from Ronnie Kerr, who asked if I was free to go to Bromley and play the American in Terence Rattigan's wartime comedy *While the Sun Shines*.

Terence Rattigan is a master craftsman. His comedies are stylish and witty, and his characters beautifully drawn. In *While the Sun Shines,* the American is a larger than life, rather ingenuous person, and I enjoyed every minute of the week's engagement. The greatest pleasure, however, was working with a producer who gave you positive direction and encouragement. The confidence you exude in these circumstances communicates itself to the audience, and I understand the people of Bromley actually thought I was an American. It was just the tonic I needed.

Ronnie was very complimentary and asked if I would like to stay on as one of the resident company. I was reluctant to go back to repertory after working in the West End, but Ronnie was very persuasive and convinced me that I still had a lot to learn. I did not know at the time that he had been a teacher at RADA, the Royal Academy of Dramatic Art. As a theatre director, or producer, he had a gift for not only managing to stage and direct a play in a week, but also for giving you limited but sufficient guidance about the character you were playing. For those who were prepared to work hard it was therefore possible, with very little rehearsal time, to give a real performance rather than simply walk through the play speaking the lines you had somehow crammed into your head.

It all begins on a Monday, with dress rehearsals all day for the production opening that night – sometimes while they are still putting the finishing touches to the set and lighting it. Monday evening, the play opens. Tuesday morning, you meet to read through the play that will open the following week, and the moves are marked out at the same time. Tuesday afternoon, you have some time to learn the lines of the new play before the evening performance of the current one. Wednesday morning, you rehearse the first act of the forthcoming play; Wednesday afternoon you run through the second act and learn more lines. Thursday morning, you rehearse the second act; in the afternoon, it is once through the third act with, you hope, more time to learn lines. Friday morning, you rehearse the third act (if it is a two-act play, it is broken down into three segments for rehearsal). On Friday afternoon you go through the whole play, and on Saturday morning you do the same again, hopefully with words and moves now in your head. Saturday evening sees the last two performances of the current production. Sunday is free, and for the conscientious there is time to become completely conversant with the lines of the new play. On Monday, the whole process begins all over again.

I worked very hard at each role every week. By listening to Ronnie's guidance, and by spending all day Sunday repeatedly going over the part until I had absorbed the words and the character, I was able to give a rounded performance on the Monday night, when the critic from the local paper was in the audience.

Ronnie was correct. I soon discovered that I had a lot to learn and the experience I gained in Bromley was invaluable. I found out quite soon that I was not very good at playing straight roles or romantic parts. My forte was character acting and comedy. The irony now is that the roles I am invariably offered, particularly on television, are very straight, which could be the result of playing a straight man to comedians for many years.

I was contracted initially to stay at the New Theatre in Bromley for twelve weeks. I then stayed on without a contract for nearly two years, and not only enjoyed it, but was grateful for the opportunities Ronnie gave me and the experience I gained. I was paid £12 a week, a good rep salary in those days. From that I had to find money for my lodgings, which were three guineas including meals at the little Hackwood Hotel in Widmore Road, extra food, and clothes. Every actor in repertory was expected to have two lounge suits and one evening suit, as well as shirts and shoes. The management only supplied period clothes. There was also make-up, laundry and fares for the occasional visit to London.

I was now running a small car again, a rather dilapidated Hillman Minx. It was a drop head, a type of car I have always loved. Once again, it cost me all my savings to buy and any extra cash from my earnings to keep it on the road, but it was worth it. I enjoy cars and over the years have owned quite a variety. In the 1960s I had a succession of Alvis cars, one of the finest British cars on the road, with a beautiful, classic line. In fact, I owned one of the last cars Alvis made before they were taken over by Rover, and wish I had kept it as an investment.

The New Theatre Bromley, later destroyed by fire and rebuilt in 1978 and named the Churchill Theatre, had not been running as a repertory theatre for long when I joined it, but we soon created a loyal and faithful following. Latterly, Ronnie mounted more ambitious productions, such as *The Barretts of Wimpole Street* and Sheridan's *The School for Scandal,* with the resident company augmented by extra actors. Kenneth Williams appeared in *The School for Scandal,* playing a comparatively small and entirely straight role. He had guested the previous week in a thriller, *The Shop at Sly Corner,* in which he played an eccentric young teenager who worked in the jeweller's shop of the title. He was an original even then, but for some reason Ronnie did not warm to him and found him difficult to cast. The more conventional, regular members of the cast could not cope with him at all, finding him odd and overbearing. I enjoyed his theatrical, camp stories, but would never have predicted that he would become the cult comedian he did.

Kenneth's gift for spontaneous humour and his ability to ad-lib showed itself on many occasions. He told me a story of the time when he was playing in an Agatha Christie thriller. The character he played was shot quite early in the play. His assailant had pulled out the gun and fired at very close range. Kenneth was supposed to sink to the floor, fatally wounded. When using guns in plays, there is always a standby in the hands of the stage manager, so if the one the actor is holding fails to fire, the spare one is fired from the wings. It never sounds as realistic, as the shot comes after the actor has pulled the trigger and spoken the line, and the noise comes from offstage, but at least the audience are aware of what has happened. On this occasion, the gun on stage failed to go off, as did the stage manager's. Silence. The actors on stage were transfixed. The audience were whispering; some were laughing. Kenneth saved the situation. He hissed to the actor with the gun, 'Throw it at me.' In desperation, the actor did as he was told. As the gun hit him, Kenneth groaned, clutched his stomach, sank to the floor and came out with the unforgettable line, 'You never told me the gun was poisoned.' He died to audience laughter and applause, and the play was rescued.

An actress who appeared in a number of productions at the New Theatre while I was there was Noele Gordon. She was particularly good as Elizabeth Barrett in *The Barretts of Wimpole Street,* in which Ronnie played the father. I had one of the smaller roles as her brother.

At the time, I had persuaded Ronnie to let me photograph the show, so there were pictures in the foyer every week. I had been interested in photography ever since my father gave me my first camera, a box Brownie, at the age of eight. I wish I had used it during the War. My father had always been an excellent photographer, with an artist's eye for composition. He even did his own enlarging. He had given me his trusted Rolleiflex, which he had used for years, and this was the camera with which I photographed the Bromley shows. It was quite a challenge, as I had just half an hour after the dress rehearsal to set up, bring in extra lights, and compose the pictures. After the opening performance, I delivered the single roll of twelve photographs to a local photographer. He would have them developed by 9.30 a.m. on the Tuesday, when I would drop in, look at the negatives, choose the best, and have prints on display in the theatre foyer by evening. The theatre management, however, were reluctant to part with extra money to an actor. In addition, as business was good, a promotional exercise to increase box office returns was deemed unimportant. They gave me £2 a week and the cost of the film and prints. Ronnie also seemed insensitive to the situation, saying simply, 'Just think of the experience you're getting as a photographer.' All through my career I have noticed an unwillingness on the part of employers to admit that an actor could have any special talent, let alone an extra talent, for which he should be rewarded. It is almost as if they want us to feel that we are still strolling players, the vagabonds of society, lucky to be accepted. It is a very British trait, not to praise anyone for fear it might make them swollen-headed or, worse still, prompt the agent to ask for more money. In Britain, if a television company has a successful show, the producers are delighted and invariably say how lucky a particular personality or performer is to be appearing in it. By contrast, with a success in America, the producers shout about it and then usually add how fortunate they are to have a particular personality contributing to that success.

When I was photographing at Bromley, I was particularly pleased with the photographs I took of *The Barretts of Wimpole Street*. There was one of Noele Gordon as Elizabeth Barrett which she said was one of her favourite photographs.

I was very fond of Noele, a fine actress, a true professional and a 'real trouper'. She deserved all the television success that came later, although the part of Meg Richardson in *Crossroads* demanded little of her true talent. It was she who helped establish that show and when it was later decided to make changes to increase the soap's declining popularity, once again it was thought that the show was greater than its star and Noele was quite suddenly dropped. The series never recovered; nor, alas, did Noele.

Ronnie inspired great loyalty, but he was by no means an easy man with whom to work. There was a mildly sadistic streak in him. For instance, he had a habit of sneaking up on stage during rehearsals and singeing the back of your hair with his lighted cigarette. He only did this to people he liked and knew well, and usually to young, male members of his cast to whom he was clearly attracted. I had learnt by this time how to deal with unwarranted attention from my own sex – not that Ronnie ever made any actual advances to me. The nearest was the hair singeing. Once, I was so angry that I lifted him bodily off his feet and manhandled him into a chair in the wings. The thing was, he enjoyed it. It was just the kind of reaction he had been hoping for.

Such was our affection for Ronnie that when he had to resign from the New Theatre and later went to revive the ailing rep theatre in Hayes, Middlesex, all his regular team of actors and actresses went with him. We even helped him to redecorate the inside of the building. Subsequently, he moved back to the Intimate Theatre, Palmers Green, and again, most of his team from Bromley moved with him.

One of the greatest lessons about acting I learnt from Ronnie is the value of good diction. I have the impression that it is not something that is given much attention in drama schools now. The vogue for naturalistic acting, which you see most vividly displayed in the cinema and to a great extent on television, where the desire to sound real at all costs, whether or not the words can be understood, seems to have developed into a cult. If you cannot understand the words, how can you follow the plot? Just because people in real life may speak in a sloppy and incoherent way does not mean they have to be imitated. A character has to be drawn from life, and the accent has to be genuine, but if the diction is poor, clarity is lost and audience concentration goes. I worked hard on my diction and even went for voice production lessons with a marvellous woman called Iris Warren. These were the only lessons associated with my craft that I have ever had, and they were invaluable.

While I have paid attention to diction ever since, I have also developed a knack of speaking languages and dialects in gibberish, where no intelligible word is used, or where recognisable words are strung together to make complete nonsense. It is something I exploited when I later worked in cabaret. It was also very useful during one particular production at the New Theatre.

Ronnie had built such an appreciative audience that he was able to undertake a most ambitious production for a weekly repertory theatre, a Shakespeare play. For this, some of the cast with the longer parts rehearsed for a fortnight; those of us with smaller parts were given the normal week. The first production was *Othello,* in which Ronnie himself played the title part. Following its success, a year later he presented *The Merchant of Venice*, in which he cast himself as Shylock. It was an incredible feat to run a theatre, direct plays and now and then perform a huge Shakespeare role every night.

My embarrassing moment in this production, when speaking nonsense turned out to be a real asset, came one evening in the last scene. I was playing Gratiano, the friend of Bassanio and Antonio the merchant. After Portia has successfully defended Antonio against Shylock's charges and returned to her home at Belmont with her maid Nerissa, both now dressed again as women, they are talking in the courtyard when suddenly in burst the three men with tales of what happened in the courtroom. On this particular evening, however, the three men did not rush on stage; two of them had missed their cue. I was the only one waiting in the wings. There was a pause on stage, which turned to silence as the two women looked despairingly towards the wings. I whispered to the stage manager, 'Get the others,' and then, with an air of supreme confidence based on blind ignorance of what I was going to do, swept on to the stage to greet Portia and Nerissa. I bowed to them and launched into what can only be described as Shakespearian gibberish. Keeping the rhythm of blank verse, and using Shakespearian phrases and words taken at random from other speeches, I ploughed on in a continuous, meaningless monologue. Jocelyn Parlane and Ann Castle, the two actresses on stage, were at first transfixed, then got the giggles, for which I took them to task in more stylised unintelligible nonsense. I kept going for what seemed like fifteen minutes, but was probably only four or five, until Bassanio and Antonio came running on, flushed and utterly confused at hearing Gratiano speak lines they had never heard in the play before. It was difficult to get back to the correct text and move the scene forward, but we did it and I think some members of the audience never realised anything was wrong. The more observant guessed what was happening and clapped, but I do not know whether it was to acknowledge my ingenuity or my downright cheek at trying to ad-lib our national poet. In my one-man show I re-create this situation with a great deal of embroidery, but fortunately there is none of the tension and panic that drove me to do it the first time.

7

. . . .

The Challenge of Cabaret

FTER working for nearly two years at the New Theatre in Bromley, followed by a stint at Hayes and then Palmers Green and Maidstone, I decided that it was time to try to get some work again in the West End. I did not have an agent, but the Spotlight Casting Directory was very good, sending me for jobs and letting me know when shows were being cast. With my repertory work I had proved to myself that my strengths lay in comedy and character roles, but invariably the parts for which I was now considered were those referred to as 'wet juveniles'. At the time, around 1950, there were a good many dreary, anaemic male juvenile roles in plays, and while I might have looked right for the kind of character that enters through the French windows and says in a very English voice, 'Anyone for tennis?', I was not very good at playing them.

In desperation to prove that I had a broader talent than might be judged from my features, I decided to put together a cabaret act. I had met Joan Ling's nephew, Peter Ling, who wanted to become a scriptwriter once he had completed his National Service. (He later became very well known as the author of *Crossroads*.) I had the idea to take off the popular films from Europe and Japan by acting out scenes in gibberish, keeping the music of the language but not speaking a coherent word. Peter helped me put together a routine, for which I think I paid him £9. It is a routine that I have worked on over the years and it has become a significant part of my cabaret and stage act. It is one that I have never performed on television in this country, because once you have exposed material that has been polished to a few million viewers, its originality is lost in one fell swoop.

A chance to try this material came when the Under Thirties Theatre Club, of which I was a member and whose aims were to promote the work of those starting in show business, required a cabaret for a party they were having in a London club. I volunteered. I realised, however, that I needed music for some of my other material and spoke to another member of the club, a talented young student actor called Leslie Crowther. An accomplished musician, he was extremely helpful, and we struck up what was to be a long-lasting friendship.

I was extraordinarily nervous: I had never performed a cabaret act before and the material was all entirely new. In fact, it was to a great extent due to Leslie's reassurance that my material was funny, that I had the confidence to stand up and perform. It went surprisingly well for a first attempt and I was encouraged to write to a man called Frank Shaw, who ran a very smart club called the Cavalero. It was exclusive and intimate, catering principally for the young people who moved in smart circles – the men tended to be members of the Brigade of Guards; their girlfriends, invariably debutantes, would often appear in the pages of the *Tatler*.

Frank Shaw booked me a number of times, both at the Cavalero and then, later, at his new club, the Caballero. It was while working here that I had the idea for what was to be one of my most successful 'point' numbers, which was written by a clever lyricist-composer friend, John Hurst. It was called 'Up Guards and At 'Em' and was an affectionate send-up of the typical Guardee types who patronised the club. They were distinguishable in civilian life by their rolled umbrellas and their bowler hats with a slightly enlarged crown, worn at a rakish angle over their eyes. With a rolled umbrella in my hand and with the right kind of bowler tilted forward, I performed the number, which always went well, particularly with the audience at whom it was poking fun. Of all the material I worked, the Guards number most reflected the social climate of the 1950s, and seems very dated in today's more egalitarian society. The verses described what it was like to be a member of the Brigade of Guards, with some topical, satirical references to their behaviour on and off parade. One of the choruses ran:

Up Guards and at 'em,
That's what the ladies cry,
I've never met a Guardsman yet
Who knew the reason why.

So up Guards and at 'em,
The soldiers of the Queen.
Put down that sublieutenant, dear
You don't know where he's been.

One evening Princess Margaret was at the Caballero with a group of people, some of whom had a distinctly military air. Frank Shaw came up to me with a worried expression, saying, 'Nicholas, I think you should drop the Guards number since there seems to be a Guards officer in Princess Margaret's party.' Knowing the British ability to laugh at themselves, I thought he was being over-sensitive. I asked the manager if he could tactfully find out exactly which regiment the officer was in. He said he thought it was the Blues and Royals. So I made out that the character I was portraying was a member of the Coldstream. Whether I got it right or wrong, the number went over very well.

Working in cabaret, and regularly returning home in the early hours of the morning, you see the other side of life in any large city. Prostitutes were still walking the streets, though it was against the law. It was not until the 1960s, when a great effort was made to crack down on women offering themselves for hire on the street, that their services were advertised in newpapers and magazines. Certain areas and streets of London were known as places where sex could be bought, and apparently the prices varied from place to place, depending on the standard of service on offer. Jermyn Street was very smart; Shepherd's Market was noted for kinky sex; Gerrard Street in Soho was middle-of-the-road; Lisle Street, also in Soho near Leicester Square, was where you found what were described as 'cheap tarts'; and the Bayswater Road was even more downmarket.

I discovered a great deal of this when I struck up a conversation with a prostitute one night after she had accosted me. I told her that I was not interested in paying for sex, but I was interested to know why she was prepared to sell herself in this way. The girl turned out to be a former nurse. She said, 'I got fed up looking

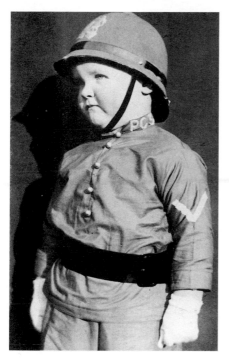

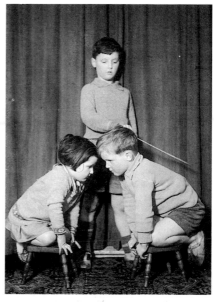

The budding actor aged three

The circus: John as ringmaster with his two horses, Patricia and myself, in the nursery at Grantham

The very young juvenile

An early character role

Above On holiday in Studland with my mother, John, Patricia and Polly the dog

Right With my father and John during the war

Keeping up with the wartime news

Noele Gordon as Elizabeth Barrett in *The Barretts of Wimpole Street*
photographed by me at Bromley Rep, 1948

First Shakespeare role, Montano in
Othello at Bromley Rep, 1948

Trying to be the young matinée idol,
1949

With Beryl Reid in the revue *First Edition* at the Watergate Theatre, 1954

As an elderly character in a sketch in *First Edition*

With (left to right) Kenneth Horne, Dora Bryan, Richard Murdoch and Sam Costa in *Much Binding*, 1954

With Richard Attenborough in the film *Brothers-in-Law*, 1957

With Mylène Demongeot in *Upstairs and Downstairs*, 1956

With Arthur Haynes and Maria Pavlou receiving some production notes from George Black during *Get Happy,* 1956

Arthur Haynes as his famous tramp character with the Reverend Parsons

Playing it straight as a policeman outside Number 10 with Arthur Haynes and Dermot Kelly as dustmen, 1960

With Arthur Haynes in the unusual role of an army officer challenging another officer to play Russian roulette, 1963

Dr Parsons coping with Arthur Haynes as a difficult patient, 1957

With Aileen Cochran and Arthur Haynes relaxing between rehearsals, 1958

Showing off my newly acquired Alvis outside Elstree studios to Arthur Haynes, Leslie Noyes, Michael Henry and Dermot Kelly, 1962

With Denise as two Martians in the award-winning commercial for Blue Cars Holidays, 1960

after the needs of men who were lying in bed. I thought I'd get into bed myself and look after their needs that way – and make a much better living.' She was very knowledgeable about the problems of walking the streets, of the hazards of working alone and not having what she called a 'manager'. It was a glimpse into another world.

My cabaret work flourished. A variety of places featured cabaret, some consisting only of a single act; others a full floor show. There were clubs with an exclusive membership, nightclubs, which charged an entrance fee, and restaurants, where there was also dancing. In the late 1950s, Al Burnett, who ran the Stork Club, opened the Pigalle and presented a glamorous floor show of over an hour's entertainment featuring a star name. This was in Piccadilly, but like nearly all the other clubs and restaurants featuring cabaret, it has long since disappeared. To some extent they were of their time, mirroring the exclusive, sophisticated world enjoyed by those with money.

Typical of the larger venues that died a natural death was Ciro's. It disappeared in the early 1950s as it was too large to survive simply as a restaurant. A beautiful, elegant room, with high ceilings and quite a large dance area, it appeared even then like a relic from another age. In prewar days it had no doubt boasted expensive floor shows with glamorous girls. It catered for the rich and well connected, with a magnificent wine cellar and amazing cuisine. The latter still existed when I worked there, but all they could manage in the way of entertainment was a single act, usually someone comparatively unknown, like myself. The salary for the week was about twenty pounds, but included a free dinner with wine after the show. This must have cost far more than my fee, and for a week I dined as never before, and tasted wines about which I had previously only read. Later, when the club was about to close, a number of previous cabaret performers were asked back to give a free show and dine at the management's expense. For nostalgic reasons, I was happy to accept. I appeared there on the Saturday, and can boast that I performed the last cabaret at Ciro's. Less generous friends say that after my last act there, Ciro's *had* to close.

This country has no tradition of cabaret, which you find on the continent, particularly in France. We have a tradition of music hall, which is much broader and more brash, and caters principally to a less demanding audience. Those who sought more discerning entertainment found it in the legitimate theatre. Cabaret was always very much a no-man's-land between legitimate theatre and variety in our country, where you strayed at your peril, as the audiences were not conditioned to show respect for the entertainment in a restaurant. The performer was often treated as just another item on the menu, which they could enjoy or ignore as they wished. I worked in cabaret in Paris once and was deeply impressed with the way the audience gave their undivided attention while you were performing. It was more like playing to a theatre audience who had come to enjoy the entertainment and, if they liked what they saw and heard, showed their appreciation before returning to the other attractions of food and wine.

The only room from this period that survives today is Quaglino's, but that has the advantage of being in a thriving hotel. My first engagement at Quaglino's was the cabaret break for which I had been working. Based on my performances at the Caballero and other, less fashionable restaurants, I was booked to appear there for a month in August 1954. This was the quiet time, when less well-known artists were booked. The room was not easy to work, as it was rectangular and the cabaret stood in front of the band, with the diners mostly on either side and only a solitary row of tables facing you. If you played to one side of the room at any time, those on the opposite side only had your back view. The audiences were always appreciative, if a little quiet on occasions, but then I was young and unknown and had to win them over. The cabaret at Quag's always doubled with the little Allegro room downstairs, where the audience were more my age and related to my material more quickly.

I had one unfortunate incident at Quag's. I used to do an encore if the act had gone well, which consisted of Winston Churchill, one of my most successful impersonations, giving a talk on cooking, a subject which had suddenly become popular on television, describing how he made a cabinet pudding. He was then Prime Minister, and all his ingredients were facetious comments about various members of his Government, especially those in the public eye. It was political satire at a time when it was not usual to send up leading politicians, let alone impersonate respected public figures. It usually went well, particularly with the young crowd. On this occasion, I returned to a warm reception, introduced the item and launched into the impersonation. Instead of the usual ripple of applause that greeted the opening, a man with a powerful, military-sounding voice suddenly shouted from the gloom, 'How *dare* you!' The audience went very quiet. I stopped and turned to face the dark area from where the voice came. 'I beg your pardon,' I said, which was pretty tame, but I could think of nothing else. The voice came back, even louder, 'How dare you, sir. How dare you take off the great man, you scalliwag.' Having regained some composure, I said, 'Why? Can you impersonate him better?' This only incensed him further. 'If you carry on, you impudent toad, I'll come up there and knock your block off.' The audience was now deathly quiet – the British always become embarrassed when someone makes a scene. I could not change my act just because one individual did not like it. I turned my back on him and tried to carry on, but my legs were shaking. There was a scuffling behind me. My bluff had failed. The irate, possibly drunk, man was storming towards me. The orchestra leader shouted a warning and I swung round to find a very tall man making a lunge at me. My early boxing training had not been in vain. I parried his fist, but stopped myself from hitting him. I could see the headlines the following day: 'Cabaret entertainer knocks down customer.' The slippery dance floor saved me, for as I fended off his attack, he lost his balance and slid to the floor. He was up immediately, but further embarrassment was saved by his lady companion who, with another friend, dragged him back to their table. What amazed me was that nobody in the audience said a word. They simply returned to their food, or pretended the whole thing was not happening. In America, they would have shouted; in France they would have taken sides; in Italy they would probably have joined in, and in South America they would have started a riot.

My problem now was to finish and make my final exit. Today, I would probably ask if there was anybody else who wanted to express an opinion; then, I was too inexperienced. I tried a couple of throwaway jokes, but the audience were completely withdrawn. I walked off to polite applause, which was followed the next day by a request from the management not to aggravate the customers, even if they were drunk. It is amazing how attitudes have changed. I cannot imagine anyone today threatening to hit a performer if they impersonated Lady Thatcher or John Major, or any politician. And when you think how often the royal family are now impersonated – if anyone had tried that even thirty years ago, they would probably have been strung up on the spot.

One restaurant to which I returned frequently was the Royal Court Theatre Club, which was on the top floor of the Royal Court Theatre in Sloane Square and was owned and run by Clement Freud. A trained cook who had served his apprenticeship in the kitchens of the Dorchester, he was an expert in the culinary arts, as well as a very shrewd businessman. He also found time to be a sporting journalist.

When he started his club at the Royal Court in 1952, he was not a speaker in the raconteur sense, and probably had no aspirations to be one. When I first worked there in 1954, he used to step forward onto the small dance floor at midnight and say simply, 'In cabaret tonight, we have Nicholas Parsons.' By my second visit, he had stretched this introduction to, 'Before I introduce the cabaret tonight, I thought I would tell you a story.' Then, with his head slightly on one side, a dead-pan expression and rather lugubrious delivery, he would tell a rather suggestive joke. The audience enjoyed it, and he gained confidence. By my next visit, he was telling two or three stories, and they were getting broader. So it continued, until he was almost doing a comedy routine before introducing the cabaret.

I would return frequently to Clement's club. It was always the same money, but it was a marvellous venue to try out new material. There was a nucleus of young entertainers whom Clement called upon – Rolf Harris, Thelma Ruby, Lance Percival, Jimmy Thompson, Noel Harrison and Peter Reeves with Brian Blackburn. David Frost, then a researcher at Associated Rediffusion, did some of his first cabarets at the club; Dudley Moore and Jonathan Miller also worked there. Jonathan Miller's act was particularly esoteric. I remember Clement saying to me, 'He wasn't really right for this audience. And it's difficult to respond to someone who walks out to entertain in his bare feet.'

An engagement from Clement always began with a telephone call and a kind enquiry as to my availability in two weeks' time or, sometimes, the following week. If I was free, I would say yes. Money was never discussed. It was always ten pounds a week, which was quite good in those days. There was never any need for a contract or letter. It was all done as show business used to be conducted, on trust, and you were paid in full on your last Saturday. There was no nagging for fees weeks later.

By the late 1950s, Clement had become so assured in his story-telling that it became difficult to follow him. His clientele were used to his style and expected some outrageous stories. One evening before he introduced me, he finished by telling a long and very coarse story that I had last heard from my workmates on Clydebank. After he delivered the crude pay-off line, through the laughter he said, 'Would you now please welcome, Nicholas Parsons.' I went out to try to make the audience laugh with some gentle, subtle material. It was almost impossible and I asked Clement if he could tone down his routine before introducing me, as it was sometimes difficult to bring the audience round when I followed so rapidly after his string of stories. He was very understanding. From then on, he only engaged me when he was taking a holiday.

The success of any restaurant or club is entirely dependent on the personality of the individual running it. He or she needs to be a first-class host with shrewd business acumen and a strong per-sonality. Clement was all of these and made a huge success of his club, and it was very sad when the theatre failed to renew his lease in 1962, saying that they wanted the room for their experimental theatre work.

Some people patronised the club for the atmosphere, some for the cuisine, and some because they enjoyed the personality of the patron, whose agile brain and quick eye never missed a thing. He was always courteous, but could never suffer fools, and was never afraid to be candid in a subtle way with those he found unpleasant. On one occasion, a difficult customer complained to the waiter about the wine. The waiter reported it to Clement, who immedi-ately went up to the man's table and said very politely, 'You have a complaint?' 'Yes,' said the man. 'This wine is disgusting. It tastes like vinegar.' 'I'm so sorry,' said Clement. 'I'll bring you something else.' He took the bottle and the man's glass and returned with a glass, full to the brim. 'Would you like to try that?' he asked, in a very concerned manner. The man accepted the glass and took a large gulp. Almost immediately, he spluttered his mouthful all over the table. 'Good God, what was that?' 'That was vinegar,' said

Clement, with a wry smile. The man never returned, and Clement was perfectly happy.

I reached what seemed to be a peak in my cabaret career in 1956. The finest cabaret room in London, the Café de Paris, on a corner of Leicester Square, which had received a direct hit from a bomb during the War, was refurbished and opened again in 1955 to much publicity. Mecca, the leisure group, had bought the premises with the idea that even if the costs were not justified by the returns, any losses could be set against profits elsewhere, and they had the laudable aim of bringing back to the West End this wonderful venue and recapturing the style and sophistication for which the club had been famous.

No room could have been better designed for cabaret. Of reasonable size, it had a small dance area in front of the bandstand, and dining tables on three sides. There was a magnificent balcony with a wrought-iron balustrade all round, and to reach the dance floor, you came down one of the curved staircases on either side. This was also the staircase down which the cabaret came to perform. What a magnificent entrance it afforded.

There was a glamorous opening night, and thereafter the very best performers were engaged. Noël Coward did a season there, as did Marlene Dietrich, Maurice Chevalier, Jack Buchanan, Danny Kaye, Hermione Gingold and Hermione Baddeley. It was intended that the cabaret would be the main attraction, as it had been in the past. People would book a table because they wanted to see the artist, not simply because they wanted a meal out with entertainment attached. It was soon discovered, unfortunately, that the costs of running such an expensive restaurant did not cover the fees that name artists could command, and the public for this kind of entertainment had dwindled since the War. They might pack the restaurant for Coward, Dietrich or Chevalier, but other names did not have the pulling power, especially at the prices the restaurant was asking.

The management came up with an idea to attract custom and keep down costs. They announced that they were going to have a season of new, young, talented performers. I was booked on the strength of my previous work, principally at Quaglino's, and went along to see the room and absorb the atmosphere. The first in this season of new talent was a very young Shirley Bassey, who had been discovered in her home town of Cardiff and had recently appeared at the Adelphi Theatre in London's West End in a show introducing new performers. She was performing the night I visited the Café de Paris. She had what can only be described as raw talent. While her style was immature, there was no doubt that she would go places. Her singing at the time reminded me of Eartha Kitt, possibly because her big number had a rather suggestive lyric about burning her candle at both ends. The style of Shirley Bassey today is very different from the talented newcomer I saw then.

I was engaged at the Café de Paris for two weeks. It could have been intimidating, but there was something about the magnificent room that inspired confidence. Working there was one of my biggest show business successes to date, and it seemed as if it could be the springboard to greater things as a solo performer. Little did I realise that I was witnessing the end of an era. Shortly after the season of young cabaret artists, the Café de Paris closed, defeated by the cost of trying to run such an expensive establishment for a public who no longer wanted to dress up to go out, were less interested in stylish entertainment, and for whom there was more television of an increasingly high standard. Mecca turned the room into a dance hall, and so it remained for many years. What a sad end to one of the most elegant rooms in London.

In the late 1950s the larger clubs were slowly fading away. Some hung on for a while, like the Colony in Berkeley Square, a large room with a huge rising platform in the middle of the dance area from which you performed. The club had boasted a full floor show in its heyday, but had now lowered its sights and presented one artist in cabaret. It had a moneyed audience and a great many foreign visitors, which it attracted because of its prime position in a very fashionable area. I worked there more than once, performing the same type of material as I had at Quaglino's, but the audience was tougher. In my last appearance there in 1962, I had begun to work a lot of jokes and stories into my act, although I still leant heavily on my tried and tested routines about laughter, foreign films and the Guards number. It is interesting that of all the routines that I have ever worked, the only one that still makes any impact in the 1990s is the film routine, which was my first ever cabaret material.

The early 1960s was probably the true peak of my cabaret career.

I had the material that the late-night diners enjoyed, and there was a style and sophistication in the West End, which reached its height at the turn of the decade. I was engaged to work at the Savoy Hotel, which had always featured cabaret in their restaurant. The entertainment consisted of a mini floor show with dancers and a singer, and a name artist. Sometimes, the last was a visiting American star, occasionally a British star; but more often a successful performer from the cabaret circuit. As the audience was fairly cosmopolitan, I devised a new comedy routine about London, with topical verses and music written by John Hurst, and satirical jokes or quips about the city in between. We called the number 'Let's Take the Lid off London'. At the time, it had all the feel of the slick, clever material that was then popular in nightclubs; today, it simply sounds dated.

The atmosphere at the Savoy was similar to that at the Colony, the difference being that the former was a hotel and a much larger room, and certainly not easy to work. The whole dance floor rose for the cabaret and there was space for a well-disciplined dance routine followed by the comedy spot. If you worked down stage, you had about half your audience behind you on either side. If you worked in front of the band, you had an expanse of dance floor directly in front of you.

I bought a new number for this engagement, written by Alan Reeve-Jones, a gifted writer of monologues. It was all about Lady Chatterley – a topical subject given the recent obscenity trial over the book's publication. The monologue was witty, but also very suggestive. The management of the Savoy was horrified, and after the first performance I was asked to drop it, or I might be dropped from my engagement. They said that the number was lewd and a witty pay-off line, which ran, 'The sign on the box at the end of the drive said "For Letters" ', was, to them, positively obscene. The four-letter word had yet to be uttered in any kind of entertainment, and even a subtle reference brought the Savoy management close to apoplexy. Naturally, I dropped the number, but what a waste of effort. And all because of a management who were out of touch with changing attitudes.

A hotel audience is very different from that in a restaurant, and the management has to take this into account. I found out just how different when a party of Americans, who were presumably also staying at the hotel, took a table near the dance floor. They talked loudly all through my act and, with them sitting so near me, it was difficult to compete. They were not only ruining my timing; they were also inhibiting the rest of the audience. I paused, and politely asked them if they would stop talking while the cabaret was on, as it was spoiling other people's enjoyment. This received a round of sympathetic applause from some of the other diners. The Americans, however, became very aggressive and one of them said in a very loud voice, 'Listen, buddy, we're staying in this hotel, and we didn't come here to listen to you. You're part of the service, and we can take you or leave you.' 'I think we'd all be happy if you left us,' I replied, arousing more applause from the rest of the audience. Another member of the group then piped up in a strong southern drawl, 'Hey, kid, you got it wrong. We ain't goin', we're just leavin' you to get on with that rubbish you're dishin' out.' 'Perhaps you don't understand English,' I responded. 'We don't understand your accent,' said another. 'Then why did you answer me?' 'Oh ignore him, Horace. Get the waiter, we need more wine,' said a third. 'You'll have no luck, he only speaks English,' I replied.

I was really roused now, and the rest of the audience were clearly on my side, which helped. I then came out with a remark that created an uproar: 'What a pity, when we colonised America, we didn't teach them manners.' The place erupted, and a man on the opposite side of the room stood up and said, 'I'm an American, sir. I hope I know what manners are, and I want to say I'm enjoying your act, and hope you won't judge Americans by that uncouth lot over there.' Everyone applauded, and I said, 'Thank you. I love America and I'm touched by what you said. Every country has a few bad eggs who let the side down.' I thought some other Americans in the audience were going to break into 'The Star-Spangled Banner' and quickly asked everyone if they wanted me to continue. They responded enthusiastically, but after that kind of incident it is difficult to coax any audience back into a mood to laugh.

After the show, I expected the management to compliment me on the way I had handled a difficult situation. Instead, they took me to task for insulting some of the customers, adding, 'They've paid their money and have a right to respond as they wish.' The joys of working in cabaret!

One club that was adapting to the changing cabaret scene, and attracting a large following among a very young clientele, was the

Blue Angel, run by Max Setty. In many ways, it was the forerunner of the comedy clubs that grew up in the 1980s, but it followed the trend of the time and was run as a nightclub, where the entertainment always started around midnight. The resident compère was Noel Harrison, the son of Rex, who sang popular songs to guitar accompaniment. A number of aspiring young comedians gained their first experience in the Blue Angel, of whom the most famous today is probably Dave Allen.

I met another young performer at the Blue Angel who was also struggling for recognition – David Frost. I approached him to discuss an idea that I was hoping to pursue in cabaret with the writer and actor Leslie Randall. What we were planning is something that is now called 'improv', that is, improvised comedy, which is very popular today and performed with great skill by, for instance, the team at the Comedy Store. We would ask members of the audience for suggestions of professions, situations, ideas or words that we could then incorporate into an improvised sketch. Our intention was to try the idea out at Merrie's, a small club near Portman Square. We would work as a duo to begin with and then, if the idea was a success, bring in others, our first reserve being David Frost.

Andrew Merrie was, in many ways, courageous in allowing us to try something so original in his club. Leslie and I had every confidence that we could make it work, but it turned out that the concept was ahead of its time. We received a glowing review in the *Stage* from Peter Hepple, and some of the diners at the club did respond to the idea. Most, however, were reluctant to participate in something that was so different and, after a limited run, we sadly decided to abandon it. There was simply not an audience in nightclubs at the time for that particular kind of entertainment. David Frost never actually performed with us, but soon after that he was launched by Ned Sherrin as the link-man in the series that broke new ground in television, *That Was The Week That Was*.

I continued to work in clubs using my more 'conventional' material. All the clubs were different. In the late 1950s at the Pigalle I was the comedy attraction in the big floor show starring the singer Yana; at the intimate Society restaurant in Jermyn Street I was the solo cabaret. One of the most unusual venues was the 21 Club in Chesterfield Gardens, Mayfair. It was smart, luxurious and probably very expensive. To me, however, it was just work and more experience.

The 21 Club was owned and run by an engaging character called Bertie Meadows. He only ever booked a single act, as opposed to a full floor show, and the exclusive audience was always most attentive, and usually very appreciative. I found it difficult to understand how the club could be so successful, as it was never very full. After a while, I realised that there were rooms upstairs that the clientele could use for private functions, or to spend the night if they wished.

Bertie, who always dressed immaculately and sported expensive jewellery, and who always seemed to be surrounded by pretty girls, was a charming host to all his customers. He seemed to enjoy my cabaret material immensely and was always extremely complimentary. He paid me £20 a week, which was quite good in those days, but on occasion gave me a little extra, when he asked me to repeat my act for some small party he had organised for special guests in one of the upstairs rooms. I had glimpses of an intimate, exotic world, far removed from the gentle, domestic one of family and home that I was by then enjoying.

In complete contrast to the 21 Club – in fact, in complete contrast to any club I had worked in London – I accepted an engagement in March 1962 to work in a small club in Wakefield, Yorkshire, near the prison, called the Kon-Tiki. (When it closed a large social club bearing the same name ran successfully for a number of years. That has now closed.)

In most clubs of this kind, you worked seven days a week, and the atmosphere when you arrived on the Sunday afternoon was much the same. The air was full of the stench from stale cigarette butts; the floor and tables were still covered with beer dregs and other debris from the night before. The Kon-Tiki had a single, naked light bulb hanging over the small dancing area, and at the back were three musicians idly strumming on their instruments – this was the trio, led by the drummer, Phil Langton, who were available to play any music that I might have in my act.

When I arrived, I was greeted by a man whom I assumed was the restaurant manager, a bluff, down-to-earth, abrasive type with a strong Yorkshire accent. He greeted me with the rhetorical question, 'Oh, you got here, did you? Have you got your dots?' He was referring to my music. 'The lads are waiting to play for you.' I explained that I did not use any music except for a play-on and a play-off. He looked mystified. 'What d'you do then? A sort of straight-man act?' I shook my head. 'You're not ventriloqual, are you?' 'No,' I replied. He looked even more confused. 'It's not magic, is it?' I again shook my head. 'Well, I know you don't sing, so what the heck do you do?'

I was beginning to lose confidence at this barrage of questions. I said that I did a comedy act. He came straight back, 'What? Not patter?' I said, 'I suppose you could call it that.' He paused for a moment then, with a wealth of meaning, said, 'Really! Well, don't expect to get a laugh here on Friday.' I asked why not. 'Well,' he said, with almost half a smile, 'No bugger's had a laugh here on a Friday yet. He can't be heard. They get up at the bar there and they've had that much drink, you're lucky if you can shout 'em down.' I said, 'What happens on Saturday?' He answered in that typically succinct way that some Yorkshire people have: 'Pandemonium.'

I was beginning to think I had made a mistake. I asked, with as much tact as I could, 'Why d'you pay a lot of money to have artists come up from London, if nobody is going to listen to them?' 'I'll have you know,' he replied, emphasising his point by prodding me with his forefinger, 'we've had some of the best acts in show business die up here.' He then proceeded to give me a list of comedians, some of whom were well known, who had played at the club, and how they had fared during the week. It was like a military roll call, detailing those who had survived and those who had fallen in action. With great pride he mentioned those who had packed it in on Wednesday or Thursday, and almost gleefully those who had been paid off on Monday or Tuesday; there was even one little-known comedian who had walked off in the middle of his first performance on the Sunday.

It was with great trepidation that I began my act on the Sunday night, which the band had told me was always the quietest, as most of the potential audience had spent their drinking money the previous Friday and Saturday. I soon discovered that any of my subtle material meant nothing and I had to ad-lib my way through the evening, making comments about the venue and the audience, and dragging out from the depths of my memory the more obvious jokes that I had used in radio variety shows. When I returned to my hotel that night, I looked up a lot of my old Workers' Playtime scripts and tried to memorise any jokes that I thought could be adapted for use during the rest of the week.

The problem was that the club's management had tried to attract diners as well as drinkers by filling the room with tables where people could sit and eat. Those who only wanted to drink had to stay at the large bar at the back. As there were not many diners, the tables were mostly empty and there was a huge, noisy crush at the bar, which made it difficult for the cabaret artist to be heard. On the Monday night, I asked for a long flex on my hand-held microphone, so that I could go right across the room and actually harangue the customers at the bar who were not listening. I was living dangerously, doing an act that bore no resemblance to anything I had previously performed in cabaret in London. It was an effort, but I survived, even if I did not enjoy it. I even reached the dreaded Friday night without any real disaster, and was still on my feet at the end of a gruelling performance. I was just gathering my breath when a well-dressed character came up and invited me to have a drink with him. I thanked him and, as we sat at a table, he asked my opinion of the club. After the week I had just been through, I told him what I thought in no uncertain terms. 'They just don't know what they're doing here. They can't make up their minds whether they want a dining club, in which case they should stop the service and give the cabaret a chance, or whether they're running a social club, where they should let the drinkers come and sit at the tables while the cabaret is on. They haven't a clue what they're about.' He said, 'Thank you. I'm the owner.' 'Oh, really?' I said. 'Well, I won't be working here any more, will I?' Not that I wanted to return. He was very tolerant, and even ordered me another drink. He said, 'I respect a man who speaks his mind. I take your meaning. What you want is a bit of hush, a bit of quiet so you can get your patter over.' He paused, and then continued, 'I'll tell you what I'll do. I'll come down tomorrow night, personal, and get someone to give you a right proper introduction, get them quiet for you.' I thanked him and hoped that my last performance would not be quite as difficult as the others had been.

Saturday night arrived and, as good as his word, the owner had found someone to introduce me. When it was time for me to start my act, he went out ahead, faced the audience, and boomed, 'Now, I want a bit of hush. Tonight we have an arteeste who is very good. He's got real class. The best-dressed act we've had for some time. He wants a bit of quiet so you can hear his patter. You won't laugh at his gags if you don't hear them. Now, before I introduce him, there's just one thing I want to say to all the men. It's about the new toilets. We've had them built, and they're working. The sign's up there.' He pointed to the sign. 'Gents,' he said. 'You can read it. We want you to follow it, and bloody well use them. We're fed up with all this pissing in the car park. Here he is, Nicholas Parsons.'

It was the most bizarre and impossible introduction I had ever received in all my life in show business. The audience were so over-awed that, for the first time, there was no noise during the beginning of my act. Unfortunately, neither were there any laughs and it took me a while to get them going. It was a strange end to an unfor-gettable week. No wonder you are never confident, walking out to face an audience in a restaurant or club. You never know what will happen. The one consolation is that once you have succeeded in cabaret, nothing else in show business is ever as daunting.

8

· · · · · · · ·

Treading the Boards Again

MY efforts to prove that I had more talent than that required to play simpering juveniles in the theatre were not working as I had hoped. Instead of proving that I could play comedy and character roles, my work in cabaret simply brought me more offers of the same, and I started to be labelled a cabaret performer. Some write-ups referred to me very generously as a 'bright new comedian'. It was the British love of labels again, which has plagued my career, and presumably that of others. At different times I have been referred to as an actor, light comedian – what is a heavy comedian? – character specialist, cabaret artist, revue artist, variety artist, comedian, voice man, straight man, satire man, game show host, quiz show host ... The point is, I am all of them. In America, they praise you if you are versatile. In Britain, they are suspicious of you. When I was young, and working for Americans, they would say if they were impressed, 'That's great. Now, what else can you do?' In this country when I was young and had a success, the typical, condescending reaction was, 'You were good in that part. If you were to concentrate on that, you could do very well.'

Besides cabaret work in the early 1950s, I continued to look for theatre work, writing to all the repertory companies around London, who were now relying less on resident actors and actresses under contract and casting for each weekly show from the vast core of hopefuls available in the capital. I was offered an engagement with the repertory company at Windsor. The play was Esther

McCracken's *Quiet Weekend*, which had been a success at Wyndham's Theatre in the West End during the late 1940s. Typecast again, I was asked to play the young man, the son of the family around whom the comedy is built, and whose fiancée gets marriage jitters just before the wedding. It was more of a romantic than a comedy role, but it was still a good part in a well-structured play. More exciting, however, was the fact that the young girl playing the fiancée was an actress who was making a name for herself at a very young age – Geraldine McKeown (later to be spelt McEwan). She was only seventeen, but her work had already caught the eye of producers outside Windsor. Her natural talent was enhanced by a very distinctive voice, which has not altered over the years, just become more mature. Even at my young age, I was conscious of acting with someone special, and the fact that I was able to play the young romantic role in *Quiet Weekend* with any success was in great measure due to the confidence Geraldine's own ability inspired in me. I was also attracted to her, and a week or two after the play was over, took her out to the theatre in London. I think, however, that she was then quite keen on the resident director at Windsor, Hugh Cruttenden, who had directed our production, and she later married him.

Shortly after my appearance in *Quiet Weekend*, I was invited back to Windsor to play the police inspector in James Bridie's *Doctor Angelus*. I was far too young for the role, and can only imagine that I was cast in the part because I could do an authentic Glasgow accent. The character was a gruff, solid member of the Scottish constabulary, and though my performance may have been immature, I enjoyed playing the role because it was a character part in which I could lose my identity and feel at ease.

The outstanding memory of that week was driving down to the theatre one afternoon as a most incredible fog descended. I had by now acquired an Austin 8 saloon, and enjoyed driving myself everywhere – driving was then a pleasure, because the roads were not congested and motorways did not even exist. Fog, however, was always a hazard, particularly when, because of the pollution, it turned to smog. This was usually so dense that it blanked out everything, even street lighting, and you could easily lose your way home along streets that were normally familiar.

As I set off to Windsor on this particular afternoon about 4 p.m., the fog was mild, but it slowly got worse and when I reached the A4, the Great West Road, I was going at a crawl. Then darkness fell. I was not worried about time, however, as the curtain was not due to rise until 7.30 p.m. and even if I could not check in at the required time of 6.55, I would still be at the theatre well before my entrance in the third act.

The fog turned to smog. Cars were stopping; some were abandoned. The journey normally took me just over an hour; I had now been on the road for three. I crawled on. It was after 7 p.m. and the curtain would soon be rising. There are no such things as understudies in weekly repertory. I began to panic slightly. I could see nothing out of the windscreen and had the window down, breathing in the foul air, as I tried to steer by the white line in the middle of the road. At least, I hoped it was the middle of the road. Once, it was the line on the opposite side of the road, and suddenly I was looking into the headlamps of a huge lorry. We spotted each other two feet from impact. Somehow, I found my way back to the right side of the road and literally inched my way towards Windsor. (Next day, it was described as the worst smog ever recorded.) I had visions of the play progressing and suddenly the third act arriving with no inspector to tie up the ends of the story. It turned out that the stage management thought I was in the building, so had made no plans for my non-arrival.

It was after 9 p.m. when I limped into Windsor, by now about the only car moving on the road. I parked and rushed through the stage door. The third act had already begun. I hurried to the prompt corner, to be greeted by the stage manager: 'You're on in a minute, and you're not changed.' 'Have you seen outside?' I asked. 'No,' he said. 'I've been tied up here all day. I haven't got time for chat, Nick, your cue's coming up. Get on.'

I had no alternative. Wearing a very old polo-neck sweater, some ghastly trousers, suede shoes with crepe soles, an ancient sports jacket with leather on the elbows, with no make-up and tousled hair, red-eyed from staring into the smog and hoarse from inhaling the putrid air, I rushed on stage, pretending to be a mature police inspector of forty-odd. The cast were thrown. Some thought I might have had a temporary brainstorm and, being weekly rep, had got muddled about the part I was playing. One thought that I had been drinking in the long break before my entrance. The situation was made worse by the fact that, after what I had just been through, I forgot my lines, something I had never done before. I did the only thing possible: I began talking a kind of Glaswegian gibberish and paced the stage until my opening lines returned. It was unnerving both for me and my fellow actors; the audience, meanwhile, were trying to fathom the plot as I confused them with incoherent nonsense. The important thing about acting, however, which I had discovered even then, is that if you lose your way, keep going with confidence. Even if you speak rubbish for a spell, the audience are often fooled into thinking it is they, not you, who have temporarily lost their way.

It was a full two or three minutes before the correct lines came back. I finished playing the scene in a trance, trying to convey as much authority as I could muster, and as the curtain came down, I sank onto the stage in a heap. The specialist who had treated me after my time in hospital in Glasgow would have been horrified at what I had breathed in during those five long hours. The soot from the smog had penetrated everything. My nostrils were two black holes; my eyebrows were ridged with soot, and when I combed my hair the soot on top immediately turned it dark grey. There was no question of returning to London. I managed to find a vacant hotel room, where I was stranded, with only my soot-encrusted clothes, for three days. The theatre remained almost empty, as few people ventured out. It was not my happiest of engagements, nor, needless to say, did it lead to offers of character parts in the West End. It was back to cabaret, until I landed an audition with the top London management of the time, H.M. Tennant, run by the brilliant impresario, Hugh Beaumont, known to everyone affectionately as Binkie Beaumont.

H.M. Tennant had a subsidiary organisation called The Company of Four, which, in May 1950, were presenting a play by Rachel Grieve, *If This Be Error*, at the Bath Festival. My audition was successful and I had my first part in a West End production since *Charley's Aunt*. All the hard work in cabaret, however, seemed to be of no avail, for I was typecast again, as the archetypal middle-class young Englishman. The play, though, was excellent.

I had never appeared in a production at a festival before, and it was tremendous fun. There is not only a vast amount of entertainment of all descriptions going on, but the relaxed atmosphere that a festival generates seems to affect visitors and the local population alike. Our production was staged at the small cinema opposite the beautiful Theatre Royal, and played to capacity houses for the whole of the brief run. The Company of Four ran the Lyric Theatre in Hammersmith, which was where the production went after Bath; we then went on a short tour.

The play was extremely well cast. Mary Ellis, who had starred as a singer in the Ivor Novello musicals of the 1940s, was playing one of her first dramatic roles. The other leading female part was taken by Mary Morris, a brilliant, idiosyncratic actress. The principal male role was played by Clive Morton (I played his son); the important part of the wife was taken by a new, budding actress, Daphne Slater, and the two other main roles were filled by Gladys Henson and David McCallum.

There was a young actor there, understudying Clive Morton and myself, who, since he was losing his hair, could pass for middle-aged though he was not much older than I was. His name was Lionel Jeffries, and I remember him talking about how difficult it was to find work as, with his receding hairline, he looked older than his age. I said that I envied him his appearance, as there was a wealth of parts suited to his character features, whereas I was only being considered for insipid, juvenile roles. Proof of what I was saying was borne out shortly afterwards, when he was offered some very good work as a character actor, before moving on with great success to cinema. I, on the other hand, went back to cabaret and repertory when the play finished its tour.

Much of the work that followed was again for Ronnie Kerr, and I played some marvellous parts in some exceptional plays for him at Palmers Green and Maidstone. He was the one person who never saw me as a straight actor. In fact, he once said, 'I could never see you playing straight to anyone. Your instinct is for character; your flair is for comedy.' He was very perceptive, but in this instance he turned out to be wrong. I think, however, that it was what I learnt from Ronnie that helped me later to be a successful straight man.

In September 1950, I was offered an engagement at the Q Theatre, beside Kew Bridge, run by Jack de Leon. They were presenting *Doctor Angelus* for two weeks with an excellent cast, including my old friend from Glasgow, Molly Urquhart. It was the first time we had worked together since I had left the city. On this occasion, I was playing my age, the leading role of the young doctor, who is influenced by the domineering Doctor Angelus yet at the same time anxious that his behaviour be ethically correct. Like all of James Bridie's plays, *Doctor Angelus* is beautifully written, and the character I played is a gift for a young man, as he goes through great emotional turmoil, and even has a marvellous drunk scene.

I had no agent at the time and was uncertain how best to exploit the opportunity this role offered, in a theatre so close to the West End. As it turned out, John Fernald, then an established West End director, was in the audience one night and my performance apparently impressed him to the extent that he asked me to appear the following February in *Spring at Marino*, adapted by Constance Cox from the Turgenev novel *Father and Sons*, which he was producing at the Arts Theatre in the West End.

Working again with Molly Urquhart made me realise how much I missed having older friends with whom I could talk. My parents were little help – it was impossible to talk to them about anything personal or intimate, and a discussion about anything relating to sex, in particular, would have been acutely embarrassing, probably for all of us. My mother rarely approved of any of my girlfriends, and the strain of living at home in my mid-twenties after being on my own from the age of sixteen until I was twenty-one was beginning to tell. The time had come to find a place of my own. It was not easy, as flats in London were almost unobtainable. No houses had been built during the War and the bombing had destroyed vast amounts of property, particularly in the capital. Indeed, the housing shortage was one of the major political problems of the postwar years. I remember one of my lines in cabaret around this time: 'This housing shortage that everyone's talking about ... I think it's just a rumour that's been put about by people who have nowhere to live.' It was the era of the notorious Rackman – and others – who charged extortionate rents for dilapidated properties. When they were foiled by the Rent Act, which controlled rents and prevented speculation in the selling of unfurnished flats, unscrupulous individuals started to charge 'key money' – a huge sum simply to buy the key of the flat. When that became illegal, an owner or tenant might put a few sticks of furniture in a flat and pass it on as furnished premises, asking an exorbitant price for some useless goods. This was how I obtained my first flat in 1951. A friend told me of a very pleasant, two-roomed, ground-floor flat in Clare Court, a large mansion block in Judd Street, near King's Cross. The block was owned by a respectable property company, and they were asking a fair rent, which was about three pounds a week. The existing tenant demanded five hundred pounds for a lot of furniture I did not want, let alone like. It was either that, however, or lose the flat. Five hundred pounds was a lot of money in 1951 and I certainly did not possess it, so I asked my father for a loan. He was most reluctant, partly because he could not understand why I should want to live on my own when I had a perfectly good home. Surprisingly, it was my mother who recognised that I needed to get away, and persuaded my father to lend me the money. He explained that he would have to sell investments, so advanced me the money with an agreement that it be repaid with interest. I worked very hard over the next two years, was never out of work and, with the exception of my car, never indulged in personal luxuries. I paid my father back, with interest, before the two years were up.

I enjoyed my flat. It gave me the freedom I needed and am sure helped ease the tension that had developed between my parents and me. Living in a large, impersonal block was ideal, as I could keep my erratic hours without fear of disturbing anyone, although I must have given great scope to the gossips in the block. The only people I got to know were the porter and his family, whose flat was next door. In fact, during the four years I lived at Clare Court, I hardly spoke to any of the other residents; I certainly did not know the name of a single person there. At the time, I was too young and busy to think about it; today, I would hate such a lonely existence. The closest I come to it now is when I stay in a hotel, but there is always the compensation that home is in a country village, where you are part of a community. Even if you do not see your neighbours very often, they are around and greet you as a friend when you meet.

In February 1951, *Spring at Marino* opened at the Arts Theatre. It seemed that this could be the break for which I had been working and hoping. It was a delightful play, well-directed by John Fernald, lavishly costumed by Michael Ellis, with excellent sets by Fanny Taylor, and every principal character played by a star name or established West End performer – with the exception of myself. It was heady stuff to be working with Margaret Rawlings, playing opposite the exquisite Renée Asherson, whose looks had bewitched me across the footlights when I had seen her acting with her husband, Robert Donat, and to be keeping company with Derek Farr, Clive Morton and David Bird.

Spring at Marino was mounted with the idea that it transfer to a larger West End theatre after it had finished its five-week run at the Arts Theatre. The critics were kind but not enthusiastic and it soon became clear that there would be no further performances once the five weeks were over. It is a sad reflection on the commercial theatre that you can give a fine performance in a play that fails, and the memory of your efforts dies with that show. On the other hand, you can give an average performance in a play which is successful, and you will receive credit out of all proportion to your efforts. Though we played to capacity audiences in the small theatre, all that happened when we finished was that BBC Television mounted a production, which was directed for the small screen by Kenneth Buckley.

After this disappointment, I had a quite different experience. David Horne, a character actor who had given many fine film performances in cameo roles, usually as a typical English gentleman, asked me if I would like to appear in a production at the small Theatre Royal in Stratford-Ate-Bow, where he was running a repertory season. David was a most lovable, gentle man, who adored the theatre and acting and used his own private means to put on productions solely for his own, and his wife Anne Farrer's, satisfaction, rather than for the public who lived in that part of East London. It was not unusual, on occasions, to play to an audience of about a dozen people.

I appeared in two productions for David in 1951. The first was Bernard Shaw's *Candida*, which had two marvellous parts for David and his wife. Anne played the lead role of Candida, and David was her husband, the Reverend Morrell. I had the role of the young man, Eugene Marchbanks, who becomes infatuated with Candida. It was all great experience, but Shaw's polemic and well-reasoned argument was way above the heads of the small audience. One night, David was very excited because a whole party had booked. I said, 'Does that mean we've got a full house?' He replied, 'No, but we've got twenty-five in the audience.' Seemingly carried away with this slight increase in business, David then put on a midweek matinée, which attracted two middle-aged women who sat in the front row with their shopping baskets, discussed the play and the characters throughout, and munched their way through several bags of sweets and crisps.

I happened to bump into the women in the street afterwards, and as soon as they recognised me, they grabbed me by the arm and one of them said, ' 'Ere, young man, what was all that you was going on about in that play this afternoon?' 'Yes,' chimed in the other, 'I've never 'eard so much bleedin' talk in all me life. If we hadn't been tired from shopping, we'd've left long before the end.' It was useless to try to explain the plot to them, so I asked, 'What were you expecting?' 'Well,' said the first, 'we like a show that's got a bit of oomph. You know, got a few laughs.' 'Or a bit of love, or somethink,' said the second. 'I mean, you were all soppy about that Candy woman, but you did bugger all about it. You just swooned around like a soft cherry.' I did not know how to reply, so I asked them what shows they had enjoyed at the theatre. The first lady responded immediately, 'Oh, some time ago we saw a lovely show, *Naughty but Nice*. That really lived up to its name, didn't it Beryl?' 'Oh, yes, Rita,' giggled the other. 'That one was good. 'Specially when he did that neurotic dance. That was real saucy. Somethink to get your teeth into there.'

This last remark reduced the two to raucous laughter and I left them, wondering where my career was going. I mentioned my encounter to David and relayed the gist of the conversation. He was completely unperturbed and replied, 'They're not typical of the kind of audience I'm trying to attract to the theatre.' I did not have the heart to point out that they were the *only* audience he had attracted to the theatre that particular afternoon.

David did present a more commercial play two weeks later, *The Silver Cord*, a prewar success written by the American Sidney Howard. I had made it a policy to accept any work for the experience, irrespective of the money. It paid off on this occasion. One of the members of the cast was Graeme Muir, an actor in his thirties who, shortly afterwards, applied for a producer's course at BBC Television. It was a wise move for him, as he soon became very successful, and within a year was offered the chance to produce a new comedy show written by and starring Eric Barker. The series required a young character actor capable of playing the different parts in the sketches, and Graeme remembered me. It was the beginning of an unforgettable phase in my career.

In the meantime, I had the unexpected pleasure of working in a West End show again. As so often happens, exciting things invariably happen when you least expect them, and also at the most inconvenient time. I had decided to take a few days off to stay with my old friend from university, Ross Belch, who was now a successful manager of a shipyard in Port Glasgow on the Lower Clyde. The decision was also prompted by the fact that a very pretty American girl called Hope Griswold was staying with my family and it was a wonderful opportunity to show her something of our country, and also to get to know her better.

We had no sooner set foot inside Ross's house after the long drive than the phone went. It was the production manager of The Company of Four, asking if I could return immediately, that night in fact, to take over from an artist who had slipped a disc in the new revue show that had just opened at the Lyric Theatre, Hammersmith.

The show followed the formula of the increasingly popular late-night revues that were filling small theatre clubs. It was directed by William Chappell and the cast, drawn from the best young talent available, was headed by Graham Payn. George Benson, with other successful theatre work to his credit, was the oldest member of the company, which also included Dora Bryan, Ian Carmichael and Joan Heal. *The Lyric Revue* took its name from the small theatre at Hammersmith Broadway, where it was launched; it later transferred to the Globe Theatre in Shaftesbury Avenue. Material was commissioned from top writers of the day, particularly Arthur Macrae; Noël Coward also wrote a number for Graham Payn.

The Company of Four desperately needed a replacement for Myles Eason. It was a marvellous opportunity, even though it had arrived at a most inopportune time. Ross and his wife Jan were very understanding. Hope was disappointed, but Ross offered to put her up for a few days and show her something of Scotland, which I deeply appreciated. The very idea of immediately doing the return trip, driving over 400 miles through the night in a small car, whose top speed was not much more than 50 or 60 mph, along what were then predominantly single-lane and winding roads through many towns, did not deter me at all; today my heart almost misses a beat at the thought of what I was contemplating. How on earth did I imagine that I could complete another ten-hour journey without falling asleep at the wheel?

I arrived at my parents' home about seven in the morning, having driven over 800 miles in the last twenty-four hours. I rested for an hour, had a large breakfast, and was at rehearsal by 10 a.m. I learnt two sketches and by the evening was on stage. The following night, I was in the remaining items in which I was to appear, and by the end of the week was taking part in the Charleston number which involved the whole cast. I stayed with *The Lyric Revue* for about five weeks, until Myles Eason recovered. It was all too short a run, and once again I was on the sidelines.

It was about this time that an incident occurred concerning Noël Coward. Graham Payn, who had become very friendly with Noël, discovered that he was keen to acquire a small dog. Graham's mother played bridge regularly with my mother, who was now breeding miniature poodles as a hobby. She had two beautiful, silver-coloured bitches, Jenny and Suzette, and had recently acquired a pedigree dog of the same strain, whom she called Pierre. He was an amazing little animal, but had obviously been inbred – something certain breeders do to produce finer points for show purposes. Pierre grew into an adorable but rather dainty little dog, and my mother had problems with him from the start. One of these was that he had a restricted anal passage, which gave him no trouble if he stayed on soft food, but caused him agony if he swallowed any bones. Mother took all this in her stride. She eased his problem manually, or in advance with the necessary laxatives. The major problem, however, was of a different kind. Pierre had been acquired primarily for breeding purposes, but by the time he was fully grown it was obvious that he was more interested in his own sex than in the attractive bitches that were available. In fact, he seemed to take more pleasure in trying to bugger our large, neutered tomcat than having his way with the delectable ladies of his own species. Jenny was a particularly flirtatious bitch and, when in season, would prance around Pierre to excite him and then tantalisingly push her rear into his face. He simply snapped at her. Something had to be done. To this day, I do not know how Mother managed it, but she was always a resourceful woman and her hang-ups about sex clearly did not extend to animals. Somehow she introduced little Pierre to the joys of heterosexual activity. Once initiated, there was no holding him. When one of the bitches was in season and Mother wanted to rest them from breeding, it was a continual strain to keep them apart.

It was interesting to observe the similarities between dogs and humans in their attitude to sex. Suzette was definitely not very interested and suffered the indignity of mating with fortitude, looking up to the ceiling with resignation; but she was an excellent, if stern, mother. Jenny, the flirt, was very highly sexed. She even walked like a canine Mae West, swinging her hips. She gave everything to the activity and was always game for more. She was also a loving and sensitive mother. In fact, she was so maternal that, on one occasion, after being served by Pierre, she swelled with all the obvious signs of pregnancy, only to subside to her normal size on the date the puppies were due. It had been a phantom pregnancy, which meant that Pierre was probably not very fertile.

Mother was wondering what to do about the situation when Graham Payn's mother asked if she could bring Noël Coward to see her, as he seemed interested in acquiring a miniature poodle. Mother was thrilled at the thought of meeting Noël Coward, whom she deeply admired – she refused to believe any stories about his private life and was convinced that he was a natural bachelor. If anyone said differently, it was out of jealousy. She very kindly asked me if I would like to be there when Noël came, and of course I was delighted. She was running around in small circles with excitement. Neither of us need have worried. He arrived with Graham and Mrs Payn and was charm itself, the most urbane and naturally courteous man I have ever met. He adored the dogs and was absolutely captivated by Pierre. He kept talking about him, saying in his familiar, clipped tones, 'He's absolutely enchanting. I love the way he walks, on his toes with his head held high, like a ballet dancer. He is quite exquisite.'

Noël Coward stayed for about an hour, enjoyed a cup of tea, charmed Mother beyond words, and flattered me by asking what I was doing. Mother could not have been more excited had the King himself called for tea. Next day, she told me that she had decided to make a present of Pierre to Noël. He obviously loved the dog.

It would solve her problems with the sex life of her animals, and while she would be sad to let Pierre go, he would have a wonderful home.

The following day, the little dog was taken in state to his new master, with his own familiar bed and bowl, a list of his normal requirements, and details of his anal problems and their prevention and cure. Mother received a most enormous bouquet of flowers and a letter of thanks, which she always treasured. She also received reports from time to time from Mrs Payn about Pierre's new life, which sounded most luxurious. Apparently, there was no one in the Coward household capable of handling the anal problem as Mother had, and she was told that when a crisis arose, the little dog was placed on a soft velvet cushion and taken in a limousine to the nearest vet.

It seems Pierre was very happy in his new home and enjoyed all the pampering. He must, however, have been missing the delights of the flesh to which Mother had introduced him. One day, the phone at home rang. My mother answered, and was amazed to discover it was Noël Coward. He said, 'I thought you would like to know that the little four-legged ballet dancer has settled in very well, and seems to enjoy his new home and all the fuss and attention. However, he did disgrace himself the other day. We had a luncheon party to which we had invited our local bishop. Pierre was summoned to meet the assembled guests. He came trotting into the room in his usual coquettish way, caught sight of the Bishop's silvery-grey gaiters, rushed straight over, and started to perform a quite obscene act upon them. I was torn between embarrassment for my guest and sympathy for what the poor little chap must be missing. To preserve some decorum, the little fellow had to be banished to his quarters.'

Poor Pierre. He may have enjoyed a lifestyle few other dogs could have experienced; but there were certain frustrations that went with it.

9

Radio Days and Going Solo

THERE were many variety shows on the radio in the 1950s, both at midday and in the evening and, unlike today when nearly all radio comedy is performed by a team with a script, or is a game show which is spontaneous and unscripted, radio comedy then came largely in the form of variety shows with solo artists. Even scripted shows leant heavily on a music-hall style as so many of the top comedy names had come from that world. There were, however, a number of great innovators in the 1950s; in some ways it was the golden age of radio comedy. The classic example must be the Goons – it is amazing, in retrospect, that the show ever came to be accepted.

The Goon Show was piloted in 1949 by a clever and maverick producer, Pat Dixon. He had started the innovative *Breakfast with Braden*, starring Bernard Braden and Barbara Kelly, whom he brought over from Canada, as well as the equally original *In All Directions*, with Peter Ustinov and Peter Jones. He only got the latter on air by selling it first to Radio 3 – then called the Third Programme.

No one on the management side at the BBC seemed interested in *The Goon Show* and it was passed by the Light Entertainment Department to a young, energetic producer, Dennis Main Wilson, to promote and try to sell. Through sheer persistence he eventually succeeded, as he did with other radio and, later, television programmes. He had that rare skill of being able to perceive what the public will enjoy, and was prepared to back his judgement with dogged energy until he broke down resistance. Sadly, there are not many of his kind around today. With too few contract producers in the media, particularly in television, and with increased costs, it is even more of an uphill struggle to promote new and original concepts.

The senior executives did not even like the name 'The Goons', saying, in typical Auntie-BBC-speak, 'No one will know who they are.' They suggested calling it '*The Crazy People Show*, starring the junior crazy gang'. Even when it eventually found its way onto the airwaves, it was never understood by the network bosses and there is the famous story, now almost apocryphal, of a memo from them asking, 'Why is this unintelligible "Go on" show on the wireless?' Spike Milligan, who wrote the script and, of course, starred in the show, along with Peter Sellers, Harry Secombe and, in the early series, Michael Bentine, broke new ground in comedy and *The Goon Show* developed a cult following with the young. The proof of their success is that the programmes are still enjoyed by audiences today, some of whom had not even been born when the show first started.

Another great innovator in 1950s radio comedy was Eric Barker with his *Just Fancy* shows. Eric had worked at the Windmill Theatre for years before the War when, according to him, it was a delightful little revue show. He wrote and appeared in sketches, and also met his wife, Pearl Hackney, there. He moved on to work in radio and then spent five years in the Royal Navy. On his demob, he was commissioned to write and appear in a new radio show to replace the naval edition of the popular wartime *Merry-Go-Round*. He called it *Waterlogged Spa*, a programme he peopled with distinctive characters, all of whom were recognisable from life in postwar Britain: Flying Officer Kite, played by Humphrey Lestocq; Baron Waterlogged, a Cockney peer (in keeping with the new socialist Britain), played by Richard Gray, and the popular Devonshire postman, played by Jon Pertwee.

Two of the best comedy writers working in radio at this time were Frank Muir and Dennis Norden, who created *Take It From Here*, starring Jimmy Edwards, Dick Bentley and Joy Nichols. The pair developed their own style but followed in the great tradition of scripted comedy sketches, where the characters and situations were rooted in truth but were a little larger than life. This style was later developed by Ray Galton and Alan Simpson into a situation comedy format for the individual talents of Tony Hancock.

Then there was the long-running *Much Binding*, written by and starring Richard Murdoch and Kenneth Horne. This show, built round a mythical RAF station at Much Binding in the Marsh, began during the War but was so popular that it carried on well into the 1950s.

Other popular, scripted comedy shows of the period included *Ray's a Laugh*, with Ted Ray, and *Educating Archie*, with Peter Brough and his dummy Archie Andrews. The latter always boasted a well-known cast; it also launched a number of performers who became big stars, Max Bygraves, Tony Hancock, Beryl Reid, Dick Emery and Robert Morton among them.

All these shows were the shining exceptions amongst the large number of variety shows of the period, including the prestigious ones such as *Variety Bandbox* and *Henry Hall's Guest Night*, a show in the old-fashioned style, boasting a series of acts. While the latter was at its peak, directed by the skilled Bill Worsley, one of the talented group of producers in the BBC Light Entertainment Department, I appeared in it with a five-minute spot, achieved after serving an 'apprenticeship' on the midday variety shows.

At one time there were as many as five shows in the slot between 12.30 and 1 p.m.: three *Midday Music Hall's* – one from London and two from the regions – and two *Workers' Playtime's*. The last were a relic of wartime variety shows, and each broadcast always came from a firm's canteen, factory floor or other main area. Such shows were always transmitted live and the producer often had quite a task to make sure everything kept to time. He had to gauge what reaction a script might receive, and also how a particular artist worked and played to his audience by embroidery or ad-libbing around his material. Imagine trying to keep someone as spontaneous as Ken Dodd to a set time! The problem was usually solved by giving the artist a green light when he or she had sixty or thirty seconds to go, so that they could cut to the end of their act and finish on time.

The 'wireless' could create stars in the 1950s because BBC Television had only one channel, transmission time was limited, and it was still struggling to find its own style. Radio remained the premier service: more money was made available for its programmes, and, besides, costs were cheaper. It was only when commercial television began in the late autumn of 1955 that BBC Television began seriously to look at its programmes, and their style and content began to improve.

The advent of commercial television was the best thing that ever happened to BBC Television, for it shook the powers at Lime Grove, from where all the programmes were then transmitted, out of their lethargy. Money and resources were poured into television, not only from an increased licence fee, but also at the expense of radio. Television audiences increased, while those for radio diminished. Some even wondered in the late 1950s whether BBC Radio would survive, but although its budgets were cut, it continued to present quality programmes, especially in comedy. Today, it is winning larger audiences than ever, often at the expense of television.

In the autumn of 1951, Graeme Muir rang to ask me to play the young character parts in a new television series he was directing at Lime Grove, written by and starring Eric Barker. This was not only a wonderful opportunity, it was also the beginning of a friendship with an exceptional comedian and his delightful, down-to-earth wife Pearl, who also appeared in the series.

Eric, in appearance, was not an obvious comedian. Reserved by nature, he appeared more like an unassuming bank manager. A very intelligent man, a shrewd observer of people with an uncanny ear for re-creating them, he was a natural satirist with impeccable comic timing. I enjoyed both his humour and his wisdom and learnt a great deal from him, both about comedy and about acting. We were a very happy company, and Graeme Muir made work easy and fun, directing with great skill and always supporting Eric, whatever the content of a sketch.

The cast for the first show was made up of Cameron Hall, who joined Eric in his famous sketch of the two old men discussing life, taken from his *Just Fancy* radio series, Patricia Gilbert and Daphne Anderson. Ronnie Boyer and Jeanne Ravel did an elegant dance routine in evening clothes, the Malcolm Mitchell Trio did a spot and other music was supplied by Eric Robinson and the BBC Orchestra. The show was called *The Eric Barker Half Hour*, and had a different musical group and solo singer in each programme. We made six programmes in all, which were transmitted fortnightly. In subsequent series, the musical group was dropped, Deryck Guyler replaced Cameron Hall, and we had the same singer for all six shows. In one series it was Sara Gregory, in another Janet Brown, singing but not doing impersonations. Latterly, the title of the series was changed to *Look At It This Way*, as Eric's writing became more satirical. He was the first person to do 'topical satire' on television, but as the phrase had not yet been coined, and as the sketches were part of a conventional variety show, he never received the credit he deserved for his originality.

When Eric's fifth television series finished, the BBC did not renew his contract – his individualism did not endear him to an organisation which at the time liked conformity and conventional thinking. Soon, however, he was being offered some good supporting film roles, particularly by the Boulting Brothers, and his *Just Fancy* radio series continued to win a large and loyal following. Then, at the comparatively young age of fifty-two, he suffered a stroke which more or less ended his professional career. He made a good recovery, but was left with a slight paralysis on one side, and while his mind was as sharp as ever, he lost some of his sparkle. All he did in his later years was a little local radio work. He died in 1990 aged seventy-eight, which is a good age and probably exceptional for someone who had suffered a stroke so young. It says much for the love and care lavished on him by Pearl and his family.

I think the biggest impact that Eric made in his first television series was with the send-up of the television coverage of the 1951 General Election. It was the first time television had covered an election and he created a marvellous skit on the whole proceedings. We were all anxious about how it would be received, and while it was quite gentle compared with what is seen and heard today, and viewers enjoyed it, messages were sent to Eric from above advising him to be careful and not to satirise too many of his employers' serious programmes. Eric, however, continued to take off most of the other programmes on television, which gave me an ideal opportunity to do my impersonations. Pearl, too, was clever at impressions, but it was her very subtle characterisation in one short sketch that created the biggest furore imaginable, and nearly lost Eric and all of us our jobs. Above all, it illustrates how dramatically respect for authority and the Establishment has changed, and how far ahead of its time was Eric's thinking.

He wrote a short sketch in which a very regal-looking lady, wearing a coat with a fur collar, played by Pearl, is on a platform surrounded by a group of very important-looking civic dignitaries. One of the group solemnly passes her a bottle of champagne on a rope – she is clearly about to launch a ship. She takes the champagne, names the ship and lets go of the bottle. The scene then cuts to a film clip of a ship slowly sinking into the river. It then cuts back to the group and Pearl, in a very studied voice, but by no means an impersonation of our present Queen Mother, saying, 'Surely, she should have floated?' End of sketch, big laugh, and before the show was over, a major crisis. The telephone lines to Broadcasting House, Lime Grove and the national press were jammed with callers. Someone had dared to impersonate Her Majesty. The royal family had been mocked. The fact that the person in the sketch could have been anyone in the public eye, and that it was also an amusing situation with a funny pay-off, did not matter. The inference was there; the bounds of good taste had been breached. The next day it was headline news in the papers. Eric and Pearl were beseiged by reporters – they could not get out of their normally peaceful Kent cottage, and had to take the phone off the hook. Eric was asked to present himself to the then head of Light Entertainment, Ronnie Waldman, who gave him a severe lecture and a warning about overstepping the bounds of good taste. If he transgressed in future, he was told, the series would be cancelled and he would not work for the BBC again.

All television in those days was transmitted live. The cameras were also huge, heavy and difficult to manoeuvre. The production had to be carefully planned in the large studio at Lime Grove so that it could house the sets for all the items on Eric's show in such a way that the cameras could move from one set to another to keep continuity. Cameras 1, 2 and 3 might be moving to the next set, while camera 4 was taking the final shots on the item that was finishing. Also, a set that had been used for an opening sketch might be being dismantled and another erected at one end of the studio while a third was being filmed at the opposite end. Such construction work had to be done in silence, as the sound system picked up every stray noise. On one occasion, Ronald Boyer was bending his dancing partner, Jeanne Ravel, backwards in an elaborate move-ment. As her back nearly touched the floor, a stage hand dropped a huge iron counterweight. His timing was perfect. It sounded as if something Jeanne was wearing had snapped. The funniest sight, however, was the stage hand, who had dropped the counterweight on his foot, hopping about in agony, trying not to make a noise and swearing the most ghastly oaths in mime.

The camera rehearsals on the day of transmission were not only to establish positions and angles, but also to make sure that, in the time available, they could move from one set to the next and that the artists could make any necessary changes of clothes for the sketch that followed. These changes were made behind the 'flats', the backdrop scenery to any set, and there were inevitably some awkward moments, which simply could not happen in today's pre-recorded world of television. They made television much more fun for the viewers, as well as more of a challenge for the performers. If a mistake was made, you covered with a gag if you could and got on with it.

Eric was very shortsighted and after one sketch, in which he was not wearing his spectacles, he was searching for his dresser who usually led him to where he made his next quick change. They missed each other. Eric failed to see that the cameras were filming on a set near him and, instead of walking behind the flats, rushed in front, dressed in football gear and carrying the kind of clicking rattle that fans take to matches. Janet Brown was on set singing a song about some man in her life. Eric passed behind her, looked puzzled, and then realised his mistake. Janet had not seen him and kept on singing while Eric, smiling weakly at the cameras, crept up to the door in the middle of the centre flat, only to discover it was false. He then tried slinking along the back of the set, hoping the cameras would cut the other way, when his dresser rushed on and dragged him off. Viewers must have been very puzzled by this odd-looking stranger in Janet's flat, by a door that did not open, and by another man appearing from nowhere. And, of course, no explanation could be given.

I had an even more embarrassing experience in one of the shows. I had found the area where I was due to make a quick change. My dresser was waiting. He took my jacket, I released my trouser braces and then bent forward to pull a shirt over my head. As I did so, my dresser, standing behind, pulled down my trousers to speed things up. At that precise moment, a cameraman bumped his machine into a flat, which swung to one side, and in the middle of an elegant dance routine I was revealed, trousers down, with a man standing in a most provocative position just behind me. Ad-lib your way out of that one! I then had to continue in the next sketch, playing a very sincere vicar. The joys of television in the 1950s.

These incidents gave us all much to laugh about afterwards. Eric and Pearl pulled my leg unmercifully about the incident with the dresser, especially since they knew of my weakness for the opposite sex. In fact, as I had a succession of girlfriends during the five years we worked together, they decided I was something of a Lothario, which was not true. I never had more than one girlfriend at a time!

The day after the War began, the BBC re-formed their Drama Repertory Company (it had existed for a short while in the 1930s), a group of actors and actresses who were put under contract and were available to appear in any production on the 'wireless' for which a producer cared to book them. They received a regular salary and a modest amount extra if any programme in which they appeared was repeated. Producers could always employ performers on a freelance basis, but as the members of the Drama Rep were all very talented, they were in constant demand. Some of the performers who became household names in the 1940s through their work in the Drama Rep were Marjorie Westbury, Gladys Young, Laidman Browne, Norman Shelley, Deryk Guyler, Grizelda Hervey, Richard Williams, James McKecknie, Gladys Spencer and Carleton Hobbs. Others, who joined later, became equally well known: Anthony Jacobs, Denise Bryer, Patricia Hayes, Duncan MacIntyre and Richard Hurndall. These were the popular stars in the early 1950s, unseen faces whose pictures occasionally appeared in magazines, but who were known to millions usually by their voices alone.

In 1951, BBC radio decided that it was time to bring some fresh blood into the Drama Rep. The established players would still be employed on a freelance basis, but a number who had been around for many years were not to have their contracts renewed. It must have come as quite a shock to those who thought that, because of their standing in the public eye, or rather ear, they had a job for life. Suddenly, there were places to fill. Exhaustive auditions were held. I filled in the forms, stating all my experience, which was by now fairly comprehensive and looked quite impressive in print. I was called for the audition, at which I was asked to perform a piece of Shakespeare, a character role, a comedy item, and any other pieces which could illustrate my range and experience.

Standing in front of a solitary microphone with no one else in sight and a group of producers listening in a control room is a daunting way to audition. At least in the theatre, however forbidding, you are performing to a small group on the other side of the footlights. As I entered the cold, uninviting studio, a voice came over the intercom, 'Go to the microphone, announce your name, your agent's name if any, introduce each item clearly, continue for your allotted time. At which point, announce your name again and remain in the studio for any questions we may wish to ask.' What a congenial atmosphere in which to declaim a piece from *Macbeth*; get really angry, with an American accent, and then sentimental in an excerpt from *Ah, Wilderness*; play a piece of high comedy from *The School for Scandal*; and display my ability with dialects and comedy in two other extracts, one of which was a speech from *The Cure For Love*.

I finished, gave my name again, and said I had no agent. A deathly pause. Had they gone to sleep? Had they gone home? Were they waiting for me to go, too embarrassed to say anything? Eventually, the unseen voice said, 'Thank you, Mr Parsons.' No comment, no encouragement, no indication of success or failure. I stood there, not knowing what to do. I thought they might be discussing me. I began to feel like an object in an antique shop, with the customers debating whether I had enough class to blend with their other possessions. At last the voice came back, 'Mr Parsons, what have you done recently?' This was a hopeful sign. I told them and then asked, 'Do you want to hear something else? I have more prepared.' 'No thank you, Mr Parsons. That will be all. We'll let you know.' They could as easily have said, 'Don't phone us, we'll phone you.'

They did telephone, and I had the job. Beginning in the new year, I would be a member of the BBC Drama Repertory Company. Unfortunately, 1952 was not a good time to join. The producers had money in their budgets to spare and were not obliged, as now, to cast contract players and only occasionally employ a freelance performer. Most of those who had left the Drama Rep were still engaged to perform, which was natural as producers knew their worth, and some of them made more money than they had under contract. The new intake, which included such talented people as Mary Wimbush and Garard Green, who are still broadcasting regularly, had to work hard to earn their position in the Rep.

I found it all very frustrating. My greatest joy was working for the producer Raymond Raikes, who during his time at the BBC created some of the most brilliant radio productions, particularly of the classics. He had a unique policy with newcomers. He cast them in principal parts in the early read-throughs and rehearsals of his major productions, which had a longer rehearsal time, before the arrival of the star actors he had engaged. This served three purposes: he could iron out his technical problems without boring his main players, save money on their fees, and discover the newcomers' abilities. I enjoyed these 'audition' performances. They gave me the chance to play some magnificent roles that I might not have been offered on the stage; they also paid off professionally, as Raymond later cast me in some very good parts in his productions, long after I had left the Drama Rep.

One of my first engagements after joining the Drama Rep was in a Wednesday matinée, a short play which was a regular feature at the time on the old Home Service. In this particular production I played one half of an engaged couple, opposite one of the young stars of the company at the time, Denise Bryer. She was charming, attractive and popular with everyone. I could never have imagined that within two years I would be officially engaged to her, especially as when I first met her she was the fiancée of someone who worked in the Music Department at Broadcasting House.

In general, I was not being given much exciting work during this period, nor was I making much of a living. Most of the productions in which I appeared were not repeated, and you only make a reasonable living in the Drama Rep if you get repeat fees. On my audition sheet, I can only imagine that someone had written, 'Good at dialects', because most of my parts during the first few months were supporting roles, playing characters of different nationalities. At various times I played an Italian waiter, a Greek seaman, an Egyptian camel herder, a Scottish ghillie, a Welsh miner, a Yorkshire farmer, a Chinese coolie, a Croatian freedom fighter, a London taxi driver and an Indian immigrant, amongst others. As a result, I earned a reputation as a 'voice man'. Another label. How was I to break away from this professional pigeonholing?

I had a chance to appear in a late-night revue at one of the little theatre clubs springing up around London and went to Val Gielgud, the Head of the Drama Department, to ask if I could accept the engagement as it would not in any way interfere with my work in the Drama Rep. We were rarely in a studio in the evening, and never after 9.30 p.m. We also had days off and were entitled to four weeks' holiday a year. (The Drama Rep was the only organisation in show business at the time that gave paid holidays to actors.) Val Gielgud refused permission on the grounds that I would be too tired for my BBC work. I said that I was rather tired from the limited demands that the Rep was making on me, and that the stimulus of a vibrant show every night would probably make me much more alive for the radio work during the day. He was not convinced and I had to turn down the revue.

After nine months of playing innumerable character roles, I resigned from the Drama Rep. Ironically, I was immediately offered some leading roles in major BBC productions, but could not accept all of them as Eric Barker had begun his second television series in the autumn of 1952 and I was happily working with him every other week until the end of the year.

My life did now seem to be settling into the world of comedy. But if this was true, I had to tackle the next most challenging work after cabaret, that of the stand-up or solo comedian in the theatre. If I could do this, I thought, I might finally prove my versatility and be offered comedy roles in plays, which was where I felt my natural talent lay. There was only one place where I could work as a stand-up comedian in London, and that was at the famous Windmill Theatre.

I had still not committed myself exclusively to one agent. I was finding work on my own, and accepting solo engagements from whichever agent cared to contact me. An agent who had seen me work in cabaret, and who specialised in looking after cabaret performers, was a strange woman called Irma Warren. I gathered that she had once run a nightclub herself, and rumour had it that it was not all that salubrious. You cannot, however, always trust rumour. The most surprising thing about her was her physical appearance. When looks were being handed out, beauty was in short supply where she was concerned. Nevertheless, her partner – in every sense of the word, I believe – was a most handsome man with a charming and aristocratic air. His name was Ulick Brown, and I think he was a lord. It was Irma who asked me if I would like to work at the Windmill. The audition was fixed and when I was successful, Irma negotiated a very good contract. I was to receive my highest salary ever, £35 a week, but had overlooked the amount of work I had to do in return – six performances a day, six days a week, for six weeks.

The Windmill was run by a very shrewd businessman, Vivian Van Damm, and it was he who auditioned me. I performed part of my cabaret routine and he liked what he saw and heard. This was lucky, because later I came to realise that Van Damm was not one of the world's greatest judges of comedy. He knew what he liked, but was no judge of what would make audiences laugh, especially Windmill audiences. It is ironic to think that such a man should have been running a theatre whose reputation is now based on all the famous comedians who first worked there.

Van Damm had been very clever. He had marketed the theatre in a most imaginative way, all over the country. As a result, the Windmill had a nationwide reputation as the home of a very racy, provocative, exciting show with lots of pretty girls, scantily clad and sometimes, it was said, not clad at all. To millions throughout the British Isles, the Windmill was the best-known theatre in London.

This image of the Windmill, however, as the mecca of sexual naughtiness, bore little if any resemblance to reality. Compared with the kind of shows that are presented today, it was gentle, charming and almost antiseptic in content. Van Damm had to walk a very difficult professional tightrope, as these were the days of that ogre, the Lord Chamberlain. There were many hilarious stories of plays being submitted and having words taken out or, indeed, sometimes left in because the Lord Chamberlain's officials did not know what they meant. The Windmill's reputation, however, was not based on the spoken word, and even the most sheltered Lord Chamberlain would have had a basic knowledge of the female anatomy. Van Damm therefore devised a very shrewd plan. On the Sunday night before a new show was to be put on, he would invite the Lord Chamberlain to a special performance. It was always a full house, attended by relatives and friends of the cast and staff and other invitees. The fact that the Lord Chamberlain never delegated his responsibility to an underling on these occasions suggested that he did not find the visits irksome. It also meant that Van Damm had won the first hand. For his second hand, he dealt out the hospitality in no small measure, so that by the time the curtain went up, the Lord Chamberlain was in a very amenable mood. Van Damm's ace followed. Girls who would normally be rather economically clad would be covered in yards of tulle and flimsy lace. Whatever disappointment 'his lordship' was feeling inside, outwardly he had nothing but praise for the show and went away saying how absolutely charming it was, and giving it his complete approval. It would be six weeks before he would be seen again at the Windmill. It would also be six weeks before the tulle and flimsy lace were seen again.

To see female flesh naked in the theatre was one thing. To see it move was another, and it was this that was strictly ruled out by the Lord Chamberlain. The girls, if unadorned, had to remain completely motionless. In the words of a well-known revue number of the day, 'It's all right to be nude, but if it moves, it's rude.' Even Van Damm did not dare break this rule. The period of total exposure in the show was, in fact, very brief and, again, very much out of proportion to the image that had been created. Had the Office of Fair Trading existed then, it might have had a lot of raincoated gentlemen queuing up outside its offices to complain in the same way that these men eagerly queued every morning in Windmill Street, with their rolled umbrellas and newspapers, in the hope of finding that titillation the advertising had promised.

The scene so many of them wanted to look at took place during the fan dance. As the dancer performed, another girl would stand, totally naked, in a delicate pose on a pedestal at the back of the stage, one leg placed strategically forward, slightly crossing the other. On one memorable occasion, the naked girl on the podium was suddenly taken with a fit of coughing which got progressively worse. The fan dancer was forgotten as the naked girl's coughing was exchanged for a spasm of sneezing and everything on her very pleasing form began to wobble in all directions. Nothing like it had ever been seen on the Windmill stage before and there was a thunderous round of applause. The stage manager, too, became highly disturbed, but for a different reason. The nude's uncontrollable oscillations were in strict contravention of the censorship laws and, in desperation, he brought the curtain down. Such was the power of the Lord Chamberlain's office.

Apart from the rules laid down by officialdom, the Windmill had its own house rules, which were displayed to the audience at each performance. An enormous notice would appear on stage at the interval, drawing patrons' attention to the theatre's three golden rules which, if broken, would result in expulsion and blacklisting. The first stated that the use of cameras was strictly forbidden; the second advised customers that they must not survey the goods through binoculars, and the third stressed very firmly that patrons must not climb over seats to get nearer the stage when places became vacant. This last rule was occasionally broken, and there was always a lot of movement as customers rushed for seats that had been vacated. The Windmill was run like a cinema, with continuous performances throughout the day. Customers sat wherever they chose and many stayed on, hoping to be able to get nearer the stage next time round when, possibly, one of the fans might slip, or the girl on the podium might unexpectedly move, or a bluebottle might land on her anatomy, which could wreak havoc. On many an occasion there was complete pandemonium.

That the Windmill Theatre did not live up to its much-publicised reputation cannot be blamed entirely on the Lord Chamberlain. The shows contained very little in the way of originality except in the three guest spots, and the novelty element, apart from glimpses of female flesh, was virtually nil. With one or two exceptions, the girls Van Damm employed were not particularly talented; if he was attracted by a girl's looks, and she had a modicum of personality, then he would engage her. An amazing woman, Maisie Cryer, would take the girls under her wing, teach them a few rudimentary dance steps and try to get them to sing or speak one or two simple lines in time to music. The more experienced girls, who were the backbone of the company, took the leading roles in the standard routines, which consisted of ballet, tap and the fan dance. Even these skills, however, were fairly basic. Assisting Maisie was a former male dancer from the Royal Ballet, Keith Lester. He used to put the girls through some simple ballet routines which he would introduce from time to time, often taking part in them himself in the actual show.

At every show, there would be opening music, with girls singing and dancing, followed by a speciality act, booked for a six-week period. A tap dance routine would follow, after which a girl would sing some corny song as best she could. After another speciality act and dance routine, we would be at the interval. So, during the first half of the show, the audience might, if they had been alert, have seen occasional glimpses of female flesh. After the break, the ever-expectant customers would be entertained with another song, which was followed by the famous fan dance. This was normally performed by one of the more experienced dancers, but not all of them were prepared to do it, since they were actually going on stage completely naked, protected only by two large fans. Here Van Damm could be rather devious. From time to time he would ask one of the less experienced girls to do the fan dance, thinking that she might make unplanned errors, get her fans in a twist, and briefly reveal all.

Between the fan dance and the closing song and dance routines came the comedian. It has been said many times that the Windmill was the birthplace of up-and-coming comics. To those who had to go on and perform immediately after the fan-dancer, a more apt word might be graveyard. Many did go on to achieve great things, perhaps more in spite of than because of their experiences at the Windmill. One of them, who followed me as a resident comedian, was Bruce Forsyth. His act then was more a song-and-dance routine, but he also did a very good impression of Tommy Cooper. I remember Van Damm saying to me that Bruce had no act and would never go far.

The other speciality act on the bill during my first season was Percy Edwards, the 'bird man'. I think we helped to keep each other sane. He had an act about a day on the farm, in which he produced the sounds of all the animals. It was extremely entertaining, but nothing could have been more incongruous than Percy taking these silent male voyeurs in the audience on an imaginary journey round the farm to meet the animals. I think occasionally one or two of them saw the joke when he imitated the birds to be found around the farmyard; but most laughed for the wrong reason.

I have always said that what I learned at the Windmill was not how to make an audience laugh, but how to entertain the odd customers peculiar to the theatre. It was only after I left that I learnt how to make any audience laugh. You just longed for the later performances because they drew a mixed crowd, with some women in the audience. At the early shows, the comedian was confronted with an audience of men who had not come to enjoy a laugh, so as soon as you came on after the fan dance, some of them would pick up their newspapers and read. There would be a lot of seat-changing and some seat-hopping. On one occasion there was a stand-up fight for a seat in the middle of the front row. Not easy conditions in which to start your act. As you finished, you would walk off to polite applause and the sound of newspapers being refolded in anticipation of the next display of womanhood.

There was one comedian with the reputation of having had real success with a Windmill audience, and that was Jimmy Edwards. He adopted a very bluff, aggressive manner and actually insulted the audience in his amiable way, and they took it from him. He would sit on the stage with a newspaper himself, making cracks at those whom he had seen in the audience during the previous performances that day. It was the perfect routine which, I am sure Jimmy realised, would probably never have worked so well anywhere else.

Another comedian who was very successful was Arthur English, who appeared as a wide-boy character, brash and outrageous. He would ad-lib to the audience and mock them. He would also try to involve them, and get them to come back at him, and if someone in the audience did, he would put his victim down with some ad-libbed one-liner, much to the amusement of the rest of the crowd.

Jimmy and Arthur were just two of the comedians whose names appeared on the 'roll of honour' outside the Windmill; others deservedly sharing this 'billing' included Tony Hancock, Peter Sellers, Eric Barker, Alfred Marks and Harry Secombe. Names which might have appeared, had they not failed their audition in front of Van Damm, were Spike Milligan, Norman Wisdom and Benny Hill. Morecambe and Wise (then Bartholomew and Wiseman) did not make the board either, though they did reach the Windmill boards – for one week only. They raised barely a laugh and were paid off after six very discouraging days.

I doubt whether Van Damm ever considered that the Windmill was to serve any great purpose in the world of comedy. Despite the 'roll of honour' outside, comedy was barely mentioned in the vast quantities of publicity material. I am sure that Van Damm considered that comics were not the attraction for the type of audience he had in mind, and he was no doubt right.

When you arrived for your six-week stint, you would go through your proposed material in front of him, putting in jokes you knew would amuse him. At the Sunday night dress rehearsal, you would make a mental note of the jokes that got a poor response – often quite a lot of them, which came as no surprise – and then surreptitiously change them for others as the week progressed. This would lead to endless messages from him running, 'What happened to the joke about so and so?' Fortunately, he never remembered the whole act, but there were often quite a number of jokes which he had appreciated and made a mental note of.

For some reason Van Damm always liked to be known by his initials, V.D., which had even more horrendous associations then than they do today. Everyone – staff, management and artists – was expected to use this abbreviated form of address. He had a tannoy system installed in every dressing room and frequently there would be a 'click', followed by 'V.D. here.' The messages would always take the same form: 'V.D. here, Nicholas – you've put back that joke about the monkey nuts, which I didn't like. Please take it out. Susan, I think we had a little too much slip showing. Veronica, try to get a little more energy into your dance with the sailor. Audrey, you can be bolder and let your dress fall away a little more. The censor didn't disapprove. V.D. signing off now.'

If what happened 'out front' had been widely publicised as 'naughty' and 'improper', it was just the opposite backstage. It was certainly not what one might imagine in a show in which there was nudity and titillation. For example, whenever the fan dance was about to take place, no one was allowed backstage. The girl would arrive in her dressing gown, slip it off and quickly pick up her fans. The only male allowed anywhere near was the stage manager. He had to work the curtains and give the necessary signals, and as far as I know, succeeded in keeping his mind on his work. The strict rules extended to visitors, and none were allowed beyond the stage door. If I had a friend arrive to see me, I would be called over the tannoy and would have to go down and take them to the nearest pub or café. Dressing rooms were strictly out of bounds for visitors, though it would have been difficult to squeeze more than one person into them anyway. You could sometimes get permission to take a visitor up to the canteen, but the visit would be strictly monitored.

Everyone at the Windmill was expected to work very hard, and working hard for thirty-six shows a week was very demanding. Doing just one spot, as I did, was not so bad, except that you still had the strain of trying to drag laughter out of your audience, if only as a matter of pride.

The hardest workers were the two pianists, who supplied all the music from their base in the orchestra pit. The only breaks they had all day were fifteen minutes between each show and a ten-minute interval, with a pause while the comedian was on. The pit was well below stage level and just below the level of the audience, whom they could see through a grille. They quite often saw the approaching army of seat-grabbers and hoppers as they made their advance to the front rows in what became known as the Windmill Steeplechase. For the pianists, it was almost like sitting in the commentary position at a boxing match, since on many occasions grown men would actually struggle with each other to get a better seat.

Despite the hard work, life backstage was always very pleasant. The girls were delightful and Van Damm and his team tried to create a family atmosphere. At times it was almost cosy, though you always had the impression that if you became too friendly with one of the girls, V.D. would resent it. His fatherly attitude to them almost amounted to possessiveness, which perhaps is under-standable, since each girl had been personally chosen by him, but this did not stop me taking one of them out for a while.

When my third season at the Windmill came to an end, I was ready to move on. I did not regret leaving. In fact, I was pleased to be released from the pressure of six shows a day. It had given me a wonderful opportunity to polish my routines and material. It was as if I had been working in the variety theatres of old, when comedians would be on tour for fifty-two weeks of the year, each week in a different town. They would try out new jokes, reject some old ones, find better ways of telling them, until every phrase and nuance in the act was really working. It was an experience I would hate to have missed.

Van Damm ran his little empire with great skill and business acumen, inspiring loyalty and devotion from his dedicated team who helped him run the theatre, and also from the great majority of artists he employed. He knew what he wanted, and he knew what the public wanted, and he gave it to them year after year. Even in the hard years of the war and the London Blitz, he carried on and there was a period when the Windmill was the only theatre in London open. It was a courageous action, summed up in their immortal slogan, 'We Never Closed'.

10

· · · · · · · ·

Working With the Best

A s 1953 drew to a close with another successful series with Eric Barker, suddenly everything seemed to happen for me. A career in show business rarely rises steadily: it is a series of peaks and troughs. For no apparent reason there will be a sudden surge forward and you become 'the flavour of the month'. The temptation is always to imagine that you have arrived', and start living accordingly. With rare exceptions, however, every surge tends to be followed by a quieter, fallow period; moreover, the greater the success, the deeper the dip that follows. In a profession I regard as a survival course, the most valuable thing is to keep a sense of proportion when things are going well. That way, you can survive the setbacks. There will be other opportunities; sometimes you can create your own, and you may bounce back even higher than before. This is certainly true with comedy. But there are no infallible formulae, no surefire routes to success. Some have a gift – and the confidence – for indefatigable self-promotion which, together with talent, has kept them at the forefront of the profession. I have always preferred to concentrate on developing new ideas. The most I can say is that I have never been out of work for long, which is in itself something to be proud of. My career has followed a path a bit like that of a roller-coaster, and I am certain that, as you get older, it becomes more and more difficult to keep the roller-coaster surging forward.

Someone who went through this roller-coaster existence was the late and much-loved Frankie Howerd. In the early 1950s he had been riding high on his radio successes, particularly in *Variety Bandbox*. Only a few years later he had hit a low, and when I met him by chance walking down Holland Park, he was wearing a shabby old coat, looking very forlorn. We talked and he was soon bemoaning the fact that he had no work, and no offers. I tried to reassure him by saying that show business was going through one of its upheavals because of the arrival of commercial television, and the changing styles in television comedy.

He was still at a low ebb in the early 1960s, when he secured an engagement at the new and successful Establishment Club in London's West End, where all the new young comedians were presenting modern revue and political satire, now the censorship of the Lord Chamberlain's Office had disappeared. Frankie courageously stepped into an environment that was totally new to him, and was an immediate success. He was relaunched, and booked to repeat his performance on the cult late-night satire programme, *That Was The Week That Was*. He was equally successful, and won a new audience from a different generation. I will always remember the opening line of his act at the Establishment. He stepped out, or rather ambled out, to the centre of the stage of this club for the young smart set and said, 'I know you're used to people coming out here and being very rude and swearing and talking dirty. Well, I have to say right away, if you're expecting that from me, you'd better piss off now.' He brought the house down, and never looked back. With that one line, which I do not think even in those days he could have repeated on television, he had won the audience over and been rediscovered.

Frankie was a thinking comedian, who worried things to success, though his style rarely gave this away. Every hesitation, however, had often been meticulously planned. I worked with Frankie in one of his last engagements, a commercial for R. White's lemonade. We had both been asked, as recognisable faces, to appear in separate commercials for the drink, but the format was the same as that which had previously made the commercial popular. Unlike the clown most people thought him, Frankie had his usual worried expression when I arrived at the studio. He said immediately, 'Have you read the script? It doesn't work. Not for me.' He then went into an animated conference with the producer and writer, revamped what he had to do by changing the clothes, and made it very funny for himself, while keeping the essence of what the client wanted. I did the original version, which worked for me. The two commercials were shown initially in one television area, were popular, but were never transmitted nationally because of Frankie's sudden death. I am sure the stresses inherent in our profession can only have contributed to his untimely end.

At the beginning of 1954 I was suddenly rediscovered by Leslie Bridgmont, one of the senior producers in BBC Radio Light Entertainment. Leslie had produced, among other shows, *Much Binding*, starring Richard Murdoch and Kenneth Horne. The programme was now in civvy street and, along with its two stars, retained one of the show's originals, Sam Costa. Maurice Denham supplied all the character voices and in 1952 Dora Bryan was engaged to play the scatty telephone operator in the office occupied by Murdoch and Horne.

Maurice Denham had been offered a film engagement which took him to the Far East, so could not appear in the new series. Whether it was my work as a character actor in the Drama Rep or my appearances with Eric Barker that had brought me to Leslie Bridgmont's attention, I do not know. I was invited to meet Richard and Kenneth, who had as much charm in private as they displayed on stage. What impressed me, in particular, was the ease with which they wrote the scripts, including the humorous lyrics for the song that finished each week's show. Kenneth, in fact, was really a successful businessman, a director of Triplex, the glass manufacturer. To him, show business was a hobby, which he fitted in between company commitments. He was the most untheatrical man I have ever met, always immaculately dressed, usually sporting a buttonhole, very modest and naturally courteous. Even when he retired from the world of business, and worked solely as a performer, he never changed. He was the epitome of the conventional straight man, and had a natural instinct for comedy – something he exploited magnificently in the classic comedy shows *Round the Horn* and *Beyond our Ken*.

He and Richard put together the script for *Much Binding* each week in about a day and a half. They would meet in Kenneth's office and by the end of the day would have most of it done. They had been doing it for years, so the style was quite easy, but to keep up the standard for weeks on end (radio comedy shows ran much longer then) was a real challenge. They met next day to tie up any loose ends, and compose the rhyming stanzas for the finishing songs. They could not work longer as Kenneth had to return to his business. They were both quite shrewd, however, for they encouraged Sam Costa to bring a little piece of script for himself each week. He enjoyed this as it guaranteed his big comedy moment in the programme – it also meant they had less to write.

When I first met Richard and Kenneth, they asked if I had any particular voices or characters that I thought would fit well into *Much Binding*. I made a number of suggestions, some of which they liked and worked into the script. Two of them they brought in regularly, and then Kenneth said, 'Why don't you write a little piece for that Bristol character and bring it along each week?' I was delighted, and grateful, that I was to have my own moment in the show, but that was typical of Richard and Kenneth. They were not comedians who worried if their supporting players got laughs, because it all helped the show. (It is significant, though, that after a week or two, the Bristol character, whom I called Mr Greenslade, was going so well that they did suggest he should appear only on alternate weeks.)

Mr Greenslade was a very excitable character who, when asked by Kenneth what had particularly troubled him during the week, would go into a long description of some situation in which he had been involved, and how he had extricated himself or resolved the matter. He would speak faster and faster as he became more excited, and always finished with the same phrase, 'Oh, I never let the grass grow under my feet,' which became so popular with the audience that it soon aroused spontaneous applause.

My mother's home was Bristol and as children my brother, sister and I had often visited and stayed with my grandfather in Westbury-on-Trim. I used to enjoy those visits and particularly looked forward to going to grandfather's firm, B. Maggs and Co., and being taken round by my mother's cousins. The younger of the two, Bertram, of whom I was very fond, had a slight Bristol accent and it is possible that the excitable Mr Greenslade was an exaggerated version of him. My mother was on the telephone immediately she heard the character on the air. In her usual direct way, she told me, 'You must drop that character immediately. It's obviously based on Bertram, and he and the family will become a laughingstock throughout the whole of Bristol.' I tried to calm her by explaining that there was only a vague resemblance and, besides, people did not take things as literally as she imagined. Furthermore, who knew that my mother had a cousin in Bristol? Even if Bertram had heard the broadcast, I knew from experience that people never recognise themselves, even when it is an exact take-off.

After the second show featuring Mr Greenslade, I was proved right. Bertram rang to congratulate me on my part in *Much Binding* and to say how much he had enjoyed the Bristol character. He added, 'You've got him to a tee, including the accent. That's something I could never do, and I was born here. I meet people like him all the time.' I told my mother, but she was not convinced. The most important thing for me was that Bertram was happy. He was so happy, in fact, that the next time I stayed with his family, he took me on my usual visit to B. Maggs and asked if I would do a quick impression of Mr Greenslade to some of his staff. That was a bit embarrassing. I had to say that the inspiration for the character had been my grandfather's gardener, who was now dead.

In January 1954, an engagement with tremendous possibilites came my way. I was asked to star in a late-night revue show with Beryl Reid, which was opening in March at the little Watergate Theatre in Buckingham Street, off the Strand. The show was devised and directed by Ronnie Hill, an experienced producer who had been in the Light Entertainment Department at BBC Radio until he left to concentrate on writing music. The show was staged by Ian Stuart, who went on to become a successful television director, and the material was drawn from a number of talented writers of the day, including Diana Morgan and her husband Robert MacDermot, Peter Myers and a young Canadian actor called Donald Harron. John Hurst wrote a very witty number about a woman who had changed her sex, which was brilliantly put over by Beryl. It was quite daring for its time, but you could get away with more in a club, as clubs were not subject to the rigorous censorship rules of the Lord Chamberlain's Office. This particular number received incredible press coverage, as, a few days before the show opened, one of the first sex-change operations on a woman was headline news in the papers. It was a happy coincidence, for John had written the number a year or more earlier for Hermione Baddeley to perform in cabaret. Beryl's superb delivery of the opening line brought the house down every night. As a hearty lady dressed in tweeds, she strode on, came centre stage, said 'Hello' and went straight into the lyric:

> I changed my sex a week ago today, [huge laugh]
> I don't know what my friend is going to say, [huge laugh]
> Though she can be cute,
> She's naturally astute,
> And it's not easy to explain the thing away. [huge laugh]

The verse that amused me most ran:

> I suppose I ought to notify the Income Tax officials
> That my records are open to some doubt.
> Although I haven't changed my name or altered my initials,
> My particulars have all gone up the spout! [huge laugh]

Beryl Reid had become a star name through her work in variety. Perhaps her most successful stage character was the naughty school-girl, Monica, which she also performed in variety broadcasts and for a spell in the *Educating Archie* radio show. She later developed another popular stage character, Marlene, an empty-headed creature who hailed from Birmingham and who was very popular with the public. Beryl was a superb actress and comedienne, but suffered from the same syndrome as I did – the dreaded British labelling disease. She always wanted to be accepted for her all-round talent and star in a revue in the West End. She obviously hoped, as I did, that this revue at the Watergate, called *First Edition*, would be sufficiently successful to transfer to a major West End theatre. It is ironic that she only became a national star as a result of the dramatic performance she gave sometime later in the play *The Killing of Sister George*.

I brought some of my own material to the revue, including my routine about the different ways people laugh. I was expecting to do my foreign film act, but Ronnie Hill preferred a routine I had developed about foreign garages, which incorporated language gibberish. I also included a number about the 'Windmill Blacklist' and a send-up of animal programmes on television.

Before the rehearsals began, Ronnie had a meeting with me to discuss material and the show generally, in the course of which he asked if I had any suggestions for the sixth member of the cast. Robert Bishop, Ian Stuart and myself were the male contingent; two girls were required to make up the female team with Beryl Reid. I remembered the very talented actress whom I had met in the BBC Drama Rep, Denise Bryer, who could not only play comedy well, but was good at dialects and had a natural singing voice. I agreed to contact her. When I rang, her mother answered and immediately gave me the number of the flat to which her daughter had just moved. Denise was completely taken aback when I spoke to her. Apparently, her mother had been under strict instructions not to give her new telephone number to anyone as she had taken the flat with the idea of being on her own for a while. Nevertheless, she agreed to meet Ronnie and myself. I did not realise how futile our professional quest was going to be. Producers at BBC Radio had regularly recommended Denise to theatre impresarios for revues and musicals, but she never went to the interviews or auditions. She did not enjoy working in front of an audience, preferring the immediacy of radio, which relied more on inspiration and spontaneity than the severe discipline of stage work. She later became extremely successful at doing voice-overs for television commercials, supplying character voices for any number of products, as well as for cartoon characters and puppets. She was the voice of Noddy in the first children's television puppet series based on the Enid Blyton stories.

Denise turned down the invitation to appear in *First Edition*. She did, however, accept my invitation to take her out one evening. I had discovered that she was no longer engaged and, although she was very reluctant to become involved with anyone again, I pursued her with ardour and lots of daffodils. Within three months I had proposed marriage, and we became engaged.

The two young girls who made up the team for *First Edition* were a pretty blonde called Valerie Carton, and a very attractive, dark-haired Welsh girl, Petra Davis, who had a lovely singing voice. The show was well received, we had excellent reviews, did packed business, but no transfer to a major West End theatre followed. The Watergate management then decided to capitalise on their success and followed with *Second Edition*. Valerie was not available, so

Barbara Leigh joined the cast, and Ian Stuart left to be replaced by James Gilbert, who later joined BBC Television as a producer and eventually became head of comedy programmes. A young dancer with a most ebullient personality was brought in to stage the show – Lionel Blair. He was full of boundless energy and thrived on the adrenalin derived from his work. He still does today – he is a true survivor in our business.

Second Edition was a success and the management were still hoping for a West End transfer, perhaps with the best of the two *Editions*. It was not to be, in spite of continued capacity business. A third show followed, and Beryl and I were dropped, which was difficult to fathom since we were the only ones at the time with any name or reputation. Perhaps it was thought that we created an imbalance and that an unknown, talented team would make a greater impact. If that was the reasoning, it did not pay off, for while the young cast did well, the business was not as good.

I continued with my radio broadcasts; I also worked with John Hurst on the cabaret material he was writing for me, which led to my first major cabaret engagement. I was booked for the whole of August to appear at the Allegro and Quaglino's.

Prior to receiving the booking for Quaglino's, Denise and I had fixed the date of our wedding, and it fell on the Saturday of the third week. It was impossible to change as everything had been planned and the church booked. It just meant that we were not going to have a proper honeymoon. We had obtained permission to be married at the Queen's Chapel of the Savoy, the exquisite little church off the Strand, and the father of a friend of Denise's, Prebendary Cottrell, who was one of the vicars at the church, conducted the marriage ceremony, to which we had invited just close family and a few personal friends. When they heard that I had to work at Quaglino's that evening, a large number came to dine in the restaurant. Saturday was often a quiet night at Quag's, but on this occasion it was full, more than half the diners being family and friends. Their mood was infectious, and soon it began to feel like one big party. I had never experienced such incredible audience reaction in a restaurant before. At the time, I had limited material at my disposal, and after forty minutes had come to the end of my repertoire. I returned to the microphone and said that there was only one thing more I could add. I said, 'I was married today.' The

British are so delightfully sentimental. The audience rose to their feet and shouted for the bride. Denise was acutely embarrassed, and as she hurried towards me, tripped over her wedding dress, which she was still wearing, and slid on her bottom across the dance floor, finishing at my feet. If she had rehearsed beforehand, she could not have performed more spectacularly.

At the end of the evening, we took Ross Belch, who had been my best man, and his wife Jan back to my flat where they were staying. Denise and I changed and set off for a little hotel outside Bray, called Monkey Island, where we were to spend the rest of the weekend. It was now about 3 a.m. and as we left in my Ford Popular, a fog descended. It was not too thick, but bad enough to slow us down. An hour later, we were stopped by the police. Apparently, a Ford Popular had been reported stolen and my car fitted the description. The police asked us what we were doing. I replied that we were just married and on our way to Monkey Island, which all sounded too improbable for words. The officer's response was very logical: 'Most newlyweds are comfortably tucked up in their bed by 4 a.m. on their first night together. And if they're awake, they have better things to do than get stuck in a small car in the fog on their way to an island of monkeys.' We reasoned for a little, then I remembered that Ross had given me the marriage certificate just before we left. It was only after I had showed it to the police that they reluctantly let us go.

It was 5 a.m. before we arrived at the hotel and it was locked, with no key left out as arranged with the owners the previous week. I prowled round the building. There was one window open on the first floor. I climbed the nearest drainpipe, now a little scared that I might frighten someone in the room or be caught for breaking and entering. I called quietly to anyone who might be inside, but there was no reply. Grabbing the windowsill, I hauled myself in. The room was empty. I fumbled my way downstairs to the front door and let Denise in. The whole thing was beginning to feel like a scene from a French farce, but we were too exhausted to see the funny side. We went up to the empty room, past caring whether it was ours or not, stripped off our clothes, threw ourselves joyfully on the bed . . . and fell fast asleep.

The two-day honeymoon over, it was back to London, where I moved into Denise's large flat near Regent's Park – which was much more attractive than the one I had in Judd Street – and back to work. It was primarily my variety work and cabaret performances that were making the biggest impression. Together with my appearances in the revue at the Watergate Theatre and the character roles I was playing in Eric Barker's show, they were emphasising my image as a comedian. As such, I was again being dismissed by those in serious, 'legitimate' theatre as lightweight, 'illegitimate'. Today, comedy receives the respect it deserves, and our top comedians are admired for their unique talent and accepted as part of the theatrical establishment. There is now the Dead Comics Society, started in June 1991 by David Graham, of which I am a founder member, and which commemorates the work of great comedians such as Charlie Chaplin, Peter Sellers, Arthur Haynes, Benny Hill, Tony Hancock, Frankie Howerd and Sid James, by putting up blue plaques on houses where they lived. While their work may be more transitory than that of the artists, sculptors and scientists who are also so honoured, they brought as much, and often more, joy to more people and deserve to be remembered.

While my cabaret performances did not lead to serious theatre work, they did lead to something completely unexpected. I was working at the Royal Court Theatre Club when, one evening, I was asked after my performance to join someone at his table. It was Dennis Main Wilson, who told me he was producing a new Sunday night variety show, *Star Bill*, for the Light Programme (later Radio 2). Top names would guest every week but, having seen my solo act, he wanted me to compère it. I was thrilled. To be the regular principal artist in a one-hour show at peak time was a marvellous break, and this was at a time when radio could still create stars.

The show's generous budget allowed for Geraldo and his Concert Orchestra, a large choir – the George Mitchell Glee Club – six acts, and sketches in which I appeared with some of the star guests. I wrote some of the script and, as there was enough money for two more writers, I recommended two friends, Richard Waring and Lionel Harris, both of whom had written good material for my cabaret act. Dennis persuaded some top names to appear, including Petula Clark, Jewel and Warriss, the Beverley Sisters, Kenny Baker, Semprini, Bruce Trent, Tony Fayne and David Evans. In the second show, top of the bill was the legendary Jack Buchanan.

The programme had a great deal of advance publicity and good reviews. Just as it was becoming popular, and I was gaining confidence in my new role, Dennis left. His responsibility had been to launch and establish *Star Bill* and, that done, he was committed to the next series of *Hancock's Half Hour*, following the success of the first series the previous year. His successor was Douglas Moodie. He was a senior producer and, perhaps because he was unhappy at taking over a show someone else had begun, was keen to make his mark. He asked me to his office for a meeting and I went, expecting to discuss some possible alterations to the show. His first words were, 'I'm making some changes. The first one is you. I'm not renewing your contract.' I was speechless. What made it worse was that I had the impression that it actually gave him pleasure to see me hurt and bewildered. There was no explanation, no apology, no gentle let-down. I asked him why he was dropping me when the show had been well received. 'It's old-fashioned, not well conceived, and the humour doesn't work,' was the abrupt reply.

I still had to cooperate with him on two more recordings, realising he disliked me, found me unfunny and believed I only had the job because, according to him, 'Young Dennis likes to try to turn inexperienced people into stars.' They were the unhappiest two shows of my career.

The loss of this marvellous job was very difficult to come to terms with. It had been my first starring role on radio and I had, in effect, been sacked. The cavalier way in which the matter had been handled also affected my personal pride, especially as neither I nor others thought that I had failed in what I had contributed. It is interesting that the programme subsequently became old-fashioned and, I thought, humourless – the very things Moodie had accused it of being before he took over.

There was some consolation in that, shortly after my exit, I was back at Lime Grove working with Eric Barker in the next series of *Look At It This Way*. Unfortunately, it seems that the BBC were not prepared to look at it Eric's way, because it was soon conveyed to us that this was to be the last series. I can only assume that Eric's individual style, and probably his satirical writing, was no longer to the liking of BBC Television, who at that time were more interested in conventional, mainstream comedy.

To a great extent, the BBC had their head in the sand when it came to the future of television. In the spring and summer of

1955 the Commercial Television Bill was being hotly debated in Parliament, and there was a powerful pressure group working hard to have it made law. BBC Television was complacent; it was also rather patronising towards the possible rival. Its attitude was almost, 'How could they possibly hope to succeed at something we know and understand, and have been doing successfully for years?' They were soon to discover the truth. When the Bill was passed, the Independent Television Authority was set up, franchises were applied for and granted, and the BBC suddenly found a large number of their staff deserting them for more challenging work with the new companies.

It was around this time that I decided perhaps I would be better served by having a full-time agent. I had met Richard Stone through his wife Sara Gregory, a singer who had been in one of the Eric Barker television series. He had a 'stable' of young male comedy performers, including Benny Hill, Ian Carmichael, Jon Pertwee and Lance Percival, and was very well-respected within the profession. I liked him very much personally, and admired his honesty, not only in business matters, but also in the direct way in which he dealt with people in the profession, including his clients. I was, however, surprised when I signed an agreement to join his agency, and he said that, while he thought he would be able to find some good work for me, it was best to be realistic and accept the fact that I would probably never achieve anything really substantial. I think that what I was really having to accept was that I do not look like an actor, let alone a comedian, and this must have occurred to Richard when he took me on.

In the summer of 1955 I suffered a kind of physical collapse. The doctors could find nothing wrong with me; I was just very run-down and lethargic. It could have been a reaction to the pressures of work, particularly the very late hours demanded by cabaret; it was probably aggravated by the rejection I felt as a result of the demise of my regular job in *Star Bill*; and it may have been reinforced by my agent's cautionary approach to my possible future. I am sure it was not helped by my having to undergo surgery. I was suffering from piles. When my father found out, he suggested I consult a friend of his who was an anal specialist and who recommended an operation which I believe is now not always necessary. It was the last thing I needed. I think I might have collapsed completely had it not been for the fact that I discovered, through psychoanalysis, a self-awareness and confidence which helped me to come to terms with pressures which, until then, had felt overwhelming. Also, I decided to take a really restful holiday. Cancelling a holiday abroad, Denise and I went to the northwest coast of Wales. My principal memories are of the magnificent countryside, the wonderful freshly caught salmon we had frequently, and of driving our car right on to the firm sand at Borth-y-Gest and forgetting to watch which way the tide was moving. We woke up from a doze to discover water lapping round the wheels of the small drop-head Morris Minor, which I managed to rescue just in time, driving with bare feet and wearing only bathing trunks.

Offers of work were a great therapy, too, and I gradually returned to full fitness. I had my first job hosting a panel game in December 1955 for the new ITV company Associated Rediffusion, called *What's It All About*, devised by John P. Wynn. It had a lot of publicity, ran for thirteen weeks, but was not really successful. It was too similar to *What's My Line*, and not as good. I was keen to do more television work and, at the beginning of 1956, felt that there must be opportunities now that commercial television was underway. I had read some advance publicity about a variety pro-gramme, *Strike a New Note*, that was to be launched by George and Alfred Black. They had taken the title from a show that their impresario father had successfully presented at the Prince of Wales Theatre, which had been responsible for discovering some great new stars, including the fabulous Sid Field. George and Alfred announced that they were going to discover the new stars of independent television. The programme had so much advance publicity, it was difficult to see how it could possibly live up to it. I made a point of watching the first show and thought it was dreadful with the exception of one person, a comedian with a round face and a moustache. I could not remember his name, but thought that he had a natural personality for television and that if they gave him some better material, he could be very successful. In fact, I said to Denise that they should give him more to do and forget about the rest.

The following week, I watched the programme again. I thought it was even worse. I did notice, however, that the man with the round face and moustache was given more to do. I also remembered his name. It was Arthur Haynes. The next morning, Richard Stone phoned. 'Have you seen the programme on TV called *Strike a New Note?*' he asked. I replied, 'Yes, isn't it ghastly?' He replied, 'They want you to join it.' I said, 'When do I begin?' All actors like to work.

It was the intention of George and Alfred Black that I should introduce the programme and perform some of the material I used in my variety act. They also wanted to use me, more importantly, as the commentator in a wonderful television idea in which a character called Oscar Pennyfeather, created by Sid Colin and Ronnie Wolf and played by Arthur Haynes, acted only in mime. I was to commentate on his actions and speak directly to him, while he mimed his responses. It was this character that established Arthur and gave the programme some badly-needed acceptability. The overall show, however, was still far from good, and at the end of six weeks George Black sacked everyone apart from Arthur and myself and built a new team round us. Today, the show would probably have been taken off after only one, or at the most two, transmissions. It certainly would not have lasted for six. In those days, however, television companies were desperate to keep programmes on the air as they were losing a fortune and it was vital to keep the airwaves open, sometimes irrespective of the quality of material being trans-mitted.

George Black was a great showman and a wonderful man for whom to work. He said he thought it would be a good idea if Arthur and I performed sketches together, having spotted the possibility of a partnership with potential, which I am sure neither Arthur nor I had realised was there. The title of the show was changed to *Get Happy*. Ken Morris and Joan Savage were brought in to do some of the comedy musical duets and Maria Pavlou was introduced as the solo singer, but the show was built around the sketches performed by Arthur and myself.

We would meet in George and Alfred's office in Half Moon Street where, along with the Blacks' production manager Roger Hancock (the brother of Tony) we would read through any number of scripts that had been sent in by writers all anxious to get into television. Having selected the ones we liked for a particular week, Jeremy Hawk, with whom I had worked when I took over in *The Lyric Revue* in the West End, then directed the sketches before we

all assembled, with the remainder of the cast, at the old Wood Green
Empire. There Peter Glover coordinated the whole production and
directed it live on camera. We repeated this process every week and
realised after a while that more and more of the scripts that we were
using came from a young writer who had previously been an
insurance salesman. His name was Johnny Speight. A young man
with a most original mind, he was to produce, over the years, some
of the most inventive comedy material seen on television.

Get Happy ran for an amazing eighteen weeks; George Black had
turned what had started as one of television's greatest disasters into
a successful show. In the process my own work changed. Not only
was I doing the commentary for the Oscar sketches, but I was
playing a character closer to my own personality, rather than resort-
ing to different voices and dialects in each sketch. Arthur, at the
same time, was slowly developing as a sketch performer. Until *Strike
a New Note*, he had only worked in music hall as a variety comedian,
but now, from these sketches, evolved three memorable characters.
One was his famous 'tramp', the second was his know-all character,
and the third was a very rough, tough, crude working-class man.
The more these characters developed, the more the parts I played
evolved into Establishment characters off whom Arthur could
bounce. I was becoming a straight man to a comedian, but neither
of us realised it at the time.

After the last edition of *Get Happy*, George Black threw a party
to say thank you, and then announced that the show had come to
an end. He hoped that we might all work together again some time,
but there would be no more productions of *Get Happy*. Sadly, we
just said goodbye and went our separate ways.

11

The Straight Man Arrives

I HAD enjoyed working with Arthur Haynes, and also with George Black. Fortunately, however, work was coming in to dispel my regrets at the demise of *Get Happy*, including a late-night television revue show, *Here and Now*, directed by Peter Croft. It featured young artists who had been successful in small theatre revue – Joan Sims, Dilys Laye, Dennis Lotis and Nicolette Roeg, for instance – as well as a great deal of the material from those shows. I performed sketches and jokes that I had used in cabaret or at the Watergate Theatre. We soon discovered, however, that while the material had been popular only a few years before, much of it now seemed dated and, furthermore, did not transfer well to television. In some ways, these shows were the swansong of that kind of intimate revue.

I was also doing 'warm-ups' for television comedy shows. Any television show that has a studio audience invariably employs someone to go out and greet them, explain how everything works, and get them in a good mood for the show that is to follow, as well as keep them amused whenever there is a delay during the recording. It is a skilled job and today there are comedians who specialise in it. Then, it was considered somewhat inferior work.

Most of my warm-ups were for shows transmitted from the old Chelsea Palace, a variety theatre in the King's Road, London, which Granada Television had converted into a studio. I felt I had some status when I was booked to welcome the audience to a cultural hour of light entertainment in which Maria Callas was the principal artist. However, when I did the warm-ups for a popular comedy show called *The Army Game*, starring Michael Medwin, Bill Frazer and Alfie Bass, I was made to feel it that it was a very downmarket job, putting the audience in the mood to enjoy broad comedy. I thought I did reasonably well and was therefore rather taken aback when the producer, Eric Fawcett, sacked me. As I did not enjoy the work, I was quite relieved, although I kept *very* quiet about it at the time, as professionally it was most embarrassing.

In November 1956, I received a phone call from Arthur Haynes. I was delighted, and surprised. He had been asked to do a guest spot in *Star Time*, a variety show produced by ATV. Since he did not want to do his stage act for fear that exposing it on television would limit its life in live performance, he had asked Johnny Speight to write a sketch and wanted me to appear in it with him. It went down very well, and Arthur's agents managed to obtain two more 'guest spots' for him in the same series, again performing with me in sketches by Johnny Speight.

Our success reawakened George and Alfred Black's interest in us and they persuaded ATV to present a series, *The Arthur Haynes Show*, which was directed by Peter Glover and transmitted live from the Wood Green Empire. Johnny Speight wrote one main sketch and some quickies for each show and we revived the successful Oscar character. There was one more main sketch; Joan Savage, with her husband Ken Morris at the piano, performed some of the musical items, and Freddy Finton appeared in a short piece as his famous drunk character.

The programme, until we reached the third series in March 1959, went out at the 'off-peak' time of 10.15 p.m. During the spring of that year, however, it was brought forward to the peak-time slot of 8 p.m. By then, the show had moved to the Hackney Empire, Dicky Leeman was the regular producer, and Aileen Cochrane, a very attractive singer, supplied the musical item in the second half of the show. This line-up lasted longer than any other and it was only later, when the shows were recorded at ATV's new studios at Elstree, that the musical items were different in each series.

By the third series, too, Johnny Speight was writing most of the material for the show; latterly, he was writing all of it apart from the Oscar sketches. His style was ideally suited to Arthur's personality; Arthur, in turn, brought out the best in Johnny's writing.

Many people are surprised when I tell them that my partnership with Arthur spanned ten years. This is probably because it began slowly and only gradually developed into the success that it was at its peak. Today, a television partnership or comedy programme does not have the same chance. We were given time to develop our characters; at the same time, Johnny Speight's stature as a writer grew. Above all, we thrived because Arthur, Johnny, myself and our different producers over the years, such as Colin Clews and particularly Dicky Leeman, all talked the same professional language.

I soon developed into a fully-fledged straight man, but only realised it when I was described as such. I was also sometimes referred to as a 'feed', which I resented. To me, this smacked of the old-fashioned straight man who just stood up and said his words, off which the comic would bounce. The straight man in those situations was just what the term expressed – a feed – whereas I was creating a character, be it a police inspector, an MP, a doctor, a vicar, or an official from the social services.

Whatever character I played, he was always 'Mr Parsons', or 'Nicholas Parsons'. Arthur, however, never called me by anything but my Christian name. This came about because, on one occasion, he called me by chance, 'Mr Nicholars', pronouncing the final syllable in a way that was guaranteed to evoke laughter. The name stuck, and the audience often waited for it, as it was a ploy used by his characters to send me up.

Arthur never enjoyed rehearsing very much and it says a lot for his talent that he emerged so successfully as a sketch comedian. It was not something he set out to do, though on television he came over as a complete natural. In the early days we would often discuss the way lines should be interpreted and how they should be balanced. I tried to impress upon Arthur that if his comments were too outrageous, it was difficult for me to sustain the credibility of my character. That essential element of truth in a broad comedy situation has to exist, or the audience will stop laughing. If you go over the top, it becomes a pantomime sketch, which is a different kind of entertainment altogether.

We had many discussions as we rehearsed sketches. Sometimes we would switch the lines round so that Arthur, the comic, would always have the 'gag' line, while the feed lines always came from me, the straight man. It is an interesting comment on Johnny Speight's writing and on Arthur's personality that, if you analyse the sketches, I am always the one who suffered indignity or was put down. In most comedy partnerships, it is the comic who is always put down and the straight man provides the aggression. Somehow we had, without knowing it, reversed the roles. I played for sympathy but not laughs, while Arthur played for the laughs through the subtle and conniving way in which he always came out on top.

The assertiveness that Arthur displayed in the television sketches, however, belied his inner feelings, and I think that his aversion to rehearsals arose partly from a lack of confidence. On the variety stage, in his summer seasons, he was on familiar ground and utterly at ease, and wholly loved the work. He was happy with the success of the television show, but was never quite sure why it was working so well. I am sure this was because he had not trained as an actor, and could not fully understand that by discussing and polishing the sketches as carefully as we did, we were creating something that would be well received by viewers and critics alike. This naivety on his part resulted in a rather unusual way of working. We would arrive to rehearse the next week's show and read through the sketches. Arthur would go through a sketch twice, making comments and alterations and then, after the second read through, say, 'Right, let's try and mark it out.' He would then put down his script and, because he had a very good memory, would already have the sense of the sketch and some of the lines in his head. I kept my script in my hand for a while as I wanted to learn all my lines, but as our partnership developed I realised I would have to learn Arthur's lines as well, because he was never sure of all the actual words. This is something which, to the very end of our partnership, we never ever discussed.

By midday on the first day of rehearsal, Arthur would very much hope that we had done enough, whereas Dicky would ask for more rehearsal in the afternoon. Even so, Arthur would always try to finish early as he wanted to get home, often to do more decorating. He was proud of his skill with the paint brush and regularly talked about it. It was an all-consuming hobby and he probably could have made a good living as a decorator if he had wanted.

Arthur may also have remained unsure of his lines because he was fearful of becoming too familiar with the material, having realised that a certain spontaneity in front of the camera produced some amazing results. We would probably only rehearse for two more days, and they were never full days by any means, and then on the fourth day we would rehearse on the set with cameras. On that same evening, the show would be transmitted live.

Many a time during these live transmissions, Arthur would forget his lines. Dicky was always prepared and had what he called a 'rogue' camera available to cut immediately to Arthur's face the second he 'dried'. Arthur had one of those faces that are perfect for television – if you put him in close-up it did not matter what he was thinking: the audience would read oceans into his look alone. Invariably, in close-up, he was looking at me and I knew full well what he was thinking – what's the next line? I would pick up the message and subtly try to feed him what he should say.

On one occasion, I was playing a bank manager and Arthur, as the tramp, had come into my office on some wild pretext and started to discuss the possibility of being given a loan. Not for the first time, words eluded him, so I said, 'Mr Haynes, I think the word you are searching for is "collateral", and you want to inform me that you don't have any.' He, as usual, did not bat an eyelid, but came straight back, 'Mr Nicholars, you've taken the very words out of my mouth. It's very intuitive of you to realise what I was going to say and I'm very grateful to you.' I found it difficult to keep a straight face and, as the audience realised that it was all unscripted, they laughed and I, too, finally 'creased'. Arthur then wickedly built on the situation saying, 'Mr Nicholars, I think it's very wrong of you to laugh in a situation like this. I've come here in all seriousness seeking financial assistance, and all you can do is snigger.' Because it was all so natural, the audience and viewers loved it.

We were often asked whether we made these 'mistakes' on purpose to get extra laughs, but this would never have worked. Television is like a magnifying glass and any prepared ad-lib always shows. Had Arthur meticulously rehearsed the sketches like a trained actor, however, I wonder whether the show would have been the success it was.

If learning the lines of the sketches was a chore for Arthur, their actual content also caused him problems on occasion. Johnny's original material would sometimes disturb him to the extent that he would even try to resist performing it. He would argue that we should keep to more recognisable and predictable material, and ask that less politics be brought in. I always backed Johnny in these arguments, knowing that our success depended on innovation. For instance, after the Oscar character had successfully survived five series and about seventy-five sketches it was becoming clear that, splendid though he was, he was coming to the end of his viable life. (By the fifth series, I was writing these sketches with John Hurst.) All the variations had been exhausted; all the jokes and situations explored. It took some doing to persuade Arthur that Oscar, with the greatest regret, should be pensioned off. He was always frightened to drop anything that was successful, and was equally averse to change. Eventually, he saw our point of view and Oscar was laid to rest. To his credit, he was the first to admit that, because of Oscar's demise, the show was better received than ever.

Another situation occurred a year or so later, when Johnny and I tried to persuade Arthur to do a continuing storyline in each show. He was very nervous of the idea, feeling far more at home with the variety format: the quick sketch, a speciality act, a major sketch, another short sketch, a singer and then the principal sketch. I pointed out that Johnny's sketches generally had to be considerably shortened and that a situation comedy, which is what a continuing storyline would be, was no more than a long sketch. The only difference was that it would feature the same characters each week, in the same environment but acting out different situations. At last Arthur was persuaded and together we came up with a format around which Johnny would write. Arthur was to be an abrasive, working-class man with a supportive wife, to be played by the indomitable Patricia Hayes, living in a dilapidated house in a street whose other properties were well cared for by their non-working-class owners. I would live next door in one of these houses, which I had done up very smartly, and would be an Establishment figure with a job in the City. I was to be enamoured of Arthur's attractive daughter, to be played by the young Wendy Richard, and he was to resent her going out with a man of my class. I, in turn, would complain about the state of his property. Arthur, irrespective of his views that it was people like me who were exploiting the working class, would regularly connive to get into my parties. Many story-lines were to evolve from this basic structure and both Johnny and I could see a great future in it.

I duly went away on a tour and returned, looking forward to the new series. When I arrived at the first rehearsal, Arthur's opening words were, 'Have you spoken to your man?' (This was his way of referring to my agent.) He then informed me that he had decided against doing the situation comedy and that we were going to do the usual style of sketch show. I was sadly disappointed, and Johnny was very depressed.

Johnny continued, however, to explore new areas for comedy: for example, our show was the first to perform sketches in which vicars appeared. Up until now it had not been considered right and proper to put a gentleman of the cloth in a comedy situation on the small screen – a hangover from the days when vicars in comedy shows on stage were always called 'comedy vicars', were rather wet, flapped a great deal and spoke with funny voices. Consequently, when, in one of the early series, Johnny came up with a sketch that involved a vicar, the script editor wanted to reject it. I felt that she should be invited to rehearsal to see the sketch performed. I explained that I played the vicar as a very genuine young man, because that was the only way the sketch would work.

This particular sketch was only a 'quickie' in which I, as a vicar, am seen delivering the Epilogue on television, appealing to people to remember others and to be generous and considerate in everything they do. As I say this, the camera pans back to reveal two rough types watching the set. As I say 'Goodnight', the two men get up and throw sacks obviously laden with goods over their shoulders. The one played by Arthur says to the other, 'We'd better be off before he gets home and finds all his best stuff's missing. [Fade out]' If the vicar had not been sincere, the sketch would not have been funny. When the script editor saw it, she was happy and we were never asked to submit material to her again.

There was only one break in my ten-year partnership with Arthur, and that occurred when the actors' union Equity went on strike against the independent television companies for better pay for all performers, but particularly in plays, where there were long rehearsals. Members were instructed not to work for any ITV company and only those who had actually signed contracts should continue to fulfil them.

When Equity went on strike in November 1961 the other performers' union that existed at the time, the Variety Artists' Federation (VAF) came out for the same reason. The heads of the independent companies, however, some of whom had close links with variety performers, recognised that if they had a nucleus of artists, particularly in the world of light entertainment, who were available to work, they could keep their channels open. They therefore made a deal with the VAF for better pay, and its members went back to work.

The strike was lost when the VAF went back, and Equity should have settled then for the best deal possible, or persuaded the VAF to present a united front, or insisted that all performers, whether under contract or not, should refuse to work. The I TV screens would have gone blank and the strike would have been over in a week. As it was, programmes continued to go out. The independent companies already had a number of Equity performers under contract. Granada, for example, had contracted actors for *Coronation Street*, as well as Bill Frazer and Alfie Bass, who appeared in *Bootsie and Snudge*. With VAF members available for other shows, they could continue. On one famous occasion, Bruce Forsyth did the whole of *Sunday Night at the Palladium* with only Norman Wisdom to help him.

The viewers' reaction was, 'Three cheers for the independent television companies for keeping something on our screens when those greedy, inconsiderate Equity members are striking.' We got little, if any, sympathy from the public because Equity showed no common sense in handling the dispute. They should never have called the strike unless the VAF had agreed to stay out as well. Having called it, they should have insisted on every single member walking out, including those who had already signed contracts.

The dispute dragged on. Arthur, who was a member of the VAF, quite understandably, got fed up waiting for me and decided to do a new series with Tony Fayne, another member of the VAF. Though I had nothing whatsoever against him personally, nor against the other VAF members with small parts in the show, I was upset. Equity was incensed. It had already stated that it would not allow someone to do another person's work, and both the television companies and the VAF had agreed. Equity said it would fight the case on my behalf. I told them they must not. I was not prepared to be the sacrificial lamb. If they fought my case, I had no doubt that they would win, but I would never work for independent

television again. I just suffered in silence while the strike lasted –
five months and three days.

Tony Fayne did a good job and I did not begrudge him his good
luck; I was just utterly distraught at my own lack of it. I received a
great deal of sympathy from people in the profession and, of course,
from my family, but sympathy does not bring in work. An irony
about our profession is that if you become well-known working
with one person, other employers do not rush to give you work if
you suddenly become available. When Harry Worth suggested to
his producer that I should join him in his television series, the
response was, 'But he's with Arthur Haynes.' Harry said, 'He's not.
Arthur's working with someone else.' The association, however,
was too well established for them to want to use me with another
comedian. The only broadcast work I had at the time was on radio,
particularly in *Midday Music Hall* from the Midlands, which I
presented fairly regularly thanks to a good producer called Richard
Maddox. You could not live on radio fees, however, even though
working in that medium is invariably a real pleasure. My mind was
turning to the problem of getting back to work with Arthur.

I came to the conclusion that my best course of action would be
to try to do a summer season with him. Up until then, I had always
resisted doing summer shows, whereas Arthur loved them. They
allowed him to do broad, pantomime-type sketches, and he was
back in the realms of pure music hall and variety, which he adored.
George Black was presenting Arthur in his summer season at Blackpool and, in spite of the fact that Arthur was working with someone
else in the television series, George preferred the idea of me doing
a summer show with him. This gave my agent a little leverage
whereby he persuaded George to agree that, if I appeared in the
show, at least one of the sketches would be written by Johnny
Speight. I considered this to be a minimum requisite, since I was
against the idea of performing in all of Arthur's broad, music-hall
sketches. George also agreed that I would do a solo spot.

While I was reassured at having a good contract, I still thought
very hard about the situation in which I now found myself. By
going into the summer season, I was moving into a complete
partnership with Arthur. Until now, I had been doing plays, film
work, radio and cabaret while he went off to his summer shows
and pantomimes. I was probably moving even further away from

the legitimate theatre which I still dearly loved. I regarded the step, however, as an investment, as a way of continuing to work with Arthur in the future which, as I had a young family now, seemed important.

The thought of spending eighteen weeks in Blackpool still did not fill me with excitement, not least because my children were very young and I did not want to be away from them. Once I had found somewhere to live in St Anne's, however, Denise, Suzy and Justin joined me and we had a really lovely time together. For my part, it was an exhilarating experience working to a Blackpool audience because they are the true British variety audience, who have come out for a good time.

There was one major problem with the show: it was too long. George Black had realised that there was too much material and was wondering what to cut. After the dress rehearsal, Arthur's response was typically blunt: 'Well, I think that sketch of Johnny's will be the one to go for sure.' I felt very strongly about this and argued very forcibly. To Arthur's credit, he listened. I said that I felt, as an actor, that the sketch would evolve and that, by the end of the season, it would perhaps be the hit of the show. Fortunately, George Black agreed with me.

We had performed Johnny's sketch on television, but never on stage. The scene was a barber's shop which I entered, as a customer. Arthur, the barber, thought I wanted a haircut. When he realised I wanted a shave and he would have to use his cut-throat razor, his hand began to shake. He regained control, but as he began shaving the shakes returned, and got worse until finally he went completely to pieces. It was a funny idea which, as I had hoped, did develop – even if not in a way I could ever have foreseen. As the season progressed, it raised an increasing number of laughs. We added business. We refined jokes. We worked on the comedy.

After every performance Arthur enjoyed having an inquest over a drink to discuss that night's show with the object of improving it and, hopefully, of finding even more laughs. One night, out of the blue, he suggested that we could actually mime the barber's sketch. He pointed out that we had cut a lot of the dialogue and that most of the laughs were coming from looks and reactions. We talked it through briefly and agreed that we needed the two opening lines of greeting. Then, once I had said, 'I've come in here for a shave,' we could possibly go to the end of the sketch without further dialogue, except for my final outburst. I said to Arthur that this needed some thought before we did anything so drastic, and that I would like to mull it over. He agreed to wait a day or two before we made any final decisions, and I put the matter out of my mind.

The next night, we reached the barber's sketch, did the opening dialogue and came to my line, 'I've come in here for a shave.' Arthur paused, looked at me, but did not come back with his usual line or, indeed, any line at all. He looked at his assistant, played by Leslie Noyes, and then back at me. He was going into the mime version without rehearsal or further discussion. The professional rapport between us was going to be tested as it had never been before. Within the confines of the characters we played, we always intuitively knew what the other was going to say, but this was an entirely new situation. We were now ad-libbing together not with words but with expressions alone. We did it. We achieved exactly what Arthur hoped we would without any rehearsal at all.

In one series of *The Arthur Haynes Show*, it was decided to feature a pop group in the musical spot each week. This was the early 1960s, and a large number of groups were springing up following the success of The Beatles. In fact, most of the best-known groups at the time appeared on the show – except The Beatles. We had Gerry and the Pacemakers, The Dave Clark Five, Freddie and the Dreamers; we also had groups who were just getting started. One of these was called The Rolling Stones. I remember them vividly. They looked completely dishevelled and unwashed but, in spite of that, had already developed an incredible following. Their dilapidated van outside in the studio car park was surrounded by young teenage girls writing passionate and erotic messages on the paintwork with lipstick. It was all new to me, and I wondered whether I was missing something. The group's number in the show was quite good. It was reasonably well received by the majority of the audience, and ecstatically by the few youngsters who had managed to squeeze in. From that one, rather immature performance, however, I would never have predicted that they would become as successful as they have.

An actor who made one of his first television appearances in *The Arthur Haynes Show* was the young Michael Caine, whom Johnny knew through mutual friends. He greatly admired his talent, which had yet to be widely recognised. He wrote a sketch in which Arthur, as a burglar, breaks into a house and is surprised to find someone else in the room he thought was empty. It turns out to be another burglar, played by Michael Caine. The two then discover that they know each other and the old hand gives the youngster a few tips. It was only a brief sketch, but Michael's talent and presence were obvious even then.

One performer whom Johnny was responsible for turning into a household name was Dermot Kelly, a skilled and disciplined actor who had originally worked at the Abbey Theatre in Dublin. He appeared in Johnny's play *The Knacker's Yard* at the Arts Theatre, and gave a fine performance.

Johnny was having difficulty thinking up new situations for sketches involving Arthur's tramp character and brought Dermot into the show as a second tramp, playing in the sketches with Arthur. He was introduced for one sketch only, but it was so successful that he then started to appear regularly – in fact, some of the most memorable sketches we ever did contained these two tramps.

Dermot was used to being in plays, where he had plenty of time to learn his lines thoroughly. He was not what is known as 'a very good study'. The pace at which Arthur worked always put him under great pressure and he never really knew exactly what he had to say by the time it came to transmission. 'Irish', the character he created, arose not out of deliberate planning, but out of necessity. He would always appear to be searching for the word he wanted to use, which was exactly what he was doing. He did it with such style, however, that the viewers, and the critics, all believed it was a brilliantly thought-out characterisation.

Of the supporting players who frequently came into different sketches, Patricia Hayes, an established actress in her own right, was undoubtedly the best. She played the cockney wife in some of the sketches with Arthur, and simply by her characterisation contributed a tremendous amount. Arthur, not being a trained actor, never really appreciated her value and often preferred to have Rita Webb play some of the character parts. Rita was marvellous at playing an outrageous cockney harridan, but had none of the subtle comic timing at which Patricia Hayes was so adept.

One person who had her first experience of television on the show was Barbara Woodhouse. She later went on to have her own series about training dogs, but at the time she had only one animal, a Great Dane called Juno, which she had presumably advertised as fully schooled by her to undertake any situation required on television.

We were doing a sketch in which I played Father Christmas in a big store and Arthur was queuing up with his family to see me. When his turn came, Arthur was to berate me for not giving his son what he had asked for the previous Christmas. The pay-off involved him calling on his dog, which turned out to be a Great Dane, and threatening that it would attack me if I did not cooperate with the presents his family wanted this year. Juno was supposed to snarl and start barking at me; I was to be so frightened that I gave Arthur anything he wanted.

Barbara Woodhouse arrived for the rehearsals with Juno (a male dog with a female name), was told what was required, and nodded confidently. However, since she had never been on television before, during the run-through she proceeded to shout instructions from behind camera to Juno, which was completely incongruous as the dog was supposed to be obeying the orders of its master, Arthur. It was explained that she would have to keep quiet and Juno was to follow Arthur's instructions while the sketch was in progress. She pleaded ignorance, then assured us that everything would be fine on the night.

The time arrived for transmission. When we came to the sketch – the last one in the show – everything was going well, we were getting good laughs, and building to the pay-off with the dog. Whether it was the atmosphere of the transmission or the fact that he could not hear his mistress's voice, we will never know. Arthur shouted for his dog, which he had assured Father Christmas would obey his every command. The dog strolled on looking extremely docile and started to sniff everything in sight. Arthur tried to get Juno to bark; instead, the dog started to lick him affectionately. Arthur was getting desperate, and the audience were loving every minute of it, since they realised things were not going according to plan. The technicians were also laughing, and I was wondering how I could help. At this point Juno spotted the Christmas tree, which was close to me and, overcome with excitement, went up to it and cocked his leg. Most of the spray hit Arthur who, acutely embarrassed, began to shout at the dog and try to get out of its line of fire. By this time, the audience were falling about. It made a good ending to the sketch, but was quite the opposite of what was intended: for once, I was not on the receiving end of the discomfort or embarrassment.

12

. . . .

Still Playing It Straight

I N 1957 Denise and I bought our first house – a milestone in
anyone's life. It was a cottage in an idyllic position on the edge
of Hampstead Heath, and was on the market for £5,750. We
fell in love with it immediately, which endeared us to the
existing owners, Dawn and David Lowe-Watson, who were
delighted that we would care for it as much as they had. In fact, the
four of us became great friends and I later became the godfather to
Dawn and David's third son, Andrew.

1957 was an exciting year: not only had we found our first house,
but professionally I was very busy. *The Arthur Haynes Show* seemed
to be established, I was offered my first film role and I was still
working in radio and cabaret. Then, later in the year, Denise told
me that she was pregnant. Our first child, a beautiful daughter,
arrived the following June.

As a father-to-be for the first time, your whole world changes.
You realise that there will no longer be just two of you; you are
going to become a family. Like thousands of couples before us, we
studied the latest book by Dr Spock. No amount of reading,
however, can prepare you emotionally for such an event. On
Monday 6 June, the day the baby was due, Denise went into Queen
Mary's Hospital, Hampstead, and I felt as if I was in limbo. I wanted
to help, yet there was nothing practical I could do. I had no
professional engagements that week and was forever phoning the
hospital, ready to rush up there at a moment's notice. I kept going
into our tiny patio garden and continually finding things to do,

usually trimming back a very prolific Albertine rambler rose, which had had its first flowering and really needed very little attention. After four days of waiting, the hospital said they were considering inducing the baby. I was not happy about this: nature has its own rhythm, and you only interfere in emergencies. On Friday the 13th our daughter, weighing 7 lb 3 oz, was born without any medical intervention. I am rarely superstitious, but the fact that our first-born arrived on Friday the 13th has made me feel that it is a special day. Whenever it occurs, I always hope something exciting might happen and, oddly, it often does.

We wanted a distinctive name for our little blonde daughter. Denise had been playing Zuleika Dobson in an adaptation for radio of the Max Beerbohm novel of the same name when we were engaged, and since we thought Zuleika both attractive and unusual, it seemed appropriate to adopt it. Knowing how children can be teased at school about their names, however, we decided that we must give her another simpler name as well and chose Suzy, after her late maternal grandmother.

When our son was born on Christmas Eve two and a half years later, we agonised for a long time about his name. We finally settled on Justin because again, at the time, it was unusual. We also gave him the family name Hugh, after my uncle.

Justin's arrival was completely unlike that of Suzy. Not only was it the middle of winter, but we were also trying to prepare for Christmas. Denise had organised everything to perfection and at 11 a.m. on 24 December I drove her to the London Clinic. I was wondering whether to wait with her when she said, 'You remember what happened the last time. Go home, and come and see me with Suzy this evening.'

Back at home around lunchtime, some instinct prompted me to ring the clinic. Denise was not in her room, and I was asked to hold on. Her gynaecologist then came to the phone and, to my amazement, said, 'You are now the father of a fine, bouncing boy, who weighs 8 lb 2 oz.' It was the best Christmas present any parent could wish for, summed up wittily by a large headline in the *London Evening News* above a picture of the three of us: 'Justin time for Christmas.'

Before Justin was born, in the summer of 1960, we decided our little cottage in Sandy Road was too small for two children, and yet we did not want to leave the wonderful position we had, so close to Hampstead Heath. A little nearer the heath, up a public footpath, was a cottage owned by an actress, Marian Spencer. It dated from the early nineteenth century and had originally been lived in by washerwomen. It was actually two very tiny cottages which had been very badly converted into one. I worked out that, by taking out most of the insides, it might be possible to reconstruct the two cottages to give us the rooms we wanted. It was a lot of work but well worth it, and we finished up with the family home we had hoped for, which we named Briar Cottage. Because of its age, we discovered two intriguing clauses in the deeds. The first, which was clearly a relic from the time when the washerwomen were plying their trade, stated that we could hang our washing to dry on the pines nearby on the heath. The second stated that we could graze our cattle on the heath. I always wanted to put this clause to the test, and be discovered by the police milking a cow not far from the cottage. The ensuing scene would have been worthy of a sketch in The Arthur Haynes Show.

The four of us settled very happily into Briar Cottage. The joy and pleasure that a young family brings are beyond words. Watching them grow and acquire language and skills is one of the greatest pleasures imaginable. It was no effort to turn down some of the work I was offered in order to spend as much time at home as possible. Children grow up so quickly that sometimes the dramas as well as the happy times help you realise how precious are the days of their childhood.

When Christmas 1962 approached, Denise suggested that, since I had been through a busy and sometimes stressful year, with the summer season at Blackpool and other work, as well as the Equity strike, it would be a lovely idea to spend Christmas abroad. As I had never skied as a youngster, but had always wanted to, she booked a family holiday in a little Austrian ski resort not far from Innsbruck. We arrived three days before Christmas with all the children's presents, including those for Justin's birthday.

Denise was not interested in skiing and said she was quite happy to wander with the children, and rented two small toboggans for them. In the meantime, I joined one of the beginners' ski classes. One day, I was with my group at the bottom of a nursery slope quite near the hotel, while Denise was with the children a little further up the hill. Suzy, who was always full of fun and very active, caught sight of me and shouted excitedly that she was going to come down to me on her toboggan. She set off. There was no one else on the slope. Due to the limited amount of snow on the ground, her little toboggan hit a bump. She was thrown off and lay on the ground crying, not really hurt but shaken by the tumble. Justin, now nearly two, had also set off on his toboggan towards me. He was taking a different track from the one Suzy had come down, but she had been thrown into his path and he was too young to be able to steer around her. I shouted frantically to Suzy to get up. She preferred to lie there, feeling sorry for herself. I was only about ten yards downhill from where she lay but since it is impossible to go uphill with skis on, I could not run to her and either pull her from the path of the oncoming toboggan, or push Justin aside. Nor was there time to unbuckle my skis. I felt completely paralysed. The agony of seeing the toboggan with a child on it going straight towards her, and being unable to do anything about it, and knowing that I could if I had not been shackled by my skis, was like the worst nightmare come true. I saw the toboggan go over Suzy's face. Having frantically unbuckled my skis, I ran to her and picked her up, to find her face completely covered in blood. I was not sure whether she was dead or alive.

Suzy was alive, but seriously injured. I carried her up to the hotel, where Denise had already rushed in to get help. I sat on a settee in the foyer while the doctor bathed her face and cleaned up the wounds. Her jaw was so badly damaged that she could not speak, and her lip was so severely cut that my heart and stomach turned over.

In our distress, we had both forgotten about Justin. He had found his way back to the hotel and was now standing forlornly in the foyer. I handed Suzy to Denise and went straight to him. The son of the hotel owner, a Mr Singer, was also in the foyer. He spoke very good English, and I said I thought that Suzy's injuries were so serious that the local hospital would be unable to cope. Mr Singer was not normally on duty in the afternoons and it was our amazing good fortune that he was not only there, but happened to have a friend, with whom he had been at college, who was now a leading plastic surgeon in Bern. His name was Professor Neuner, he was from Innsbruck, and usually came home for Christmas.

Mr Singer made a phone call and discovered that Professor Neuner had just arrived home for the holiday. The situation was explained to him and he made immediate arrangements for an operation. A taxi was called, Suzy was wrapped in blankets, I hurriedly put a few things in a holdall for Denise, and the two set off across the mountains for Innsbruck.

Meanwhile, I had taken charge of Justin, who was very shocked by the whole experience and thought the accident was all his fault. I comforted and reassured him, trying as best I could to ease his distress and explain what really happened.

Denise rang that night to say that Suzy was going to be fine. She had, however, been anaesthetised with gas, which she hated. Professor Neuner, whom we discovered later was one of the finest plastic surgeons in Europe, believed that Suzy would make a full recovery and, because of her age, would have very little scarring.

Denise stayed with Suzy in the hospital for four or five days over Christmas, while Justin and I remained in the hotel. We decided to wait until Denise and Suzy returned before we celebrated his birthday, and I simply took him for walks around the resort. I took him on the ski lifts; I also took him for rides on his toboggan.

Denise and Suzy returned. Suzy had stitches in her lip, but was once again able to speak. It was a very emotional reunion and the delayed celebrations of birthday and Christmas were all the more moving. We had been extremely lucky to find such a brilliant plastic surgeon. You would not know today that Suzy had ever had an accident when she was so young.

We had to stay in Innsbruck on our way home so that Suzy could visit Professor Neuner before we returned to England. The present we gave him when we settled his account seemed woefully inadequate for the miraculous operation he had performed, and we will always be eternally grateful. It is tragedies such as this that bind you close as a family, and the memory never leaves you. It also helped me to put major professional disappointments into perspective, because however upsetting they might be, nothing could compare with the near-fatal disaster that occurred that Christmas in Austria.

I spent as much time as I could with my family, particularly when Suzy and Justin were growing up, and was reluctant to take on any work that meant I would be apart from them for very long. For

Arthur Haynes, however, work was always the priority. In many ways, I think, he was a lonely man. He had a charming wife, Queenie, to whom he was completely devoted. She, however, did not enjoy the social life of the show business world. In the years Arthur and I worked together, I met her only once or twice, so never got to know her well. Arthur sought the company of fellow professionals – one, in particular, Leslie Noyes, became both a friend and right-hand man. Leslie had come into the series from the world of variety to play small parts and, although he had a family of his own, was extremely loyal to Arthur, going everywhere with him.

Arthur had never been interested in holidays, and since Queenie was quite happy to stay at home, he simply worked continually. The more successful he became, the greater became his thirst for work – not simply for its own sake, or the money, but because of the insecurity that I believe builds up in all comics the more successful they are. If they are not in constant demand, they feel lost and rejected.

While holidays meant little to Arthur, they meant a great deal to me, and it was this subject that gave rise to the only occasion when he and I had strong words. It occurred during the television series in 1963 that followed the Blackpool season. That show had been incredibly successful, breaking box-office records at the Winter Gardens. The television series was going even better than the previous year and Arthur and I had been asked to appear at the London Palladium in a musical variety show called *Swing Along* in May. Arthur was top of the bill, then came the Australian singer Frank Ifield. I had a good billing – along with Susan Mangham and Joan Savage – and would be doing my solo spot in addition to appearing in sketches with Arthur, which included the now famous barber's sketch. To make it all the more pleasurable, there would be a two-week gap between the end of the television series and the start of rehearsals at the Palladium. I had made plans to take Denise, Suzy and Justin to a little *pensione* on a beautiful, completely unspoilt beach in the north of Ibiza at Portinatz, which I had discovered the previous year when making a travel film for Sky Tours, and was looking forward to it enormously.

Then one day, Arthur came to rehearsal and said, 'Have you heard from your man? We're opening at the Palladium a week earlier.' I said, 'You're mad. What d'you mean?' He replied, 'They've been let down by one of the American artists and they've asked us to step in. It's a great compliment.' I could not restrain myself. 'You really are an absolute fool, Arthur. If you go on working like this, you'll have a heart attack. You need a holiday. You should take a complete rest and go away somewhere.' His response was typical: 'If you don't want to do it, don't bother. We'll get somebody else.' I replied, 'Arthur, of course I'll do it – but I still think you're a fool.' I was deeply disappointed. All I had now was a break of five days, which Denise, Suzy, Justin and I spent in Dorset. We had a lovely time, but it did not compare with that distant haven in Ibiza.

I did not realise how prophetic my remarks to Arthur were going to be. Half way through the Palladium season, he had his first heart attack. It happened on August Bank Holiday weekend, which made it very difficult for the management to find a replacement. Hardly any agents were in their offices, but eventually a comedian was tracked down and booked temporarily to take Arthur's place. Derek Roy came in on the Monday and did a solo spot, while I performed one sketch with Arthur's understudy. To have performed the barber's sketch, however, would have been out of the question, for that was a completely personal performance between Arthur and myself.

On the following Tuesday, I was called to rehearsal again and discovered I was to be working with Tony Hancock. It was an exciting prospect, as I had always admired him. Tony deputised for Arthur until he returned nearly three months later, looking somewhat thinner and more rested than I had ever seen him. The heart attack had not been a serious one and he was now sufficiently recovered to work, although he had been warned not to overdo things. He stayed out of the opening sketch, in which his understudy was by now fairly proficient, and we rested the barber's sketch for a while. Arthur concentrated on his opening, one other sketch, and his closing routine. His illness, however, had not changed his attitude to work one iota and it seemed that he had no intention of curtailing any of his former activities in show business. I again thought he was foolish, but this time thought it wiser not to stress the point.

The season at the Palladium continued until the middle of

November and *Swing Along* became the longest-running variety show ever staged there. Afterwards, we went without a break straight into rehearsals for yet another television series. I was sure that Arthur was still overdoing things and I was struck by how tired and drawn he looked. I did not remark on his appearance, but did tactfully ask whether he was perhaps doing a little too much. He said he had been doing one or two 'dinners', which meant doing his act as a cabaret spot, generally at company functions. I know from personal experience that after-dinner speeches can be particularly hard work and this must have been especially so for Arthur. Most speakers write their own material or adapt their routine to suit the occasion or audience; Arthur relied purely on his variety act regardless of whether it was wholly appropriate or not, which can only have induced more stress. Even though he claimed he was fully fit, deep down this was perhaps just one of the anxieties that was troubling him. His lack of confidence as a sketch performer was magnified by his state of health, and he also knew that Johnny Speight was finding it more difficult to come up with amusing and original sketches.

Another matter that may have unsettled Arthur was something that may sound strange to the more rationally minded. Rationality, however, does not necessarily count for a great deal when it comes to analysing the mind of the comic. Arthur was a loyal member of the Grand Order of Water Rats. He attended meetings whenever he could, and was rewarded by being elected King Rat. He would report to me after these meetings that his fellow Water Rats had been most complimentary about his straight man, saying that he would be wise to keep someone who contributed so much. This was too much for Arthur: he needed to feel he had achieved his success without help from anyone else. I used to feel very uncomfortable when Arthur told me someone had commented on his straight man. It needed no great psychological insight to realise that he resented such comments, and I rapidly came to wish that people would stop making them.

Arthur always had to outshine his fellow performers, and he always liked to be in control. He had a particularly idiosyncratic attitude to directors and producers, whether he was working on television or radio. Since he knew what he wanted in a sketch he would take charge of the read-through, and in the television series he was lucky to have someone like Dicky Leeman who would go along with him. Once Arthur had got a sketch reconstructed as he wanted it, he would turn to Dicky and say, 'Right, it's all yours now, Dicky, where do you want us to move?' Arthur never appreciated Dicky's talent enough or his contribution to the success of the show. I know that Dicky was hurt by this and could not understand it. Arthur only came to appreciate what a director could contribute when Dicky was not available because of other commitments. On one occasion Josephine Douglas, who had at one time been a television presenter, was assigned to direct the show. She was one of the first women to do this demanding job, and did it well, but presumably did not have much experience working with comedians. She certainly did not understand Arthur. At one point in rehearsal she said, 'No, I don't think you should do it that way,' and got up to demonstrate how she thought the scene should be performed, taking Arthur's role, and then responding with mine. I looked at Arthur, his face said it all, and we both started laughing. She never knew why. I think she thought it was her acting. This was the only occasion when Arthur asked for his director to be changed.

When a series of thirteen radio shows was made, also called *The Arthur Haynes Show*, the producer was a young man called Richard Dingley. I think this was one of his first jobs as the producer of a comedy show. Unfortunately, he was unaware of the personality of the man with whom he was about to work.

Richard called us to rehearsal at the Paris Studio and was anxious to get straight on to the microphone to time the show. Arthur, however, insisted on sitting in the little 'green room', reading through the scripts and getting them exactly as he wanted them, ignoring Richard and giving instructions, as he normally did at a read-through, to everyone concerned. Eventually, he said, 'Right, Richard, we're ready to go to the mike – it's all yours.' By this time, poor Richard was in a dreadful state. He only had time now for one run-through, and since he was not very experienced, he got very nervous. He subsequently collapsed and the next thing we knew he was in hospital. Arthur and I went to visit him, Arthur never realising that it was he who had probably put Richard there in the first place.

Meanwhile, other Light Entertainment producers were sent

down to direct the shows, and word soon got round that Arthur was a special kind of character whom you did not try to direct – you just let him do it and edited the finished product afterwards. During the thirteen programmes we had no fewer than nine different producers. Even Arthur saw the funny side of this. He put up on the wall of the green room a roll of honour of producers for the series. It became quite something in the Light Entertainment Department to be listed on it. We used to wonder who was going to arrive for the next recording, to replace the hero from the previous week who had fallen in action.

The following year, another radio series was commissioned. Richard Dingley, now fully fit, was again to produce and one of the first things he did was to say that we would not be using any of Johnny Speight's sketches because all he was doing was adapting or recycling his television scripts. Whether this was a directive from the departmental head, or whether it was Richard's way of trying to have more control over the programme, I do not know. It is now accepted practice to use television scripts for radio: *Yes, Minister* and *Dad's Army*, for example, were transferred to radio virtually unaltered. In the days of *The Arthur Haynes Show*, however, material had to be original.

Richard Dingley's hopes of directing Arthur in a new series with new writers never materialised. Arthur could not or would not change his ways – if anything, he spent even longer in the green room getting the scripts to his liking, because they were not the ones he had done before. Poor Richard became more and more anxious and, after the second week, he left. We never saw him again.

Following our successful television series in 1964, Arthur and I were booked to do a summer season in Scarborough. This is one of the most beautiful resorts in the British Isles, with its parks, its magnificent open sandy beaches and the Yorkshire moors nearby. The chill of the North Sea is well compensated for by the lack of Blackpool-sized crowds and Blackpool-type concrete. Denise, Suzy, Justin and I stayed in a small house on a farm just outside the town and enjoyed exploring places such as Robin Hood's Bay, Ravenscar and Hayburn Wyke. When I was not working or with my family, I learnt to water-ski, which subsequently became one of my favourite sports.

About the middle of the season, Arthur asked me, as he often did, to drop in to his dressing room after the show for a drink and a chat. I assumed that he wanted to discuss any little points that had arisen during the evening's performance. On this occasion, it was quite different. Expressing himself very clearly, but pleasantly, he told me he had given the matter a great deal of thought, and said that it was obvious to him that I wished to go my own way. I was taken aback. I pointed out that this was not what I wanted. The only reason, I reminded him, why I took on individual work was that I had to keep my options open as we did not always work together. He, for instance, had accepted a small part in a film and gone to Hollywood for a spell; he also did pantomime. I would accept other work while he went off on his own, but I was quite prepared to turn it down to help build our partnership. He said that was not what he wanted. He would, however, for the time being, like me to do the next television series with him and then join him on his trip to New York, for *The Ed Sullivan Show.* It was the first time he had been asked to appear on American television, and he obviously wanted to go in strength. This work would take us through to the following spring, when our partnership of some ten years would end.

The trip to New York helped to take my mind off our impending split. It was my first visit to America, and my appearance on *The Ed Sullivan Show* was to be my first on television there. I had been told by my agent Richard Stone that, for the sake of convenience, Arthur's agent was arranging the whole contract, and this would also simplify the process of getting the necessary work permits. I thought nothing more of it. Arthur helpfully said I would need what the Americans called a 'tax lawyer', who would work out my tax on the spot before I left the States, otherwise I would have to pay tax twice – American and British.

When I visited the lawyer in New York, I explained my working relationship with Arthur in Britain, and that I was an artist in my own right. He found this confusing, because it did not tie up with the way I had been booked. He advised me to speak to American Equity, who had sanctioned my work permit. I duly phoned them and was asked some very searching questions, which I found unsettling. The union representative then perturbed me further by saying, 'Mr Parsons, I don't like the sound of what you're telling me.

Where are you placed? The Blackstone Hotel? OK. Stay right where you are. We're coming straight round.'

I was extremely alarmed and wondered what on earth I had done. It did not help that just before leaving England I had seen that magnificent film *On the Waterfront*, with Marlon Brando and Rod Steiger, about the corruption-riddled New York docks and the gangster union bosses who ruled them. I had visions of a couple of heavies in big black coats bursting into the hotel room and snarling, 'We don't like it. Get the hell out of here right back on that boat to England. Some other guy should be doing the job you're doing.'

The two representatives arrived. They certainly were not happy with the situation. After I had answered their questions, it dawned on me what Arthur had done, and in what an embarrassing position he had placed me. I back-pedalled rapidly, not only to save further embarrassment, but also to safeguard my job in New York.

Arthur, in order to bring over Leslie Noyes as well as me for the fees on offer, had asked his agent to book us as 'Arthur Haynes and Company'. I was not even named on the booking form and contract. This was the reason, I now learned, why I was on such a modest salary. If I had been listed by name and given the status of a performer in my own right, I would have needed a different kind of work permit and would automatically have commanded a higher fee. I had no option but to play Arthur's game. I was there, I wanted to appear on *The Ed Sullivan Show* and, for the sake of harmony, I did not even bother to raise the matter with Arthur.

On the show, I was not introduced by name. Things, however, worked out in my favour in the end. As soon as the first show finished, Ed Sullivan came straight over to me and, in front of Arthur, said, 'You're one of the finest straight men I've ever seen. I just had to congratulate you.' Arthur's face was a study, but there was nothing he could say.

Despite this problem, I enjoyed my first trip to New York immensely, and as there was a two-week break between the two recording sessions, Denise and I were able to explore the city.

Denise never really liked Arthur. She admired his talent, but never warmed to him and felt he took advantage of me. I have always accepted people as they are. I knew, for example, that Arthur had some difficulty in parting with money, but used to accept that this was just the way he was and, for the sake of the partnership, did not say a word. An incident during dinner together in New York, however, made Denise very angry. Arthur had suggested we meet with him and Leslie at a French restaurant he knew. We had an excellent meal. When the waiter arrived with the bill, he presented it to Arthur who took it, studied it carefully, put it back on the plate and said, 'Yes, that seems in order. Will you give it to the gentleman over there?' I was the 'gentleman', though that was the last thing Denise thought Arthur at the time. I did not want a showdown, so I settled the bill.

News of the split between Arthur and myself became public in April 1965, during the rehearsal period for the West End play *Boeing-Boeing*, in which I was taking over the lead. True to my word, I had not said anything to the press and Richard Stone had secured a clause in my contract to the effect that, should the play continue to run beyond nine months and Arthur Haynes required me for another television series, I would be released. Richard always felt that the break-up had been caused by an aberration on Arthur's part and that we would eventually get together again.

Some people have described a comedy partnership as a form of marriage, and there is a great deal of truth in this. Some of that truth came out when Arthur announced that he was taking a new straight man in his next television series. His statement to the press was not as he had promised it would be when he had first suggested the split. It came over as that of a jealous partner who felt let down by the other, and who was piqued that I should be moving into what was obviously a very prestigious and successful position in the theatre. I was hurt by what he said, as well as bewildered, because it was not what we had agreed.

The first I knew of the stance he had taken was when I was in the middle of a rehearsal for *Boeing-Boeing*. The stage director asked if I could take an urgent phone call from the *London Evening News*. This was to be the first of many calls from newspapers that day. I had not realised how popular *The Arthur Haynes Show* had become. The split was headlined in every paper. Even the quality press had a piece about it on their inside pages. The first person to speak to me was James Green, a professional and fair-minded journalist. He told me what Arthur had said, and for a moment or two I was completely dumbstruck. James wanted my side of the story, so I stuck to what I had promised Arthur I would say: it had been a mutual agreement; I was always happy working with him and hoped that the occasion might arise again in the future. I stressed, however, that it had originally been Arthur's decision and not mine that we should separate. James Green presented the story on the front page of the *Evening News* both objectively and amusingly. Other papers seemed to take one side or the other. Either I was an ungrateful cad who had walked out on his partner for something better, or he had become unreasonable, foolish, and had got rid of a straight man who had made a large contribution to the success of the partnership.

At the time of the announcement of the break-up, Arthur had started rehearsals for his new series with Tony Fayne in my place. The series did not prove to be as successful as previous ones. There must have been something in our relationship which had developed over so many years, which was lacking when he worked with someone less familiar with his style. Arthur probably realised this and the tension began to build inside him. In the summer season that followed, he displayed his anxiety by taking with him, for the first time, Dermot Kelly and Rita Webb from the television series. He went back to the Winter Gardens where together we had broken box-office records. The season was not a success.

I heard later from Tony Fayne that Arthur would complain during the day of indigestion and hardly eat. Then, after the euphoria of two shows, he would feel better and go out for a huge meal. I have little doubt that the pains he thought were indigestion were symptoms of his earlier illness.

Arthur finished his Blackpool season and went straight into rehearsals for yet another television series. By now his agent realised things were not going well, and for the first time advised him to do a 'storyline' – a situation comedy instead of a sketch show. If he had done this much earlier, the decline in his success and, indeed, his health, could perhaps have been avoided. It was also decided to drop Johnny Speight. The new scripts teamed Arthur with a woman. There was to my mind, though, something about Arthur's personality that bounced better off a man. One step in the right direction was to bring back Dicky Leeman to direct. He told me that the new scripts put Arthur in a domestic situation that was not ideal for him; nor did he think the overall concept was very good.

All of this must have been very stressful to someone of Arthur's temperament.

During the first week of rehearsal, Arthur suffered a second heart attack from which he never recovered. His death at the early age of fifty-two was very sad and a great loss. He was an exceptional comedy performer as well as a great comedian. He loved his work and was at his happiest when he was facing an audience. If it is any consolation to those close to him, it is that if a man like Arthur Haynes, who is driven by his work, dies working, at least we know he died as a result of what he loved most.

13
· · · · · · · ·

On the Big Screen

D
URING the years I was working with Arthur Haynes, I appeared in a number of British films. In the early years of our partnership there were reasonable breaks between each television series; it was only after 1961, when I agreed to do summer seasons with Arthur, that I became committed to working with him almost full-time and so had little opportunity to accept other work. I had not appeared in a film since *The Master of Bankdam* in the late 1940s. The way I obtained my film role was quite remarkable.

For a number of years I had been having my hair cut at a traditional barber's, Trumper's, in Curzon Street, Mayfair, which is still popular. My regular barber was an engaging Scotsman called Jock Johnson. I enjoyed his conversation and stayed with him until he retired in the 1960s. Jock lived near Penge, not far from Bromley. When I was working in repertory there, I often used to give him my two free tickets and, over the months, he saw me in a number of different roles.

Jock, it turned out, also cut Roy Boulting's hair. In the early 1950s, the Boulting brothers, Roy and John, were reaching the peak of their film-making careers. They were identical twins, almost impossible to tell apart, which sometimes made working for them very confusing. I am sure, however, that it was their empathy as twins which allowed them to work together so well. They shared the responsibilities equally: when Roy was directing, John would produce, and vice versa. They made a number of very successful comedy films including, in 1955, *Private's Progress*, which made a star of Ian Carmichael.

Whenever I visited Jock to have my hair cut, he would tell me in his strong Glasgow accent, 'I had Roy Boulting in and I told him about you. How good you were. And I said to him straight – he should use you in one of his films.' I asked Jock to stop. I thought that if a top film producer was having a comparatively unknown performer promoted by his barber, it would put him off that actor for good. I used to say, 'Leave it to my agent, Jock, please. That's his job.' Jock would reply, 'Well, I don't think your agent is doing a very good job. I happen to know Mr Boulting's casting again. Why doesn't your agent send you along?' I was touched by Jock's loyalty, but genuinely thought his constant singing of my praises would be counter-productive.

One day in 1957, the telephone rang at home. A Scots voice said, 'This is Jock.' I said, 'Jock who?' I had never heard my barber's voice on the phone. He replied impatiently, 'Jock Johnson, your barber. Now listen.' He then became very businesslike and spoke exactly like a theatrical agent. 'I've fixed it with Mr Boulting. He wants to see you. This is the number. Take it down and give him a ring. He's expecting you. OK? Got that? I'll see you soon, and you can tell me how you got on.' Then the money ran out in the call box.

I could not believe Roy Boulting had told Jock to tell me to contact him. If my agent could not fix an interview, how could my barber manage it? For three days, I ignored the message, then thought there was nothing to be lost in trying. As soon as I was put through to Roy Boulting he said, 'I've been expecting a call from you. What happened?' I replied that I thought, as Jock had been talking about me for years, I would be the last person he would want to see. He said, 'I was getting a bit tired of hearing your name, but thought someone couldn't be so persistent without reason. Also, I realised if I did see you, I could then have a haircut without your name always being worked into the conversation.'

Roy and John Boulting were casting a new film, *Brothers-in-Law*, from a novel by Henry Cecil, a comedy about two young men – played by Richard Attenborough and Ian Carmichael – starting in the legal profession. I was being considered for the part of their friend, who was not connected with the law, was mad about motorcars, and who eventually walks off with the girl they both fancy. It was a very attractive supporting role. I was tested, given the part, and also offered a contract with options on my services for future films.

It was a time when artists were put under exclusive contract to a film company, a relic of the days just after the War when the Rank Organisation had tried to build a British film industry and, emulating the great days of Hollywood, signed up many aspiring young performers in the hope that one or two would develop into stars and they would reap the benefit. They even started what became known as the Rank Charm School, where completely unknown performers, some not even in the profession, were taught to walk, smile, dress and, presumably, act. These starlets would be trotted out at film premières and other high-profile occasions so that they could be seen by the public. Some were utterly untalented and it took the men at Rank, who were not steeped in show business, some time to understand that there was plenty of talent in the profession without them having to go searching for a face that might do nothing more than photograph well. The only name I know who graduated with distinction through the Rank system was a young girl from Swindon called Diana Fluck, who wisely changed her name to Dors, or had it changed for her; but she would undoubtedly have succeeded anyway.

By the mid-1950s, all film producers in the country began to realise that, as their industry was based near the centre of an entertainment profession where a wealth of talent already existed, unlike Hollywood, which had only a cinema industry producing cinema-trained performers, long-term contracts were unnecessary. The contract the Boulting Brothers offered me was probably the last of this kind that they signed. When it expired, Roy and John were very loyal, and I subsequently appeared in good roles in a number of their films.

Some may wonder how my barber managed to obtain an interview for me when my agent appeared to have failed. Richard Stone may not have pushed me as hard as Jock because, quite simply, he may not have had great confidence in me as a performer. As I have already said, I do not look like an actor. We had a very warm relationship, however, and I always felt he was the ideal man to represent me (even when, on one occasion, out of integrity, he did not push me for a job that I wanted because he thought some other artist, represented by another agent, was better suited). After the expiry of my first contract with him, our association was built entirely on trust, a simple handshake, and that is how, sadly, it finished in 1988.

In *Brothers-in-Law*, the young actress who supplied the love interest, and who drives off with me in my old jalopy at the end of the film, to the chagrin of the other two men, was Jill Adams. She was most attractive, with a look of Marilyn Monroe. I always thought that she had the potential to become the British equivalent of the great Marilyn, but no one in this country seemed interested. I am sure that in America, someone would have put her under contract and groomed her for film stardom.

After *Brothers-in-Law*, Roy and John demonstrated their faith in my abilities by casting me in their next production, *Happy is the Bride*, an adaptation of the highly successful Esther McCracken play *Quiet Weekend*, in which I had played the lead in the early 1950s at Windsor Rep. The leading roles in the film were played by Ian Carmichael and Janette Scott. Cecil Parker played the bride's father, Edith Sharpe her mother and Joyce Grenfell her aunt. John Le Mesurier was the bridegroom's father, and I was the brother of the bride, who returns home to be best man, accompanied by his very hip girlfriend, played by a young Elvi Hale. Other actors and actresses, who might be called part of the Boultings' 'team' and who were cast in this film, included Terry Thomas, Eric Barker, Irene Handl, Athene Seyler, Miles Malleson and Joan Hickson. Roy and John liked to employ performers who had worked in variety and music hall, such as Terry Thomas and Eric Barker. They really launched Terry Thomas on his film career, and tried to find something for him in each film that they made. Above all, however, they engaged players whose talent they respected, and who had served them well or been successful in their previous films. They gave Peter Sellers, another performer who hailed originally from the world of variety, his first major cinema roles, and teamed him with Terry Thomas in *Carlton Browne of the FO*, in which I also had a supporting role. I worked with Terry a good deal, including in the Betty Box film *Too Many Crooks*, in which he played the lead. He was not the kind of man you could get close to, or share a joke with. Larger than life, and a fine comedy performer, he knew what he wanted for Terry Thomas, and pushed hard for it. He was one of those unusual comedians who understood comedy and how to get his laughs, but who did not seem to have much sense of fun.

Working on *Happy is the Bride* was like being part of a very creative family. The young star, Janette Scott, Thora Hird's daughter, was charming and unaffected. She had been a successful child actress, yet there was nothing precocious about her. Joyce Grenfell, who played her aunt, was one of the most atypical stars with whom I have ever worked. She was the least theatrical person I have ever known, and looked as if she had wandered into show business by accident. Yet she was wholly professional and greatly talented, with the most exquisite sense of timing and that particular gift, granted to few, of making even a straight line sound funny. It was her 'ordinariness', however, the impression she gave of being no more than an inspired amateur, that endeared her to the British public. For there is something in the psyche of the people of this country which makes them vaguely suspicious of anyone who appears too professional. If you can convey that what you are doing has been achieved with the minimum of effort, even though it is the result of great skill, the British will warm to you far more than if you come across as an obviously dedicated professional.

It was on *Happy is the Bride* that I learnt my most valuable lesson about the technique of film acting. It was Roy Boulting who guided me. Most directors then would not have bothered, or would have been unable to bother. In my opening scene, I arrive home full of excitement and enthusiastically greet my parents and introduce my pretty girlfriend. I came on the set and, at the first run-through, gave the scene all the panache I could. Roy gently took me aside and said, 'The feeling was fine. We want the excitement and the enthusiasm; but try to convey it using only twenty-five per cent of the effort. You've been working a lot in theatre, where your job is to project your performance so that it appears natural to someone sitting at the back of the dress circle. In the cinema, your audience is just behind the camera lens. You don't have to project any further than that.' It was the basic lesson, which I have never forgotten.

Apart from working with the Boulting Brothers, I was lucky to be offered many attractive film roles by other producers. I was also fortunate in playing opposite some very attractive actresses. In *Eye Witness*, a film made by Sydney Box for the Rank Organisation and directed by Muriel Box, I played the part of a young doctor, and there were two lovely creatures, playing nurses, with whom I shared scenes. One was the gorgeous Belinda Lee, a voluptuous blonde with limited talent but outstanding beauty; the other was Susan Beaumont, another beautiful blonde, less sensuous than Belinda, but with more personality.

In *Too Many Crooks*, the Mario Zampi film, made for Rank, my leading lady was the lovely Rosalie Ashley. She played Terry Thomas's daughter in this comedy thriller and I played her fiancé, whom she brings home to meet her father. He is indulging in some pretty shady deals and I turn out to be a tax inspector, which created a lot of fun. Once again, I was cast as a pillar of the Establishment and, in a way, I was playing the straight man role, giving Terry Thomas plenty of opportunity to indulge in some manic reactions every time I appeared in a scene with him. At least I had the consolation of playing some love scenes with a beautiful girl, though many of those moments were left on the cutting-room floor, as they did little to keep the comedy moving.

I worked a lot for the Box family and, to an extent, felt as if I was part of a team. Betty Box, who also produced films for the Rank Organisation, which were directed by her husband Ralph Thomas, cast me in one or two of her films. In *Doctor in the House*, I was once again cast as a doctor. Perhaps I looked convincing as a medical man because I had unconsciously absorbed a number of my father's professional mannerisms. It was certainly a role I found comfortable to play.

The most memorable part I played for Betty and Ralph was in *Upstairs and Downstairs*, which starred Michael Craig, Anne Heywood, James Robertson Justice, and a most delectable French actress, Mylène Demongeot. She was blonde, gamine, with a bubbly personality and great sex appeal. She played the part of a Swedish au pair who causes havoc in the English household where she has come to work. I was only in one short scene with her, in which Daniel Massey and I, along with several others, vie for her attention. I also fancied her like mad in real life. I find the natural sophistication and chic possessed by many French women irresistible. Mylène was very warm and friendly, and when it came to shooting the scene, all the young men tried to chat her up between takes. The next day Betty Box said to me that she had been amused by our behaviour

Suzy, just sixteen, photographed by me on holiday in Menorca, 1974

Suzy and Justin aged three and fifteen months, photographed by me in the South of France, 1962

With Suzy and Justin, thirteen and eleven, and our Jack Russell, Tunky, on Hampstead Heath, in 1972 when sideboards were fashionable

With Denise, Suzy and Justin being energetic around Hampstead Heath, 1975

Trying to be Eamon Andrews with
Benny Hill as a surprise guest in a
skit on *This Is Your Life* with
Robertson Hare playing the
unsuspecting subject, 1969

With Benny Hill in his sketch
sending up the film *Bob and Carol
and Ted and Alice*, 1971

With Benny Hill and Bob Todd in one of Benny's medieval costume sketches,
1970

The five girls who shared the hostess responsibilities in *Sale of the Century* in 1978: (clockwise from top left) Sophie Batchelor, Eunice Denny, Laura Beaumont, Caro Greenwood, Christine Owen

Celebrating after the final recording of *Sale of the Century*, with Carole Ashby and Karen Loughlin launching me back to the theatre, 1983

Top With three of the original *Just a Minute* team, (left to right) Clement Freud, Kenneth Williams and Peter Jones, 1975

Above With Dora Bryan and Cyd Charisse, when we appeared on Denis Norden's afternoon programme during the run of *Charley Girl*, 1986

As Rev. Wainwright in 'The Curse of Fenric', with Dr Who, Sylvester McCoy, and his assistant, Sophie Aldred, 1989

As a pantomime dame

As a punk rocker for a promotional advertising campaign

With Alice Cooper when he appeared on 'The All New Alphabet Game' in *Night Network*, 1987

Unveiling the plaque the Dead Comics Society put up to Arthur Haynes in 1993, with (left to right) David Graham, David Lodge, Johnny Speight and Jack Douglas

The Nicholas Parsons Campaign

THE FOLLOWING PEOPLE HAVE GIVEN NICHOLAS THEIR SUPPORT. IT'S YOUR TURN THIS THURSDAY

| Jonathan Ross | Tim Brooke-Taylor | Rik Mayall | Barry Norman | Barry Cryer | Bill Tidy | John Benson | Robert Powell | Willie Rushton |

NICHOLAS PARSONS

Nicholas Parsons was unique in launching his Rectorial Campaign on National TV (Night Network) last Friday, and followed that up by mentioning St.Andrews the following night on The Noel Edmonds Roadshow. This Tuesday, he again plugs St.Andrews on National TV ("Prove It" ITV 6.30).
It is this sort of media exposure we need, and Nicholas can deliver.
Within the first few months of being elected he will attempt to regain the World Record for the longest after-dinner speech in St.Andrews and the subject of the speech will be "St.Andrews and the Future". The media coverage this will produce will highlight our position.

But certainly the most important job that Nicholas will perform is arguing our corner on the University Court. As a graduate of Glasgow University, he is familiar with student views. His national work as a fundraiser for hundreds of charities will be put to good use in attempting to raise funds for The Crawford Centre and other St.Andrews projects

Nicholas Parsons is commited to the task ahead. He is in St.Andrews all this week - come and let him pull you a pint in Ma Belles this Wednesday !.Nicholas is ready to throw all his weight and energy behind St.Andrews.Perhaps that's why Frank Muir, and Tim Brooke-Taylor have endorsed him.

Nicholas Parsons. Ready to be Rector from Day One

Above A poster designed by my team when I stood for the Rectorship of St Andrew's University, 1988

Right With some of the team who represented the Lord's Taverners in a special game at Lord's to celebrate the fortieth anniversary of the founding of the charity, July 1990. (Left to right) Chris Tarrant, Tim Rice, Willie Rushton and Henry Kelly

As the Rev. Green in *Cluedo* in 1993 with (left to right) Liz Smith, Leslie Grantham, Jerry Hall, Joanna Lumley and John Bird

Above With my grandchildren Annabel and Tom, three and a half and two, when they lived in Jersey, 1992

Right With Annie, after a graduation ceremony at St Andrew's University (wearing my Rectorial gown), 1991

Below Relaxing with Annie when working on the *Canberra*, 1986 and then added, 'But you were the one she asked about. You made a hit there.' I was most flattered, and surprised. If I had not been married, I might have tried to follow it up. It is one of the joys and sadnesses of show business. You meet someone, you work briefly together, a chord is struck, and then you both move on.

In the British film industry, one very clear-cut example of a team being formed was that of the *Carry On* films. It was a deliberate policy on the part of the producer, Peter Rogers, and the director, Gerald Thomas (the brother of Ralph, with whom I had worked so happily). They also had a quite specific approach to the film-making itself. Each *Carry On* film was made on a more modest budget than a big feature and the production schedule was intense. The team, therefore, had to be made up of very talented performers who could all be relied on to work quickly and, it was hoped, get everything right first time. Some felt that they were not paid as much as they might have commanded in a major feature production, but their reward was the loyalty shown to them. Once part of the team, wherever possible a part was found, or even created for them, in subsequent films.

Through Richard Stone, I was offered a supporting role in one of these films, *Carry On Regardless*. Unfortunately, I blew any opportunity of working again with Gerald Thomas. I failed to grasp the professional ground rules by which these films were shot. I had been working with the Boulting Brothers and others on higher-budget films, where there was more time and retakes were often common to get a scene as polished as possible. This was not how Gerald worked, and I should have had the common sense and professional instinct to realise it. After a take of a long and complicated scene which featured Joan Sims and myself, Gerald, in the gentle, courteous way he had of speaking, asked me how I felt. I replied quite truthfully that the run-through of the scene in rehearsal had been better. He agreed, but said that he was satisfied. My reaction should have been, 'If you're happy, Gerald, that's great.' Gerald then asked me if I would like to go again with the scene, to which I should have replied, 'No, not if you're satisfied.' It was my big moment in the film, however, which finished with Joan Sims pouring a bottle of wine over me, and I tactfully replied that I could make my part funnier. Gerald considerately said he would do another take, which we did, and he admitted it was better. The following day, however, Richard told me that I had been reported as being fussy. If only Gerald had behaved like a conventional director and had said quite firmly that he was thoroughly satisfied, or that time did not permit a retake. I had accidentally put my head into a professional noose, which had tightened round me, and I never worked in another *Carry On* film.

The situation came back to haunt me a few years later, but fortunately without disastrous results. I was working in a film called *Don't Raise the Bridge, Lower the River*, which starred the American comedian Jerry Lewis. It was made in this country by Walter Shenson, for whom I had worked before. The director was Jerry Paris, who had directed most of the *Dick Van Dyke Shows* in the States, and I assumed that this was one of his first cinema assignments. He was the typical ebullient American, who was always wisecracking and who generated a warm, friendly atmosphere on the set. The only problem he had was with Jerry Lewis, who was dour and difficult. He was suffering from what I call 'comic's melancholia' – I never saw him smile once, and there was always a sombre feeling when he was around. Even the most sensitive director cannot get the best out of a comic's talent if the melancholia in his system is fighting the extrovert side of his nature.

The situation on the set that brought back unhappy memories occurred in a scene where the character I was playing is in bed feeling very unwell. It was a short, funny scene, which came to a climax with me apparently throwing up. We rehearsed, and went for a take. I put in some funny business, but there was a technical problem, so we went for another take. Jerry was happy, and then asked me how I felt. I told him I thought that the previous take had been better. He agreed and said immediately, 'Let's go again.' Then, in his usual jokey manner, he said at the top of his voice to amuse everyone, 'We're going again. Mr Parsons is not happy. It's Mr Shenson's money, but he's not bothered ...' Panic-stricken, I interrupted him. 'Jerry,' I said, 'forget it. I don't want to go again. If you're happy, we'll leave it.' He looked at me, mystified, and asked what was up. I briefly recounted my previous experience of being offered a retake to make something funnier. He looked at me with genuine concern. 'I was only gagging, Nick, you realise that. Never forget this: it's your face in front of that camera, and if you can do a better one, that's good for you, and that's good for me.

That way, we're both winning.' Then, with a twinkle in his eye, he said, 'But, it had better be a better one.' We did another take. It was a much better one. He came over and put his arm round me. 'That's my boy,' he said. 'How I love a professional.' I may be very British, but I enjoy the enthusiasm of the Americans, and the pleasure they take in working as hard as possible to get everything as right as possible.

In 1960 I formed my own production company. I had been wanting to do some independent productions for a while, but an opportunity arose when a travel firm called Blue Cars, who were principally concerned with coaching holidays in Europe, and for whom I had written and appeared in three television commercials the previous year, asked if I would write and appear in three more commercials the following Christmas. The managing director was a man called Ken Fox, the brother of Robin Fox, one of the directors of the Grade Organisation and father of the actors William and Edward and the theatre producer Robert. I accepted the offer to write and appear in the commercials, but asked that my own production company should make them. (I did not say at the time that the company had not, as yet, been formed.)

Ken Fox backed his instinct and, as he liked what I had done for him the previous year, and as we had a very happy working relationship, he readily agreed. I discovered that, besides the three commercials, he also wanted a thirty-minute advertising film that could be distributed to travel agents to promote Blue Cars Holidays, as well as a special thirteen-minute film with an original story that he wished to place in the Advertising Magazine slot that then existed on commercial television. The material for the two films was to be shot on location in Europe.

First, it was necessary to decide on the format for the three commercials, which were to be shown over the Christmas and New Year period. I thought of three different themes, and took them to Ken. Instead of using a storyboard, however, I described each of the three verbally, acting parts out where necessary. Two of the themes were quite conventional, but the theme for the other triplet was completely way-out. After I had given my 'performance', I sat down. Ken looked at me. 'Well,' he said, 'of the three ideas, there's one that definitely appeals more than the other two.' I said, 'You mean the safe one with the pretty scenic shots?' 'No,' he said. 'I mean that crazy idea with all the gibberish.'

Then came the problem of negotiating the budget, which, in fact, turned out to be very straightforward, as Ken told me that all the money he had available was £3,800. While this was worth considerably more in 1960 than it is today, it was still an extremely small amount out of which to make three commercials, an advertising magazine programme and a travel film. As I already had an income from The Arthur Haynes Show, however, and wanted a contract in order to get my production company off the ground, I accepted. I then had to decide whose production facilities to use. Here, I was very lucky. In fact, I did not realise how fortunate I had been until after I had negotiated the deal.

The previous year, I had worked for Gerry Anderson of A.P. Films. Gerry, who later became famous for his space puppet series such as *Thunderbirds* and *Captain Scarlett*, had a film studio in Slough, where he had made other children's puppet series, which included *Twizzle* and *Four Feather Falls*. Denise had supplied some of the voices for the former. In developing the voices with her for the second series, I had read the part of the hero in *Four Feather Falls*, Tex Tucker. As a result, Gerry asked me if I would play the part in the series, which I was thrilled about. I still think this series is one of the most delightful and original children's puppet series ever made. It was set in the Wild West, and had all those magic ingredients that children love.

At the time I approached Gerry about the Blue Cars contract, he was going through a difficult time. He had just heard that the contract on *Four Feather Falls* was not being renewed, and was trying to develop a different series called *Supercar*, which required a fair amount of investment in the puppets before the idea could be sold. I told him what was required; I also told him the exact amount of money in the budget. He very sportingly agreed to split the budget, in return for which we could use his studios and technicians, and he would design all the sets and direct the commercials. I agreed to pay all the artists who appeared in the films and luckily was able to persuade Arthur Haynes, for a very modest extra fee, which Blue Cars agreed to pay, to make a guest appearance in the advertising magazine film.

The commercials ran for a minute each. For two of them, I

devised dramatic scenes for two characters that, respectively, looked and sounded like part of a French and German film. The dialogue, however, was an unintelligible yet authentic-sounding gibberish of the relevant language. Denise, making one of her rare appearances before the camera, played the female character in each commercial. Being a voice expert, she could speak the gibberish with total conviction, which was just as well, since I could not have afforded to employ an actress outside the family. As in a foreign film, the scene depicted in each commercial had subtitles which, purporting to be a translation of the dialogue, were all about the incredible Blue Cars Holidays.

The third commercial in the trilogy was set not in Europe but on Mars, with two Martians looking through a telescope, fascinated by a sudden flurry of activity on earth below. They discuss what they see, and discover that the interest is all to do with something called Blue Cars Holidays. As with the first two commercials, the gibberish was translated with subtitles.

Gerry Anderson and his team had been most inventive with the Martian clothes and headgear, but when we came to film the commercial, we ran into difficulties. We unexpectedly became inhibited by the whole idea. I began to think that we had been too clever and was convinced that it was not working. Gerry was beginning to feel the same, and then showed his astuteness as a creative director by saying, 'Before we all get overwhelmed by this, let's go back to first principles. When Nicholas first dreamt up this idea, we all thought it was funny and original. Let's get that feeling back and go from there.' He was right. We did another take, with Denise and I throwing ourselves into the Martian gibberish as if it was the funniest thing we had ever done. Gerry said, 'Cut', and then added, 'That's it. We've got it. It works.'

The three commercials were edited, timed and dubbed, and the carefully composed subtitles added. Ken Fox viewed them and liked them immensely, and they were delivered to Associated Rediffusion, who were transmitting them. My favourite was always the French one, and I felt that the Martian one was not perhaps as effective as the other two. I think Ken Fox agreed, but I remember Gerry saying that we ought not to underrate it.

The commercials were transmitted over the Christmas period and during January 1961, which is the peak promotional time for travel firms. From the reactions, comments and criticisms in the trade press, as well as the public response in the form of holiday bookings at Blue Cars, it seemed that they achieved their purpose.

About this time, *Television Mail* announced that they were going to present the first British Television Commercial Awards. Since our commercials had created some impact, I had been asked to write an article for *Television Mail* about the making of them, which made me think that it might be worth entering them for the awards. I did not think that we had much chance of winning anything, but hoped that we might get a mention in one of the categories, which would be helpful to a young production company. The presentation was due to take place in the spring at the Hyde Park Hotel in London. As the day approached, one of the directors of *Television Mail*, Derrick Baker, rang to ask if I was going to the banquet. I told him that I had not thought about it – actually, I was trying to economise after putting so much money into the company. He suggested that it might be a good idea if I did come, and added that it might also be nice if Gerry Anderson could be present as well. Gerry agreed to join me, and I booked a table for our wives and ourselves, and also invited Ken Fox and his wife.

The banquet was enjoyable, with that slightly over-animated atmosphere which seems to exist whenever a large number of people connected with the media – most of whom know each other – are gathered together for the giving of prizes. The presentation of the awards was very well handled, with the chairman of the judging committee announcing the first three in each category, and an award being given to the advertising agency and production company responsible for each winning commercial.

We were already in a slightly embarrassing position, since no advertising agency had been involved in the making of the Blue Cars commercials. It was a direct contract between client and production company, which is perfectly all right, but not popular in the industry, since advertising agencies quite naturally like their clients to think that it is their experience which is going to produce a winning commercial for them. Anyone, therefore, who has the presumption to make not one, but three, commercials through direct contract, on a shoestring budget, without any previous experience in that area, is unlikely to win friends and influence people. Nevertheless, the applause was very generous when it was announced that the French commercial had been placed third and the Martian commercial was the winner in the Consumer Services category. To be fair, there was not much competition. Gerry and I, as joint producers, went up together to receive the plaques.

We sat down, excited and surprised by our success. After the category winners had been announced, the chairman of the judges made a speech to introduce the Grand Prix awards. He explained how their decisions had been reached and that every aspect of advertising had been taken into account in choosing the final winner. He also emphasised that it had been a unanimous decision on the part of the judging panel, which seemed a little laboured, but in retrospect was probably his way of trying to pre-empt a lot of the emotion that he knew his final announcement would arouse. The judges' choice of the best ten commercials for 1961 was then announced in ascending order and shown on the film screen in turn. Before the announcement of the Grand Prix winner there was a long pause while the chairman of the judges made the most of the occasion. The moment is indelibly etched on my mind, and I genuinely had no idea what was about to happen. In fact, I was still thinking which other outstanding commercial I had already seen that evening would be taking the prize, when onto the screen came the Blue Cars Martian commercial. The result was so unexpected that Sylvia Anderson gave an audible gasp, Gerry's jaw dropped visibly, Ken Fox started to clap enthusiastically, and Denise instantly slipped down into her chair, trying to look inconspicuous.

When the commercial finished, instead of the usual tumultuous reception, the applause was subdued, almost desultory. Gerry and I stayed glued to our seats. The chairman had to invite us to come to receive the plaques. We rose sheepishly, to no more than polite clapping. Talent did not come into it. We had done the unforgivable: we had entered somebody else's domain and, without any experience or track record in the area, had taken the major prize. How presumptuous! How tactless! How unfortunate – for us. It is said that winning awards is the kiss of death. This certainly turned out to be true for Gerry and myself. Flushed with success, we both hoped that requests to make more commercials would follow. I spent a fair amount of time and money trying to build on what I had gained. Nothing happened. My company did not receive a single enquiry, and even Blue Cars decided to trade on the success they had had with their 1961 commercials and cancelled their plans for new commercials in 1962. Such is the unpredictability of the advertising world, and the irony of the entertainment profession.

Nothing in show business, however, is ever lost or in vain. I subsequently made a few industrial films, which turned out to be quite profitable, and later moved on to make documentaries and entertainment shorts for the cinema – which are not profitable. Gerry Anderson's company survived, and *Supercar* was sold to ATV television. Both it and his subsequent space series have been enduringly successful.

My short-lived success as a writer and producer of commercials did not prevent advertising agencies from offering me work appearing in commercials. Over the years, I have performed in quite a few, and in all of them, I now realise, I appeared as the straight character in a comic situation. There was only one set of commercials that I turned down. These were not humorous, and were worth a great deal of money, and I still wonder if I did the right thing. It was the early 1960s, I had become well known through *The Arthur Haynes Show* and was asked to appear in a series of commercials promoting OMO, the popular washing powder, in which the presenter asks housewives in different parts of the country which of two piles of washing they think is the whiter. The commercials were very simple, very direct, and sold a lot of OMO.

At the time there was a reluctance among legitimate actors and actresses to appear in commercials. It was considered almost infra-dig to endorse or advertise a product on television, and probably harmful to your professional career. No one would ever cast you in a play again. If you worked in light entertainment it was not so bad, especially as it was unlikely that you would be offered work in drama, such was the distinction between the two areas of entertainment. Nowadays, it seems that well-known performers from the 'legitimate' side of the profession are only too keen to appear in commercials, and cash in on this lucrative area of show business.

I discussed the matter with Richard Stone, outlining my anxieties and stating that I still wished to work as an actor. He considered it acceptable for someone in my position to appear in a commercial advertising most goods or services ... but not a washing powder. That was too downmarket and could damage my chances of being taken seriously as an actor or comedy performer. How times have changed! If the opportunity arose now, my attitude would be quite different; but such offers usually only come once in a lifetime.

I appeared in one or two advertising magazines, and in a commercial with Arthur Haynes for Fox's Glacier Mints. The only other product I endorsed was a dog food called Stamina, a contract I was happy to accept as the commercials were to be humorous and therefore in keeping with the comedy work I was doing at the time. I now realise that I was appearing as a straight man to a host of dogs. There is a saying in show business that you should not work with children or animals. I like working with children, especially in pantomime, but animals can be difficult. I should have known better than to take on a whole pack of them.

The storyline of the commercial was that I appeared on a desert island, incongruously dressed in black jacket, pinstripe trousers and wearing a bowler hat – clothes I often wore on *The Arthur Haynes Show*. I had to say, 'Alone at last! Now I can tell you all about Stamina . . .' As soon as I mentioned the word 'Stamina', innumerable dogs of all shapes and sizes appeared from every direction and leapt all over me to try to get at the dog food. This was not going to be easy to film.

I went to a small studio in Bushey, where I met the director who introduced me to an animal trainer who had brought a large collection of dogs. I changed into my suit and spent some time getting to know the animals. This dog handler assured the director, and everyone else concerned, that the dogs would respond to his commands and, on the given word, rush forward and leap all over me.

We tried a rehearsal. The dogs seemed more interested in exploring the studio. We tried more rehearsals, with the dog handler exhorting his animals to 'attack' and 'go fetch him, boy'. The director then pointed out that, as they wished to record only my dialogue and the dogs' barking, the dog handler would have to keep quiet. It was then decided that I should have some food smeared over my hand, in the hope of luring the dogs towards me.

Before we did the next rehearsal, the dogs were given the scent of the food, after which it was hoped that they would all leap forward for more of the mushy stuff, which was now oozing out between my fingers. Two or three of the more intelligent dogs got the hang of it, but the remainder still went sniffing round the studio. After many more rehearsals, between which dog food was smeared on my clothes as well, and attempts at some takes, which took most of the day, it was decided to abandon the filming and try again the following morning.

When I arrived at the studio the next day and put on my city suit, which now smelt of stale dog food, I was told that a different group of dogs had been brought in, and I was introduced to their trainer. A tough-looking character with a strong Cockney accent, he did not make me feel very confident. 'Don't worry, Nick. I've been starving 'em since last night. They'll be ready to 'ave a go as soon as I give 'em the word.' More dog food was smeared over my suit jacket, along the arm, round my hand and underneath the tin of Stamina. The director decided to try a take right away in the hope that, with the dogs fresh, it might all happen. It was not much better than the previous day. The dogs were affected by the atmosphere and the lights, and while most of them could smell food, they were puzzled as to where to find it. More dog food was smeared over my black jacket, which was now becoming saturated and rather evil-smelling. We tried further takes. Some of the cleverer dogs were now getting to know their part and jumped up to lick my clothes. I decided the best way to act the scene was to pretend to fall down when the dogs jumped up, so they could crawl all over me and appear to be licking the tin of Stamina in excitement. I would then shoot up from the midst of this canine mêlée to proclaim the virtues of said dog food.

One of the stage crew then said that dogs went mad for aniseed, so somebody went in search of this dog-provoking substance while we broke for lunch. I was not very hungry, and no one wanted to sit next to me, as I smelt disgusting. After lunch, I climbed back into my jacket, which was now as stiff as cardboard, and the aniseed was added to the already pungent smells that were issuing from the ruined material. Being black, it still looked quite presentable.

We tried another take. More dogs got the idea. This encouraged the dog handler and the director to smear more aniseed on me, and really cover me from top to toe with dog food. It was pushed down my collar, behind my ears, around the rim of the bowler, on my trousers, into the pockets of my jacket; some was even put under the rim of the bowler so that it got into my hair, in the hope that, when my hat fell off, the dogs would lick my head. With me in this revolting state, we began the next take. By now, some of the dogs went for me on cue; others still could not understand that I was 'food'. They barked loudly, but refused to leap.

The director was now desperate. More food and aniseed, and this time some bacon fat for good measure, was smeared over me and lumps of meat and bacon lodged wherever they could be concealed. I will never forget the next take. I stepped into camera shot and spoke the opening line. The dogs were released and more than before came bounding towards me. I fell to the ground as if knocked over by the rush, and all seemed to be going well. I tried to tell the viewers about the quality of Stamina, while covered with frantic canines of all descriptions. Then two of the animals, which had not yet had a lick, or a bite, leapt forward for their share. Unfortunately, they had picked up the scent from my lower regions, on which they both landed together with great force. There began a dog fight for the meat that was clinging to my trousers which threatened to endanger my life and limbs. I leapt to my feet before the two ferocious creatures could cause me irreparable damage and ruin my married life into the bargain. In the true tradition of show business, the director simply shouted, 'What was wrong? Why did you run away? It was going so well.' I explained, and while he was mildly sympathetic, he asked if I would do it again as quickly as possible now that the dogs were in the right mood. I said I was not very happy about the mood of one or two of them, and asked if anyone had a cricket box that I could wear. Since none could be found at short notice, and it appeared that the dogs were straining at the leash to get back at the evil-smelling, food-encrusted suit, I compromised and put on two jockstraps.

Now feeling very nervous, I lined up for another take. Even more food and aniseed were smeared over me and, for good luck, they also put some chocolate in with the food, so once the dogs discovered the source of supply, they would continue to enjoy themselves. With my hand barely able to hold the tin of Stamina for all the gooey dog meat in my palm, and smelling like something that had stepped out of the filthiest rubbish tip, gritting my teeth yet trying at the same time to look happy and relaxed in front of the camera, I stepped forward on the word 'Action'.

On cue, the dogs were released. Praying that this was the take that would work, I threw myself into action. With dogs leaping all over me, I pretended to fall to the ground. As I was licked all over, my bowler was knocked adrift and one dog found the food in my hair. I got out the lines extolling the qualities of Stamina, rose to my knees with the dogs still barking, and delivered the pay-off line. The job was finished. I rushed to change and shower, but the smell of dog food remained with me for days, so vivid was the memory. The commercial had taken two days to shoot, had cost a small fortune in film stock, and was thirty seconds on the screen. It was very successful and ran for quite a time, and though I was well paid, I felt I had earned every penny.

I did not appear in any commercials while *Sale of the Century* was running, as the Independent Broadcasting Authority was very sensitive in the 1970s about someone who was in a programme offering goods as prizes endorsing products of any kind on television. They thought that there could be a conflict of interest. I thought this was absurd, as I did not choose the goods in the quiz.

In the 1980s, I appeared in one commercial in which my performance received the most surprising reaction. The commercial, brilliantly directed by Nick Lewin, was for Renault cars, and I appeared as a quiz-show host in someone's nightmare, driving his car at speed around an underground car park. It was a clever and funny commercial, and I treated the job as an actor. I wore a flamboyant evening suit and gave an over-the-top performance, trying to create a caricature of a game-show host who might appear in someone's horror dream. The commercial was a great success, and I was praised for sending myself up. This surprised me, as I felt that I was doing a straightforward acting job. I have never taken myself seriously, so it seemed natural to take off the image of the personality I must have projected when hosting a quiz show. This confused the press, as it did not fit neatly with the labels they like to use when writing about me. Fortunately, it endeared me to the young audience that I was now building, as it seems they warm to anyone of the older generation who has the ability to laugh at himself. Once again, it was the unexpected and modest engagement that created the most impact.

14

·······

Playing for Laughs

THE break-up of my partnership with Arthur Haynes made
me sad, because I felt that we could have gone to greater
heights together. I was given little time to dwell on the
loss, however, as I was offered a marvellous part in a
successful and popular play, *Boeing-Boeing*, taking over from Leslie
Phillips when the play moved from the Lyric Theatre in Shaftesbury
Avenue to the Duchess Theatre, off the Strand. What I did not
know at the time was that John Gale, who was presenting the show,
had decided that the play had probably all but finished its run in
London. After all, it had been on for three years. Apparently, one
of the reasons he was pleased to cast me in the lead was that he had
estimated that the stay at the Duchess Theatre would probably be
very short, after which the play could go on a national tour, helped
by the fact that the star name was someone well known to television
audiences. The fact that I would be appearing in the play in London,
even for a short while, meant that he could advertise the show in
each town not only as a 'record-breaking success from the West
End', but also with the West End cast. Had I known all of this, I
might have been a little unsettled. The move to the Duchess
Theatre, however, was far from disappointing. The play eventually
ran for another eighteen months in the West End, though I stayed
with it for only fifteen. Peter Byrne, who took over from me, went
on the provincial tour.

Boeing-Boeing had a very chequered history. A clever farce, it was
originally written in French by Marc Camoletti, and was only an

hour long. It had run for a long time at a small theatre in Paris and had subsequently been translated and extended into a two-hour play by Beverley Cross for performance in this country. John Gale had bought the rights, cast David Tomlinson in the lead, and invited Jack Minster to direct.

The play opened to very poor reviews in its try-out week in Oxford and Jack Minster, who had invested in the production, had grave doubts about bringing it to London – it is even rumoured that he tried to sell his shares. It needed great courage on the part of John Gale to continue with the play. On Thursday 20 February 1962 it opened in London, received good reviews from *The Times* and *Telegraph*, but the popular press said it was dreadful. Bernard Levin, writing in the *Daily Mail*, even went so far as to say that the only things missing were the sick-bags on the backs of the seats for the audience.

Word of mouth is what creates a success, but you need audiences to start the ball rolling. The two good reviews brought some custom to the box office, and this was boosted by J.W. Lambert on the Home Service on the Saturday following the opening. He stated that the play was a 'true, blue French farce'. The final boost that put the seal on its success, and confirmed John Gale's faith in the play, was an unexpected piece of good luck which occurred during the second week.

Around this time, the BBC was presenting excerpts from West End shows live from the theatre. It was not great television, but wonderful for the box office of the show from which the excerpt was taken. The BBC always chose comedies and, naturally, always picked the most entertaining scene. They chose the second scene of the first act from *Boeing-Boeing*, which probably contained some of the funniest moments in the play. It was one of the last trans-missions of an extract from a London play that the BBC ever presented. The next day, the box office was inundated with calls for tickets; the play was soon established.

When you have a farcical comedy and you have a director who encourages the leading players to search out areas for extra laughs, any inventive performer will always try to improve the comic potential of the part he is playing. This was certainly true of David Tomlinson, and I am sure there were more laughs in the play when he left it a year after the opening than when he began. It was also true of Leslie Phillips, who played the part for two years. I inherited all the extra material that had been inserted by my two predecessors, and introduced some more. I was encouraged by Jack, who was one of the most creative comedy directors with whom I have ever worked, particularly when it came to comedy business. I learnt a great deal from him, in particular a variation of the old show business maxim, 'Leave them wanting.'

It is always a temptation when you are working in comedy and getting laughs to push for extra ones. The show had been running for a while, during which time I had built in a number of extra laughs, principally with stage business. I asked John Gale if Jack would come back and look at the show again to approve anything I had added, and generally judge my performance. Jack's response to my request was typical: apparently he told John Gale, 'Leading actors don't really want to be told things or disciplined; they enjoy doing it their own way.' John insisted that I really was genuine in wanting his reaction. Jack duly watched the show and came back-stage afterwards. Because of my respect for him, I was slightly nervous. He had a wry smile on his face as he entered the dressing room, which put me at my ease, although I knew something was coming. He approved my overall performance and the new comedy business, but asked why I had extended this at one point with an extra line. 'Because it gets a laugh,' I replied. 'It's not necessary,' he said. 'Do the business, get that laugh, and move on.' He was right, of course. There is a fine line between indulgence and keeping the comedy moving, which is more difficult to judge in a broad comedy, such as a farce. I hated cutting any extra laughs, but had too much respect for Jack not to do as he suggested.

The unexpected can happen in any production, and while I am used to coping with most situations, a near insurmountable challenge did occur during the run of *Boeing-Boeing*.

The character I played, Robert, is up from the country visiting an old friend, who has organised his private life in a most ingenious way. He has an 'arrangement' with three air hostesses, timed so that as soon as Air France flies out, Lufthansa flies in, and as soon as Lufthansa departs, TWA arrives. Something is bound to go wrong eventually, which is, of course, the basis of the play, and this begins to happen when Robert is in the flat alone.

At the beginning of Act Two, the maid goes out to buy some

cigarettes for the German air hostess who has returned without warning, to find Robert in the flat. The two are immediately attracted to one another. The girl excuses herself and goes into the bedroom, leaving Robert alone on the stage. At that moment, the maid enters with the cigarettes. Robert immediately has the idea of taking the cigarettes so that he can give them to the girl personally. He asks the maid to hand them over, but she refuses, so Robert grabs the packet from her and then dismisses her to the kitchen.

That is what should have happened. On this occasion, I grabbed the cigarettes with my usual flourish, but did not have proper hold of the packet. It flew out of my hand, over the footlights and into the orchestra pit, which contained a single piano. My mind raced. For practical reasons concerned with the plot, we could not continue without the cigarettes. I thought of suggesting that the maid go and buy another packet, but realised that that would be impossible, as she had already established that it had taken her a long time to buy the first one. Also, what would I do while she was off stage?

I glanced into the orchestra pit and saw the cigarettes lying beside the piano. I looked puzzled, and then looked at the audience. They started to laugh, which gave me confidence. The agonised look on the face of the maid also helped.

We had established on my first entrance in the opening scene that there was a huge picture window in my friend's flat which was over the footlights, so I began ad-libbing, 'It's a pity the window was open.' The audience laughed. I pretended to look out of the window (over the footlights) and continued, 'Oh, look, the cigarettes have landed on the window ledge of the flat below.' I proceeded to climb over the footlights into the orchestra pit, lowering myself down by holding on to the edge of the stage until my feet touched the piano. The audience now applauded. I managed to climb onto the piano without doing myself an injury, jumped to the floor of the orchestra pit, picked up the cigarettes, and then climbed back the way I had come, at the same time giving a running commentary on the neighbours who lived in the flat below. My final ad-lib, to the actress Joanna Henderson who was playing the maid and who had remained paralysed on stage throughout, was, 'I hope in future you'll make sure that window is kept shut!' This not only amused the audience; it 'corpsed' her. I told her not to laugh at my misfortune and suggested that she go back to the kitchen.

The play then continued as normal – and as written.

On another occasion, the unexpected came from a member of the audience and was memorable proof of the comedy maxim, 'Laughter travels backwards.' Laughter is infectious, and while no two audiences react in the same way, if you can get the front rows laughing out loud, this is invariably communicated to the people behind. But it never works the other way. It does not matter how much the people at the rear of the auditorium laugh, they cannot infect the rows in front, and while everyone might be enjoying what they are seeing, it will be a very subdued crowd.

The incident that proved this to me was at a matinée. Suzy, who was then a lively seven-year-old, came to the show with our au pair. It was the first time she had seen me on stage, and she was very excited. Our company manager put the two of them in the box, which at the small Duchess Theatre is at the back of the stalls. Business at this particular matinée was rather poor: the auditorium was barely half full, and the audience were the quietest we had ever had. In the interval, Suzy was brought to my dressing room and pleaded with me to be allowed to sit closer to the stage. I did feel that I was being a little pompous in not letting her sit in the stalls, so I asked our manager if he could find her and our au pair seats nearer the front.

I think Suzy found her own seat, because when the curtain went up on the second act, which begins with me sitting centre stage, talking to the American air hostess, out of the corner of my eye I caught sight of a highly excited seven-year-old bouncing up and down on her seat, plumb in the centre of the front row. She was entirely surrounded by a typical London matinée audience: mostly middle-aged women.

In the scene that followed, the American girl is flirting with me and remarks on my lips, which she finds irresistible and has to kiss. The love scene progressed along these lines, until she said, 'I just love the way your lips moved when you said that. Say it again.' I repeated the phrase, 'It depends what you mean.' She said that she found it so exciting that she just had to kiss me again. I then put my hand up to hold her off for a second and, turning my head away, mouthed the phrase, 'It depends what you mean,' a number of times. She asked me what I was doing and I replied, 'Just rehearsing the lips.' There was usually a big laugh, then it was into the clinch. On this occasion, as I was mouthing the phrase, a completely uninhibited young voice suddenly shouted, 'Daddy, what on earth are you doing?' It not only made us dry up on stage; it was so perfectly timed that everyone in the audience suddenly laughed. If it had been pantomime, I would have spoken back to her, but as it was, we had to try to continue with the scene. Suzy was totally unaware of the impact she had made. It was as if this very subdued crowd had suddenly woken up to the fact that they were permitted to laugh out loud. Suzy then proceeded to laugh at anything remotely amusing that happened on stage, and the audience slowly followed her. Perhaps some of them were enjoying the comedy through her eyes, but whatever the reason, they continued to laugh in a way they certainly had not done during the first part of the play.

To the average member of the public, it seems that an actor is extremely lucky to play love scenes and kiss pretty girls with no strings attached. I will not try to pretend it is unpleasurable – unless you do not particularly like the girl, or she has had garlic for supper the night before. It is, however, a technical exercise that has to be timed with the lines. (Also, what is the pleasure in kissing a girl in public? It is something you can only really enjoy in private.) When the love scenes in a play appear during a comedy sequence, it becomes even more of a technical exercise. You have to concentrate on the timing to make sure the laughs come as planned. I do not think the public are particularly impressed by this argument, but it is true!

While I was in *Boeing-Boeing* I came very close to experiencing what must be the actor's nightmare – failing to get to the theatre on time. I have dreamt this many times, and the panic you feel is indescribable.

In the side street off the Aldwych, where the Duchess Theatre is situated, there were two parking bays in front of the theatre. The commissionaire kindly kept one of these for me every night, so I had the luxury of parking on the doorstep and just walking into the theatre. It is a rule of theatre that every artist reports in at what is called 'the half', thirty-five minutes before the curtain rises. On this occasion I left my home in Hampstead, allowing the usual time to reach the theatre by 7.25 p.m. The curtain rose at 8, and I was on stage ten minutes after that. I reached the end of Gower Street and there was a solid block of cars, which was unusual. The queue began to crawl. I was not particularly worried, as it only took me ten minutes to get ready, and if I arrived after 7.30 they would simply assume I had been delayed. The queue edged slowly forward, but the time was ticking away. It was now nearly 7.45 p.m. and I was about 200 yards from the theatre, just north of the Royal Opera House where, I discovered subsequently, the Queen Mother was attending a special gala performance, which was the cause of the traffic jam. Another five minutes passed, and I had moved about fifty yards. At this rate, I was not going to be at the theatre until after 8 p.m. I was now desperate. I could not abandon the car in the middle of the road. I was going hot and cold. I was due on stage in fifteen minutes.

In a real crisis, you suddenly find you have an authority that does not normally exist. In the car directly in front there was a man sitting in the passenger seat. I jumped out of my car, ran round to the passenger door of the car in front, opened it and said sternly, 'Can you drive?' The man nodded. 'Can you drive an Alvis?' He nodded again. I then said with supreme authority, 'Please get out of the car,' to which he meekly responded without a murmur. 'The key's in the ignition. I'm due on stage at the Duchess Theatre in ten minutes. Leave the car with the commissionaire. He'll look after it. The curtain's going up. I'm running.'

With that, I sprinted all the way to the theatre, where there was a different panic, as no one knew about the traffic jam. The curtain was about to rise and the understudy had not arrived – presumably he, too, was held up. I was ready in ten minutes; the curtain was only delayed for three. The nightmare was over.

The sense of relief lasted until the interval, when a different panic gripped me. What about my beautiful Alvis? I rushed outside, and there was the car, sitting happily in its normal place. The sense of gratitude I felt to this unknown man, who had saved me from disaster, was tremendous. Then another awful thought struck me: in my panic I had forgotten to ask him to leave his name and address with the commissionaire. I would not be able to thank him for his kindness. I live in hope that he might still contact me, and I will at last be able to thank him properly for his noble deed that day in 1965.

*   *   *

When I left *Boeing-Boeing* in mid-1966 it was the first time for a few years that I was not committed to working on stage during the summer. I received one or two new offers but turned them down, and while I would have liked to have taken over from Richard Briers in the leading role of *Arsenic and Old Lace*, Richard Stone advised against it. The show, revived at the Vaudeville, had only about three months to run and Richard, my agent, felt that, since *Boeing-Boeing* had been such a success for me, it would be a professional step down to take over a part. From a prestige point of view, perhaps he was right. I have always felt, however, that it is the quality of your performance by which you are judged and would have liked to play the role again.

Instead, I took the chance to enjoy a long family holiday on the then unspoilt island of Menorca. I subsequently bought a plot of land in one of the popular and fast-developing villa areas near the coast at Binibeca, for which I paid the princely sum of £500. When we returned to Menorca the following spring, however, we could see the way the area was being developed. I sold my plot of land and Denise bought an old farmhouse as a personal investment. We renovated it and had many very happy family holidays there over the next twelve years, until it was sold in 1980 because we were visiting less frequently. We also needed the money to bring down our joint loan at the bank, which we had taken out to buy our house in Berkshire before we had managed to sell Briar Cottage.

When we returned from our first trip to Menorca in 1966, I was asked to go and meet an American theatre producer who was planning to take a British cast to star in a Broadway production of *Say Who You Are*, the very funny farcical comedy by Keith Waterhouse and Willis Hall, which was currently enjoying a very successful run at Her Majesty's Theatre in the West End. There were two equally attractive parts in the play, one of which was played in London by Ian Carmichael, the other by Patrick Cargill. I felt it was the part played by Ian Carmichael that would suit me best (it is interesting that, in the Broadway production of *Boeing-Boeing*, he played the same part as I had in London), but the Americans wanted to consider me for the other role. In the end, I read both. They offered me the role I did not want and for which I thought I was less suited, and I turned them down. I turned down the opportunity to star on Broadway! Some people thought I was mad. Such opportunities rarely occur a second time. Would I have gone if they had offered me the part I really wanted? Perhaps not. I had plenty of work in Britain; we had just expanded and rebuilt Briar Cottage, and Suzy and Justin were settled at school. I did not want to be separated from my family for a long time and, if the play was successful on Broadway and other offers followed, I was not sure that I wanted to bring the family over, with all the upheaval for them that would involve. From a personal point of view, my instinct to turn down the offer was probably correct; from a professional point of view I probably turned my back on a fascinating and very different career in America.

Within a month or two of turning down the American offer, Peter Bridge, who was presenting *Say Who You Are* in London, invited me to play the part that I wanted in a new production at the Vaudeville Theatre. Prunella Scales, who in 1967 was not as well known as she is now, was billed alongside me, and the other two roles were taken by Peter Gray and Gillian Barge, playing her first leading role in the West End. The production opened to good reviews, but did not survive long, due mainly to the timing. Peter Bridge had finished the run with the previous company at Her Majesty's and then allowed more than a week to elapse before beginning the new production. I am sure the London public assumed it was a revival, and not a continuation of an established success with a different cast. This feeling was borne out by the fact that the tour which followed the run at the Vaudeville was an amazing success. The box office receipts in each major city we visited were excellent: in Glasgow, for instance, we played to capacity for the whole week and the money taken exceeded that which the previous company had taken on their visit prior to the show opening in London.

Following the tour of *Say Who You Are*, I was asked to appear in another West End show, *Uproar in the House*, an inventive farce written by Anthony Marriott and Alistair Foot. I was delighted: I would be reunited with two old friends; I was also being asked to play a wonderful part.

A firm of estate agents have a house on their books which they cannot sell because it was designed and built round a huge tree, which grows up through the middle. In order to sell it, the agency persuades one of their smart salesmen – the part I played – to take up residence in order to convince prospective buyers of the advantages of the property. An actress is brought in to play my supposed wife, and various members of the office staff play other characters to give authenticity to the situation. The prospective buyers arrive, and then a fog descends. Everyone has to spend the night in the bedrooms, which are arranged in a row along a half-landing. Nobody is who they say they are; all of them are concerned about their reputation. It has all the classic ingredients for a farce.

Tony and Alistair came up with some marvellous ploys to promote the show, one of which was to offer a free seat with every ticket bought by anyone in the London area with the name of Parsons. A large number of people took up the offer and many of them came backstage to greet me, some out of courtesy to say thank you, others as long-lost cousins, and a few who gave me the impression that this was to be the beginning of a newfound family friendship. I never realised there were so many people in the Greater London area with the same surname as myself. They were all different shapes and sizes, but I assured them all that, somewhere in the past, we must have a common ancestor.

The man who bore most resemblance to me was a reverend from the West Coast of America. It transpired that he and his family had come to the show not because of the advertisement, which they had not seen, but purely because we shared the same surname. Like many Americans, they were interested in tracing their ancestry and came backstage to discover whether we could be related. I told them about my father's paternal ancestors in Oxfordshire and they decided they must go and search among the parish records. They probably now know more about my ancestry than I do.

Tony and Alistair took every opportunity to promote *Uproar*. They heard, on one occasion, that some London University students were going to kidnap me and hold me to ransom as part of their rag-week fundraising efforts. In theory, it was a good idea: the theatre management would have to pay for my release, otherwise the curtain could not go up with the leading performer on a Bank Holiday matinée performance.

Tony and Alistair turned the situation to their advantage. They employed two strong Securicor guards to collect me from home and bring me, handcuffed, to the theatre in one of their sealed vans. This in itself got considerable press coverage, which was good publicity for the play. The two guards stayed with me all through the matinée, shadowing my every movement. One of them even naively asked if he should come on stage with me in case the students suddenly appeared and started to clamber over the footlights. I pointed out that this was not necessary, but suggested that one of them should stand guard outside the front of the theatre to forestall any invasion. The other decided to stay in the wings, and dogged my footsteps wherever I went throughout the afternoon and early evening. They left only after the curtain for the evening performance had risen without any sign of the students, having finished the tin of biscuits and basket of fruit in my dressing room, as well as all the beer and most of the whisky I kept for guests. They said it was the best day of their working lives.

In *Uproar*, the part of the actress engaged to be my wife was played by Joan Sims, a lovely leading lady and great fun to work with. Joan was particularly fond of spring onions. I have a sensitive nose and rarely like kissing anyone, even professionally, if they have eaten strong-smelling food. Joan had an ingenious solution to the problem: whenever she ate spring onions before a performance she would always save two, which she would then arrange to have laid out before the mirror on my make-up tray. I pointed out that, while it was thoughtful of her, I did not always feel like a couple of onions before a performance. I always ate them, however, but then wondered whether we were being considerate to the rest of the cast. There was one afternoon when I swear all the cast had eaten onions. They were all being terribly British; all taking avoiding action, rather than finding out where it started and suggesting that we should give the onions a miss before a matinée.

I had one of those truly embarrassing moments in the play that can only occur on stage. At one point Joan hurries out from the kitchen, wearing thick oven gloves and carrying a pile of hot plates. The doorbell goes and she says, 'I'll get it. You take these.' Without thinking, I immediately take the plates and, of course, scald my hands. I usually did a little jig of agony, leaping around trying to find somewhere to put the plates down. I then stood facing the audience, shaking my hands, my face expressing extreme pain. This piece of business always raised a good laugh. On this occasion, the laughter was much louder and, such is the conceit of the actor, I imagined that I was performing the business a little better than usual. I looked at Joan, stationary at the door. She looked at me, and then nodded her head gently downwards. I followed her gaze. My shirt was sticking out through my fly buttons. My acting changed dramatically; horror mixed with genuine embarrassment. I turned my back on the audience and did up the buttons, to more audience laughter, while Joan could only wait patiently. My next lines suddenly took on new meaning: 'I don't think I'm going to recover from this. Well, don't just stand there. Open the door. Things couldn't get much worse.' I can only assume the buttons had come undone while I was jigging around with the plates. Until then, I always had fly buttons rather than a zip, because if that stuck, you really were in an impossible position. Buttons had seemed safer . . . until this embarrassing experience.

While I was in *Uproar in the House*, I landed a marvellous job in an American television comedy series, *The Ugliest Girl in Town*, being made by Screen Gems. The company, based in Hollywood, had made a number of successful situation comedies and hoped that, on the strength of the pilot, this new one would be taken up by the NBC Network. They had decided to set the whole thing in Britain, as the technical costs were much cheaper over here. The story was rather bizarre: a young man, for a dare, dresses up as a girl and enters a beauty contest. He/she wins and is taken up as the latest original face in the modelling world. I was cast as the head of the British public relations agency who takes on the 'girl' and promotes her as the model with the face of the seventies. A young American actor, Peter Kastner, was cast in the lead, and Patricia Brake was his English girlfriend.

The script for the pilot was extremely well constructed and, as always with American productions, a small fortune was spent to get the show absolutely right, in the knowledge that if it was successful, a lucrative network series could follow. We spent a whole two weeks filming at Shepperton but the final result, while impressive, stretched credibility too far because we were inhibited by rules laid down, presumably by NBC, to make the story acceptable to American audiences nationwide. The young man must never act effeminate, must appear in male attire for at least one-third of the film, and must never kiss the girl when dressed in female clothes. The result was that Peter Kastner always looked what he was: a young man wearing women's clothes, and not a beautiful girl who fooled the press and public, and fascinated the public relations agent. I was amazed when I was told, some months after the pilot, that a series had been commissioned and we were to start filming later in the year.

Screen Gems signed me to a five-year contract, which contained an option after thirteen shows, another after twenty-six, and then one every year. I was paid what was then a good salary – £400 a show – with increases if the options were taken up. When the tabloid press reported the story of the contract, the headline read, 'Nicholas Parsons signs £50,000 film contract'. What they did not add was that, to earn the full amount all the options would have to be taken up, and I would have to work on the series for five years. The headline made impressive reading, but was difficult to live up to as people wonder why you have not bought a more expensive car, or started to throw lavish parties.

It was great fun working on *The Ugliest Girl in Town*. The filming, however, was not without its problems. The producer of the series, Gerry Davis, and his team had been told little about how the film industry was structured in Britain, and were obviously ill-informed about crewing. They approached the technicians' union, the ACTT, asking them to recommend people. In Britain, however, the union exists only to look after the interests of their members, not to find them work. I know from taking on crews myself that you engage technicians who have worked with you before, or invite a company that you are familiar with to crew the film in consultation with you. The priority of the union in this country would not be to find the most talented people for the job, but to obtain work for any member who was unemployed at the time. The result was that the cameraman who was booked for the first episode was unable even to get the scene in the centre of the frame. He was dismissed, and presumably arguments with the union followed.

In America, because so much money is involved in a project, the producers will sign a binding agreement with the union for the length of the production, or for an agreed period. This means that the film makers can get on with the costly work without fear of industrial action while the agreement lasts. In Britain, where the technicians earn less, if problems arise they are negotiable on an *ad hoc* basis. The Americans were not used to this and became irritated when a request they considered normal was treated by some technicians as a matter for negotiation. As a result, Screen Gems swore they would never make another series in Britain. Word would have got back to other production companies in Hollywood and a great potential source of work for film technicians in this country dried up, which is a pity because the best British crews are some of the most talented in the world. As a member of the ACTT, I saw both sides of the argument and tried to explain to Gerry; but it was too late.

It is difficult to judge whether these problems contributed to the early demise of the series. Perhaps the American public did not take to the basic idea, in spite of the excellent reaction to the original pilot. The series ran for thirteen episodes. Three weeks before filming finished, we heard that no options were being taken up and, as a result, every possible economy was introduced. The writer, Gerry Kaufman, was told to keep his storylines, as far as possible, to the four main characters under contract for the series, and not to introduce unnecessary scenes or expensive sets. This entailed some very concise writing, as well as much more dialogue for the principal characters to learn.

There is always a sad feeling on the set of a show that is coming to a premature end. It is better not to know until after the filming has finished. It becomes harder to give your best performance, but if you let your performance slip, you could be blamed for contributing to the demise of the production. Also, there is a reluctance on the part of potential employers to rush to offer you more work. They have a psychological resistance to anyone connected with a 'failure'; they may also think you contributed to it. This is particularly so in America, where the stakes and rewards of success are so much higher.

Young Peter Kastner was extremely distressed that the series was to end. It could have established him as a big name in Hollywood. Instead, the failure in a starring part could put him so far back that it might be difficult to recover. He was a talented actor with a fine sense of comedy. We lost touch after the series. He returned to America and, I understand, is now an agent in Hollywood.

15

Satire and JaM

I N the early 1960s political satire had become all the rage on
television following the success of the late-night programme
That Was The Week That Was. There was, however, nothing
comparable on radio. In late 1964 I contacted the writer
Alistair Foot, who had written wonderfully constructed, stylish
sketches for the last Arthur Haynes radio series. He had also written
some excellent material for a Ronnie Barker radio series. Together
we developed a concept for a political satire show for radio, to
which I gave the title *Listen To This Space*. We then took our
synopsis to the head of Radio Light Entertainment, Roy Rich,
whom I had known as a theatre director, and explained our idea in
more detail.

BBC Radio at the time was still influenced by its great Reithian
past and in many ways was still very prim about the kind of
programmes that could be transmitted, and particularly what could
be said or referred to in those programmes. Roy Rich, however,
had faith in the idea, confidence in us and, as a recently appointed
head of his department, was keen to explore new ground. He
commissioned a pilot programme and passed it to the most experienced producer in Light Entertainment, Bill Worsley. I knew Bill
from many shows in which we had worked together, and also knew
how good he was. It was an auspicious start.

Alistair asked if we were going to write the show together. I said
no. I thought my strength was in ideas rather than scriptwriting and
I preferred that he should find another experienced writer with

whom he would be happy to work. If the series went ahead, I would always be on hand with suggestions. (The one mistake my agent made was to fail to get me any credit for the original idea. When the show later became a success and the original writers had moved on, I had no say in, or control over, the format. New writers were introduced whom I would not have chosen, and the show disintegrated.)

Alistair Foot told me that there was a fellow writer in the office where he worked, Anthony Marriott, who was experienced and very politically oriented. He knew that Tony would be interested in the show, and he thought that they could write well together. I liked Tony and trusted Alistair's instinct, and so the team was formed. None of us realised at the time that the two would become one of the most successful writing duos of the 1960s and 1970s. Their partnership blossomed when *Listen To This Space* became a success, and later they went on to write comedies and farces for the theatre, the most successful of which was the record-breaking *No Sex Please, We're British*.

As far as politics were concerned, our opinions differed, but that was a help rather than a hindrance; professionally, we got on extremely well and made a good team. For the pilot, Denise played all the female roles in the sketches, Roger Delgado and myself, the male parts. Libby Morris sang, and more music was supplied by a great trio under Tony Osborne. There was a special item, in which we put a high-profile personality on the spot. Our 'subject' in the pilot was Robin Day, whom I interrogated about his own aggressive interviewing technique. As so often happens, he turned out to be very different from the personality he projected on television, and was urbane and very charming.

In 1965, programme producers were responsible for deleting from a script anything remotely sexually suggestive, or even mildly vulgar. Swearing was strictly forbidden and unsolicited advertising was not allowed – even the names of newspapers could not be mentioned. Lastly, the royal family was out of bounds unless the reference was respectful. The pilot show that we had devised was going to break nearly all of these rules.

Before we began, we had to obtain permission to mention the names of newspapers, since we were going to quote from them and, specifically, take passages where misprints and sloppy journalism had created humorous inferences or ridiculous meanings. This is something that is done as a matter of course now, but it started on *Listen To This Space*. We obtained the permission we needed, which was the first breakthrough; the others we decided to leave until after the pilot to negotiate.

The recording went very well and we were all optimistic. Our spirits were dampened by Bill Worsley who, while saying that he thought the show was good, did not believe that we would be granted a series because the content broke too many BBC ground rules. He had overlooked, however, the tenacity of Roy Rich, who loved the pilot and was determined to see a successful series. As far as I know, Roy had no support from the rest of his department. While he might be breaking the traditional mould in the BBC with something so different, he might also be damaging his career if the show failed. Gerald Mansell, then head of the Home Service (now Radio 4), liked it but no series was commissioned. Somehow, by what means I do not know, the pilot landed on the desk of Hugh Carlton-Greene, the Director-General who had already blown many cobwebs away from 'Auntie BBC'. He liked what he heard and sent word that a series should go ahead.

Bill Worsley was due to retire and Roy asked John Bridges to produce the shows. John had recently joined Light Entertainment from the recently disbanded Features Department and had a fine track record. There were, however, problems from the start. John had never handled an audience show, where you treat the recording as live and edit the fluffs and mistakes later to bring the programme down to the required length. Also, when playing before a studio audience, it is often possible to capitalise on a mistake and create a laugh out of the situation. John was used to working with a script prepared and approximately timed in advance, and a recording which could be interrupted if necessary to eliminate mistakes as you went along. To add to his pressures, some of our new show was written by Alistair and Tony on the morning of the recording so that it would be as politically topical as possible. The show was to be broadcast on Friday at 7 p.m. on the Home Service. The first programme went out on 12 April 1965. In order to preserve the topicality, Alistair, Tony and I had asked that we record between 5.30 and 6.15 and then do an incredibly rapid edit in forty-five minutes to have the programme on air at 7.

I think Alistair and Tony instinctively realised that John was lost and, without discussion, took over. Alistair noted on his script the sections that were getting laughs, and made notes for cuts. We could not go for the luxury of single-line edits; it had to be sections and, on occasions, a whole sketch. Tony kept the overall structure in his head, so as rapidly to endorse or reject proposed cuts from Alistair. John's production assistant, who had timed every page of script during the recording, then worked out very quickly how many minutes had been cut and kept the two writers abreast of the total time, while the recording engineer, a talented technician called Mel House, with great skill cut and spliced the tape as the edits were explained. The finished show was down to the required twenty-eight minutes sometimes with only a minute to spare. On one famous occasion, they were still editing the second half of the show while the first was being transmitted.

John Bridges was much happier in the pre-production and planning stage of the show. When Roger Delgado was unavailable, it was John who suggested someone to replace him. He was a farmer, approaching middle age, who had little professional experience as a performer but who was a naturally funny man, with a gift for dialects. His name was Bob Todd, and *Listen To This Space* marked the beginning of his career as a full-time entertainer. The thing about Bob, however, was that while he knew he could make people laugh, he never knew technically how he did it, so if you asked him to repeat something, he could not be guaranteed to reproduce the same intonation or inflexions, which often meant he was at his funniest the first time he read a script or delivered a line. He was a rare and exceptional performer and an invaluable asset to the small cast, as was Denise, who continued to play the many female roles. Libby Morris did not contribute to the sketches and, since she did not sing in every show, left at the end of her contract, when another performer was brought in. In the second series it was the impressionist Peter Goodwright, then in the following series at Tony's suggestion we engaged Barry Cryer, who was then known principally as a scriptwriter and talented warm-up comedian.

Barry Cryer could do a brilliant impersonation of Harold Wilson who, as the then Prime Minister, was obviously going to appear quite frequently throughout the run of the show. I could do a good impersonation of Edward Heath, the Leader of the Opposition,

and the two often appeared in sketches together. Barry's impersonation was the finest I have ever heard and he became a valuable
member of the team. He also became a good friend.

Listen To This Space, after the struggles to get on air, made an
immediate impact and, contrary to the expectations of seasoned
broadcasters and producers, we soon had a success on our hands.
We even received a personal message of congratulation from the
Director of Sound Broadcasting. Political satire is so commonplace
now, it is surprising to think that this was only 1966. Alistair and
Tony had the courage to be outspoken and critical in their sketches,
yet they were always entertaining. They mocked the struggles of
the Liberal Party through two elderly Liberals, played by Bob and
Denise, who were living completely in the past, recalling the great
days of their party. They also made significant political comment
on the social conditions in urban areas through a lovable family of
Indian immigrants who were trying to come to terms with the
vagaries of our Health Service, unemployment system and the
general structure of society. Poor, likeable George Brown, then
Foreign Secretary, never appeared quite sober in the show, and if
any politician said anything remotely foolish, he was fair game for
satirical comment. We had most fun at the expense of Harold
Wilson and Edward Heath, but always kept a balance. If, one week,
there was a sketch knocking the Labour Party, the following week
we would have a go at the Conservatives. We were also outspoken
about the royal family, although we were never rude or cruel, as
happens today.

I initially thought that, by fronting a show that was having fun at
the expense of those in power, I would soon be made a political
outcast, and certainly *persona non grata* with those in the Establishment. I had overlooked how the British respond to positive
criticism and to those who are successfully promoting anti-Estab-
lishment ideas. They take them over. They do not attack or deride;
they accept you into their inner circle in the hope of seducing you
away from your more radical opinions. It usually works. As the
success of our show spread, I received invitations to visit the House
of Commons from MPs who were followers of the show. They
clearly enjoyed the publicity, which was meat and drink to those in
the political public eye. I was introduced to Edward Heath when
he was a guest in a show at Television Centre. I was initially quite

nervous, but he was courteous and charming. Of course, it would have been foolish for anyone to state that they hated being 'taken off' and demonstrate that they had no sense of humour, but I did feel that his smile was being rather forced through clenched teeth.

The show's popularity grew; it even had a repeat for a time on the Light Programme (later Radio 2) on the Sunday following its Friday transmission. In 1967, the Variety Club honoured me at their annual awards ceremony by naming me Radio Personality of the Year. I was very flattered and, while not wishing to sound like every show business award winner, it is true that it could not have happened without the talented writers and marvellous team.

The most surprising thing that occurred while *Listen To This Space* was at the height of its success was an invitation for me to attend a special luncheon at Buckingham Palace. The Queen and Prince Philip occasionally host informal lunches to which they invite six or seven people from different walks of life – there is usually a representative from the world of politics, the Church, the law, medicine, industry, sport and the arts. On this occasion, I was the guest representing the arts.

One day, the phone rang at home. I picked up the receiver and a voice said, 'This is Buckingham Palace.' I thought immediately that it was a friend playing a joke, so I replied, 'Really? This is Battersea Dogs' Home. We don't have any stray corgis here at the moment.' The voice became more pompous. 'Is Mr Parsons there?' I thought by now it was probably Tony Marriott winding me up, so I said, 'Come off it, Tony. What are you doing at the Palace? Getting copy for next week's script?' The voice at the other end was now even more formal, but very patient. 'This is the Controller of the Household at Buckingham Palace. Is Mr Parsons there?' I then thought for a moment that perhaps this *was* real – but if so, why were they *phoning* me? I spluttered a little, then said, 'Did you say Buckingham Palace?' 'Yes,' came the reply. 'I'm so sorry. This is Nicholas Parsons.' There was no reaction to my embarrassment. He simply continued, 'Oh, good. I've been asked by Her Majesty to invite you to have lunch with her and Prince Philip. It would be a week on Thursday, and if you are free to join them we will put the invitation in the post.' It was genuine. What a fool I felt. I thanked him very much and said I would look forward to it immensely.

The next day the beautiful, embossed invitation arrived. The lunch was magnificent. The Queen sat at the head of the rectangular table, Prince Philip in the middle and a young Princess Anne, who was on leave from school to keep a dentist's appointment, at the other end. I was placed opposite John Surtees, representing sport, and beside Princess Anne. It was a memorable occasion and, as The Queen and Prince Philip talked to us easily and informally, it made me realise how difficult a task the royal family have in maintaining a royal presence while trying not to appear too distant in today's informal society.

I will always be grateful to Alistair and Tony, not only for their writing, but also for the way they worked on the scripts each week and saw each show through to transmission. Their work on the editing was more than could be asked of any writer, and well beyond the call of duty. It also, I imagine, left John Bridges feeling undermined and professionally impotent, which are the only reasons I can give for his subsequent behaviour. Instead of accepting that he was working with experienced performers and writers who all knew what they were doing, and then walking the corridors of the Corporation and receiving the plaudits that would be given to the producer of a successful show, he first became frustrated, and then exploded. It was about the sixth show in the first series, and we had assembled for a read through of the script. John called us all into the auditorium and then went up onto the stage. The programme had, by this time, been acclaimed and I thought he was going to congratulate everyone. Instead, he berated us for our unprofessional attitude. He finished by saying that, as someone who had led troops over the top in the last war, he could certainly lead a rabble like us in the right direction, and then swept off to the studio control room, instructing us to get on with it. There was a stunned silence and it was a while before we could put our minds wholeheartedly to the task in hand.

The next day John went to Roy Rich and asked to be released from the programme. Roy immediately asked me out to lunch to discuss the matter. I explained that John was not used to a show where everyone was very experienced, knew their jobs and were trying to make something work against time. We all made suggestions, and without Alistair and Tony working on the editing, the show would never get on air. Roy was very shrewd as always and said, 'I think I understand. Your programme doesn't need a general to lead; it requires a quartermaster sergeant to organise supplies.' I replied, 'Exactly.' Roy then asked if I would like a different producer from his department. I did not dislike John, and certainly did not want to harm his career. I said that I would be happy to work with him, providing Roy could explain what we had just discussed. John returned, clearly embarrassed about his outburst. We got along fine after that, and the show went from strength to strength. In retrospect, however, I should have trusted my professional instinct and let John go. Deep down, he was still frustrated that he did not feel in control.

After a few years, when *Listen To This Space* was well and truly established, Alistair and Tony quite rightly asked for a salary in keeping with their contribution to the show, pointing out that each script took the best part of a week to prepare, unlike most radio scripts, which could be put together more rapidly. Also, as it had to be topical, they could not finalise any of it more than a day or two in advance. They were spending the same amount of time as they would have spent on a television script, for which the money was infinitely greater.

Their request for an increase in salary was refused; John Bridges did nothing to promote their cause, and they left the series. They suggested that Barry Cryer and Dick Vosburgh should take over the writing, which was an excellent idea. John Bridges would have none of it. He saw his opportunity to take control at last. He let Alistair and Tony go, ignored their suggestions and brought in two writers, Peter Myers and Ronnie Cass, who were talented but totally wrong for the programme. They had been very successful in the 1950s with their clever, saucy *Intimate Revues*, which was a different kind of writing. The most frustrating thing of all was that John never consulted me and, as my agent had never negotiated the credit for the idea, I lost any control over the format.

I agreed to continue in the show, which was now called *Hear This Space*. We struggled on for three further series, more on the reputation of our previous success than anything else, and then I really lost heart and it all petered out. I should have left with Alistair and Tony, and started a new programme. It is never a good idea to stay with a show when it has lost its quality or style. You become associated with its decline, however good your performance may have been. A year or two later a similar programme, without a studio audience, was begun, called *Week Ending*, which was, and is, excellent and always entertaining. It is really the offspring of *Listen To This Space*.

While *Listen To This Space* was running, I was keen to do something different on radio. In particular, I thought it would be fun – and more experience – if I could become a panel member on a comedy game show. I went to see Ian Messiter, a friend and the creator of a number of successful panel and game shows, and he outlined an idea that had gone down well on radio a number of years previously. The show had been called *One Minute Please*. Ian thought that perhaps it was time to try to revive it. I took the idea for the show, now renamed *Just a Minute*, to Roy Rich, who liked it sufficiently to commission a pilot.

The producer was to be a young man new to the Light Entertainment Department who had just come down from Cambridge University, where he had worked with the famous Footlights. His name was David Hatch. He was also, at that time, appearing very successfully with his Footlights colleagues, John Cleese, Tim Brooke-Taylor, Bill Oddie and Graeme Garden, in *I'm Sorry, I'll Read That Again*. Not only did he understand comedy as a performer; he also had a flair for directing.

In consultation with Ian Messiter it was decided that Jimmy Edwards should be invited to act as chairman of the proposed new series, with Beryl Reid, Clement Freud and myself on the panel. David was keen to find another woman panellist and, recognising that it was a difficult game to play, invited a number of actresses to Broadcasting House to audition. Since Jimmy Edwards was not available to 'chair' these auditions, David asked if I would mind acting as temporary chairman. He said afterwards, 'Well, I don't know if we've found the fourth panellist, but if Jimmy is eventually unable to be chairman, I think we've found just the person for the role.'

I did not want to be chairman of *Just a Minute*. I wanted to break away from the more serious roles and straight-man image that I had established with Arthur Haynes. It was not to be. Jimmy Edwards was having difficulty freeing himself from his regular Sunday polo commitments (in the end, the BBC got tired of waiting for him) and I reluctantly agreed to be chairman for the pilot programme. Beryl and Clement were joined on the panel by Derek Nimmo and a very witty American, Wilma Ewart.

We recorded the first ever *Just a Minute* at the Playhouse Theatre in Northumberland Avenue on Sunday evening, 16 July 1967, and it was a moderate success. In that original pilot there were some specialist rounds: in one, the panellists were not allowed to use plurals; in another, they could not use pronouns; and in a third, the word 'the' was barred. We discovered, however, that this was very inhibiting and when the series was eventually commissioned, it was decided that the basic format was more than enough on which to build a show. It was a mark of Ian Messiter's genius that he could think of something so simple but also so effective.

After the pilot, we all felt that, while it had not been great, with some adjustments there was every chance that it could become an entertaining and popular show. David Hatch had every confidence in the programme, and was therefore dismayed when he was told, some weeks later, that a series would not be commissioned. It was only when he threatened to resign that the BBC, keen to keep him on the staff, granted him his series.

It was now accepted that I would be chairman when the series began recording in November. This may not have been what I originally intended, but like everything in show business, you have to find a way to make something work for you, and I think I have evolved quite naturally into a straight man for a team. It is a job I now thoroughly enjoy.

During the recording of the third series I felt the panellists had exhausted all the ploys of getting back at each other, and there was now a tendency for them to have a go at me. I remarked on this to David Hatch, who shrewdly replied, 'Nicholas, that's probably the way the show is going to develop, and I think your shoulders are broad enough to take it.' The show developed exactly as he had prophesied and I found myself performing a special kind of straight-man role, keeping the show moving and orchestrating all that takes place, as a good chairman should, while taking all the brickbats and insults that are thrown at me. It is interesting that when, sometimes, I have tried to be rude or facetious to one of the panellists, the studio audience have not usually found my comment funny. I have taken this to indicate that, as chairman, I can make general remarks that are amusing, but it is not my role to make jokes at other people; as the straight man, it is my role to receive jokes at my expense from the others.

In the first series of *Just a Minute*, the two panellists who had been particularly successful in the pilot, Clement Freud and Derek Nimmo, were naturally booked to take part. It was thought necessary to have at least one woman, and Andrée Melly was engaged, who also proved to be very successful. The fourth chair was a piece of daring and original casting by David Hatch. He invited Kenneth Williams to join the panel. Kenneth was happy to accept, but not so sure that he was right for the show. For the first two recordings, he was almost floundering; by about the third, however, he suddenly found his own way of playing the game and never looked back. Eventually it was one of the jobs he enjoyed most, and he looked forward to every new series. After we had been running for a number of years, it was decided that guests would appear on the panel, replacing the regulars from time to time. Kenneth, however, retained his panellist's seat. He appeared on every show. Perhaps this is why some people felt that *Just a Minute* did not exist without him.

Although *Just a Minute* rapidly became very popular, thanks mainly to the expertise of the regular players, Kenneth Williams, Clement Freud, Derek Nimmo and Peter Jones (who joined the show in the second series), there was always the recurring problem of finding a woman who could play the game as well as the men. Sheila Hancock was particularly adept, as was Andrée Melly, because neither of them were intimidated by the aggressive behaviour of the men, and the almost chauvinistic attitude of Kenneth Williams. Another woman who played the game with incomparable skill was the American actress Elaine Stritch. She had never heard of the show before, listened to one recording, and then took on the challenge of facing Kenneth, Clement and Derek. She was so original and amusing that not only was that particular recording one of the best ever, but at one point Kenneth remarked, 'No one plays it like she does.'

I have often wondered why more men than women have been successful at playing the game, and have reached the conclusion that this is because the average man is not afraid to be outrageous.

He is also determined to win, or at least do well, and to this end indulges in a great deal of one-upmanship against the others, rather like naughty schoolboys competing for teacher's attention. Many women, on the other hand, find this difficult. British women comedians in the early days of radio and television were almost all 'character' performers, with accents and specific roles to play. They were unused to asserting their own characters, and sending themselves up, which *Just a Minute* seems to demand. American comediennes have always had the assurance to be funny as themselves, which can now also be said of modern British comediennes. Sheila Hancock and Andrée Melly were successful because they gave as good as they got. Aimi Macdonald, by contrast, played the game successfully as a 'dizzy blonde' and came over as ultra-feminine and vulnerable. This gave the three men a very different personality off which to bounce their repartee. Sometimes they would go over the top and Aimi would appeal to the chairman for protection, which spontaneously took the game off in a quite different direction.

Aimi's appeals invariably came after some rude comment from Kenneth Williams, who was in a class of his own when it came to impudent remarks. His delivery was such, however, that it was almost impossible to take offence. He was also, in some ways, a most generous player of the game. I frequently noticed that whenever he had been particularly rude or aggressive to me, he would find an opportunity later in the show to pay me some compliment. There were times, however, when he would put me under great pressure as he became very excited or, to quote him, 'throbbing with it' .

An occasion that caused me some embarrassment was during a round in which the subject was 'snapshots'. Kenneth was unhappy at one of my decisions, and started to harass me. Peter Jones and Derek Nimmo then joined in, which only added to the pressure. In an effort to bring them to order, and to quieten Kenneth, I eventually said, firmly and pleasantly, 'I'm sorry Kenneth, I cannot agree. The subject is snapshots. You have deviated from snapshots . . . no, no, Kenneth, it was snapshots . . . You were well away from the subject. Clement has it. There are twenty seconds, Clement, snopshots, er . . . snipshots, er . . . snopshits . . . snop . . . snap . . . snip . . .' The audience roared with laughter. I simply said, 'I'm not going to repeat the subject. I think you know it . . . and I think I've just finished my career in radio.'

David Hatch said afterwards that while he might be able to edit out the fluffs, they were so natural that he was going to take a risk and leave them in. I was reassured after the programme was broadcast to receive only one letter on the subject, and that was from a Professor of English at Aberdeen University, who said he felt that I had enriched the language.

No one could ever replace Kenneth, but since he died different players have joined the panel, and while the original three still participate frequently, one or two newcomers have proved themselves to be so skilled at playing the game that they have become accepted as regulars. One such is Paul Merton, whose great contribution, to my mind, is his ability to take a quite commonplace remark from one of the other players or myself and go off at fantastical, surreal tangents that are extremely funny. Another new regular is Wendy Richard, who displays all the attributes of other successful women players of the game. She is not at all inhibited by the men; she is entirely herself and speaks forcibly and entertainingly, and is quite prepared to hand out aggressive treatment to the others if she feels she is being got at.

There is probably no comedy show that can boast a cast list as long as that of *Just a Minute*. At different times, Peter Cook, Victoria Wood, Maureen Lipman, Stephen Fry, Tim Rice, Barry Cryer, Michael Palin, Willie Rushton, Richard Murdoch, Lisa Goddard, Barry Took, Jimmy Mulville, Brian Johnstone, Tony Slattery, Sandi Toksvig and Tony Hawkes have all contributed to the fun and entertainment. From the day it began, the programme has had the most incredibly loyal following, not just from audiences but from the performers themselves.

After twenty-seven years, *Just a Minute* is going to be seen on television. Some people are amazed that this has not happened before. BBC television did try in 1981, but the pilot show was a disaster, principally because they forgot to invite an audience to come to enjoy the recording. The only people in the auditorium were twelve students that my son Justin had brought in a party from his college. Trying to perform a show that relies on laughs to a dozen people was a miserable experience, and it so frustrated Kenneth Williams that it was all we could do to persuade him to stay to the end of the recording. Perhaps this unfortunate experience inhibited the BBC from trying again.

In 1992 Mike Mansfield bought the television rights and made a pilot. He and Ian Messiter added a lot of extra ideas to make the show more interesting in visual terms but they proved unnecessary, and when we recorded the series for Carlton Television in 1993, we reverted to the original format with great success. The only difference from the radio show is that I ask the audience to suggest one of the subjects, and at another point we offer the panellists an object, which they have to describe. Tony Slattery is the regular panellist, and his sharp and original mind is ideally suited to the programme. There are three different guests in each show and, once again, I am the foil or straight man to the others' comedy. It might not have been what I originally intended, but it has been a privilege to have been associated with a show that, on radio and now television, has been running for so many years.

16

· · · · · · · ·

Comedy Greats

I HAVE been straight man to many comedians in my time. After Arthur Haynes, my longest association was with Benny Hill. Benny was one of the most considerate, gentle people with whom I have ever worked. I first met him in 1952, when he was compering *The Variety Show*, which was transmitted on television from the Nuffield Centre. Troops shows had been staged here during the War and servicemen still came to watch entertainments in its theatre.

The Variety Show was one of Benny's first major engagements after the War, and all the acts that he introduced at the time were making their first appearance on television. When I appeared, I reverted to the material with which I had begun in show business and did an impersonation act, taking off all the current sports commentators. The show had an interesting line-up of performers, including an attractive young Australian girl, Shirley Abicair, who made headlines in the papers the next day because she not only sang but also played the zither, and this was the first time anyone had been seen playing it on television. There was also a jazz band that finished the show, whom I thought were marvellous. I was particularly impressed by a young girl who shuttled on to sing a blues number with them. The band was Johnny Dankworth's, and the singer was Cleo Laine.

During the late 1950s, I deputised for Benny in his summer show for a few nights while he was in hospital having his appendix removed; I next met him in the 1960s, when he appeared in a charity show at the Prince of Wales Theatre, performing his popular sketch, a skit on *This Is Your Life*, in which a little man is surprised by an Eamon Andrews character carrying a big red book. Benny played a number of unlikely characters who are supposed to be associated with the man's life. The compère whom Benny had used before was not available. We shared the same agent, Richard Stone, and it was Richard who suggested that I might be a good choice for the role. I did an impersonation of Eamon Andrews, which got laughs at the beginning of the sketch. Apparently, this had not happened before and Benny, being a true comic who felt only the funny man should have the laughs, said to me afterwards jokily, 'I was standing in the wings at the beginning, and I heard you getting laughs. I said, "This isn't on. He's the straight man. Get him off."'

He was actually very pleased with the way the sketch had gone. In 1967 he asked me to work in his series, and decided to revive the sketch. By then, I had taken the hint, however gently he had conveyed it: he did not like me to get laughs when I was playing his straight man. However, he never minded the character performers who worked with him to have laughs. This was particularly true of Bob Todd, to whom Benny gave some very funny parts. Perhaps Benny, who had once been the straight man to Reg Varney, did not feel threatened by Bob because they were so different.

I enjoyed four seasons with Benny, which finished in 1971, the year *Sale of the Century* started. I think once I had my own show on television, Benny thought it best not to use me any more. We remained the best of friends, and knew each other very well. About two years after I stopped working with him, when *Sale of the Century* had become very popular, he did a takeoff of the show in which he did a wicked impersonation of me. He knew my little mannerisms so well that he could highlight them and make the whole sketch very funny.

Benny had worked very hard for his success. In his younger days he had accepted every engagement that came along – stage shows, radio, television. Once he became famous, however, he ceased to work obsessively and did just four or five shows a year, for which he wrote all the material. In many respects, he was the most mature comedian with whom I have ever worked. I even told him this, which surprised him. He put a great deal of energy into each of his shows, which he had carefully planned and prepared. He worked very closely with his director, who was integral to his success, as Benny knew exactly what he wanted and needed someone who thought as he did. It was John Robbins when I worked with him; later it was Dennis Kirkland, who had been the floor manager in his earlier shows and probably understood him as well as anyone.

The four or five *Benny Hill Shows* would be made over a four-month period and in between Benny would travel the world, particularly Europe. He enjoyed visiting clubs and seeing other entertainers work, which would fire his imagination with ideas that he would incorporate into his sketches and songs. He rarely told anyone where he was going, not even Richard Stone, who said to me that often he would have no idea where Benny was until he received a phone call from some foreign capital. Benny only kept in touch out of courtesy. He barely packed anything when he travelled, just a toothbrush. When his clothes became dirty, he simply bought some more and, depending on their condition, either gave or threw the old ones away.

I once asked him how he handled the problem of being recognised abroad, as he must meet many British holidaymakers. He said he always travelled with his 'prop' teeth, particularly the ones he used for the Chinese character who featured in some of his sketches. Once fitted over his own, they completely changed his features. He said, 'You can sit at Barcelona airport wearing these with hundreds of tourists milling around, and no one recognises you. You're incognito, and that's how I like to be when abroad and not working.'

Benny had a fund of knowledge about comedy routines and a book full of jokes old and new. A lot of what he wrote was well-tested variety material he had used before, recycled so that it sounded fresh. Once, when we were rehearsing, Benny said, 'Nick, the sketch is too long. We're going to make some cuts.' He then proceeded to cut lines which I thought would get him laughs, and pointed this out. He said, 'I know. But it doesn't matter. I'll use them again.' One of his great skills was the way he took old and tried material and made it different. He was fully aware of this, and not embarrassed when I remarked on it. He said, with a huge grin, 'I know. There's nothing really new. Most of the time, it's finding a way to make something sound different that's been tried before. That's why I never mind cutting. I know it'll all come back in another way in another show. Nothing's wasted.'

Benny was never anything other than professional in his work and I was very sad to read in one biography of him an anecdote that entirely misrepresented his true nature. It was a story attributed to Bob Todd. Bob's memory may have been at fault; it was never very reliable at the best of times. Apparently, Benny played a cruel practical joke on me. Nothing could have been more alien to his nature. In order to get a bigger laugh at the recording, instead of dropping a plate of food on my lap as had been rehearsed, he tipped it over my head and one of my best suits. He then supposedly revelled in my misfortune. Benny would never do anything that had not been rehearsed or prepared. Furthermore, no best suit was ruined because if you are going to have your clothes spoiled in any way, you are always supplied with some from the wardrobe department.

Benny was generous with people he liked and, on occasion, would splash out on parties for his cast. He was quite unlike most comedians I have known, who often seem to have difficulty parting with their money, which presumably becomes a symbol of their success. Benny enjoyed his popularity, but the money was incidental. Latterly, he would have uncashed cheques lying around his flat, or stuffed in his pockets – possibly some of the residuals that kept coming to him as another country showed his programmes. All this success left him completely unaffected. His lifestyle remained the same, except perhaps he indulged his love of food and wine a little more and, as a consequence, put on a lot of weight in his later years.

I realised he had a craving for sweet things when I bought him a special tin of biscuits as a present at the end of one of the series. I gave it to him after the final dress rehearsal. When he opened the package and saw what it was, he pleaded with me to take it away. He said he appreciated the thought, but if the tin was left in his dressing room, it would be empty before transmission, which would not help him at all. 'If I eat one, I won't stop until they're all gone. As a friend, take them away.' In his last months, I am sure, from all I have heard, that he was not resisting the temptation, and indulging himself too much. Perhaps it was for comfort. There is no doubt that the way he was unexpectedly and abruptly dropped by Thames Television, after many years of faithful service, surprised and hurt him. I heard it was because someone at Thames bowed to external pressure when it was pointed out that Benny's shows were not always politically correct in the way they depicted women. Benny never understood this, as his humour was of a style that has been popular for generations. It was broad, honest, at times vulgar, and with an innuendo that is no worse than the *Carry On* films, which now have a cult following. As he loved and admired women, he never understood why he was criticised for the way they appeared in his shows; he also pointed out that it was the men in his sketches who were made to look foolish, and often at the expense of the women.

Benny seems to have been very sad towards the end, failing to understand the criticism coming from people in his own country when he was so popular abroad. From all accounts, he was eating and drinking too much, especially for someone who had received a warning from his doctor about the state of his heart. Apparently he needed an operation, which he had an eighty-per-cent chance of surviving. He continued to socialise and entertain his women friends. According to two of them, shortly before he died he took them out to a restaurant, where he ate the most colossal meal – something he did frequently. Was he deliberately ignoring his doctor?

He died in his flat, alone. His heart was probably not strong enough to withstand his indulgences. What a sad end for a great comic and a gentle, loving man who brought pleasure to millions all over the world.

In contrast to Benny, and different from any other comedian with whom I have worked, was Tony Hancock. He was, by nature, a depressed man. Along with his melancholia, which he exploited in the character he presented in 'The Lad from East Cheam', I also wondered, from the short association I had with him, whether there was a self-destructive side to his nature.

Tony had always been one of my comedy heroes. The way he could handle a perfectly straight line in a script was nothing short of brilliant. I had watched him at recordings of *Hancock's Half Hour*, and when he was surrounded by the best talent available, including the incomparable Sid James, who was an exceptional foil for his humour, he was always outstanding. The comic's need to prove that he owes his success to no one but himself, however, was so powerful in Tony that he slowly got rid of all those who appeared to be shining too brightly in his shows. The first to go – from his radio show – was Kenneth Williams, and eventually he even dispensed with his writers, Ray Galton and Alan Simpson, who had written so brilliantly for him. Latterly he himself wrote part of the script for a feature film in which he starred, but without any of those who had been associated with him on his rise to fame. It was a box-office failure.

I worked with Tony when Arthur Haynes suffered his first heart attack during *Swing Along* at the London Palladium. The management were desperate to find a top comedian to take over and by sheer good fortune for everyone concerned, Tony was in the office of the agent, Billy Marsh, when he was desperately phoning to find a replacement. I was looking forward to working with someone whom I had admired so much. When we met for rehearsal, we ran through one of Tony's sketches that he had performed before. We kept one sketch in which Arthur had appeared, with his understudy taking the role, and Tony finished the show with a long solo act. When the sketch that I had rehearsed with Tony did not go very well after two performances, Tony, instead of working to get it right as Arthur or Benny would have done, gave up and decided to cut it. In the end, he just did a long stand-up comedy act at the end of the show.

I would often sit in the wings to watch and listen to his timing. He was performing material that he had used from his very earliest days, and although I knew it well, I still enjoyed listening to the way he put it over, as did the audience. The material, however, was very dated: he even included an impersonation of Charles Laughton from the film *Mutiny on the Bounty*, which had been made before the War. He frequently talked about humour, and truth in comedy, and moving forward, but it seemed that he was stuck and unable to develop his full comic genius. He was in a very low state during that season at the Palladium. I went to his dressing room more than once to talk with him, and always found it difficult. On one occasion he was seated at the end of a settee in a kind of Buddha-like position, looking even more lugubrious than usual. He had none of the fun or humour that so many comedians exude in conversation. Instead, he seemed desperately sorry for himself, like a child who feels misunderstood and is desperately trying to attract attention.

And there was nothing I could do to cheer him up.

A comedian who is quite different again is Ken Dodd. I first worked with Ken in the 1950s, when I was introducing *Midday Music Hall* from the Midlands and he was on his way to becoming the inimitable comedian he is today. What impressed and amazed me was his dedication: every joke, whether written by himself, or another writer, or borrowed from a different source, was carefully filed and annotated. He would keep notes of how each joke went with different audiences, as well as, presumably, personal comments of his own about the content of the joke, which all helped over the years to build a style of humour that was entirely his own. At the time I first worked with him, he had a devoted girlfriend who sat in the audience during each broadcast, and made notes for Ken's future reference about the audience's reaction to each individual joke in his script. Nearly all comedians keep reference books of jokes, but what was individual about Ken's method was to file jokes into categories, so that he could build a routine on a subject and then, through regular performance, polish a group of jokes or comments on that subject into a stylish whole that appeared as if it was all coming out as spontaneous thought. This meticulous application to the content of his material has given him a computer-style memory for joke material, which to my mind has made him quite exceptional.

Ken is devoted to comedy. His principal nourishment in life is derived from the applause and laughter of audiences. For this reason he is much more successful in the theatre than in the mechanical media of television and radio, and failure to get laughter from an audience is difficult for him to handle. There was an occasion in the late 1960s, when I was compering a big cabaret at the Hurlingham Club in London. It was a charity ball, in which all the performers had given their services free, and the audience was a rather smart, young, monied crowd, whom one would not automatically set down as fans of Ken Dodd. I had been informed that Ken, who was then starring at the Palladium Theatre, was arriving after his second show, just to draw the raffle. It was emphasised to me that he was not permitted by his contract to do more than that. The young audience were mostly sitting on the floor, and had enjoyed more than an hour's cabaret, which included Joan Turner doing quite a long act. After this, I went on and introduced Ken. A number of the audience had left the ballroom by this time, and Ken walked out to a very average reception, which perhaps in itself made him feel he had to prove something. He immediately began to tell a few little jokes before drawing the raffle, but they did not receive the warm reaction he expected. In spite of the fact that he knew that he did not have to prove anything, and I had already explained to the audience that he had come solely to draw the raffle, Ken proceeded to try to win over the crowd. He worked on them; he persisted; he coaxed them, and would not give up until he had them roaring with laughter. I can think of no other comic who would have risen to that particular challenge, let alone have succeeded so magnificently.

All comedians are different, and there is no doubt that in each one there is some driving force that motivates him, against all the odds. With some there seems to be a sublimation of what they may have experienced in their childhood, which is mingled with the drive for success. Norman Wisdom is someone who suffered a great deal of sadness and deprivation as a youngster, and his ability to create pathos and endear himself to an audience is quite exceptional. He is a natural clown, a great tumbler, and has the unique ability to win an audience completely and make them laugh at the misfortune he so brilliantly expresses in comic terms. Like all top comedians, he is a great professional, and working with him as I did in a slapstick mime sketch that he had devised, and which we performed at the children's *Royal Variety Show* in 1990, was tremendous fun. Once again, I was working as a straight man to help get the laughs, and I am sure that one of the reasons the sketch was so successful was Norman's generous attitude, similar in many ways to Arthur Haynes'; the audience laughed at him, but if they laughed at my characterisation too, he did not mind – it all counted towards the success of the sketch.

There is no doubt that one of the most humorous, gifted men I have ever known was Kenneth Williams. Just thinking about him, I smile as I remember his animated face with its impish grin, and hear that inimitable voice.

There is a word that has crept into the English language which is used quite frequently now: 'camp'. The dictionaries state that its derivation is unknown, but I am sure it arose in the theatrical profession. It originally meant something outrageous and somewhat effeminate. The dictionary now defines it as 'behaviour involving the adoption of false attitudes and false values for purposes of ridicule or to amuse'. Kenneth could have been said to have commercialised 'camp'. The character he portrayed in the *Carry On* films and in the radio comedy shows in which he appeared all had an element of 'camp' in them. It was this indefinable element in his performances and his character to which audiences instinctively responded.

In one of Kenneth's obituaries it was pointed out that he was very friendly with flamboyant homosexuals. That says nothing about his sexual proclivities, since he was also friendly with flamboyant heterosexuals. He did not, in fact, ever want an intimate relationship with anyone. He enjoyed the company of theatre people, some of whom were his best friends. Joan Sims, with whom he worked on the *Carry On* films, was one of them. When Joan and I were working together in *Uproar In The House*, she told me that on one occasion Kenneth actually proposed marriage to her. He was very fond of her and the feeling was mutual. He said, however, that if they were married, they would have separate bedrooms and bathrooms, and that there would be none of that embarrassing 'sex stuff'. She told him that was fine for him: he was getting what he wanted, a companion and someone to cook and run the house. What about her? The proposal was gently but firmly refused.

The only person who was close to Kenneth was his widowed mother, who religiously came to every recording of *Just a Minute*. He was very fond of her, and always referred to her by her Christian name, Louie, and provided her with a flat not far from where he lived, near Regent's Park. Few, if any, people visited Kenneth in his flat. In his private life, he enjoyed being alone with his books and his thoughts. One of the reasons for this was his fastidious attitude to hygiene. As he said to me once, 'I can't bear the thought of someone else's bum on my loo seat.'

Kenneth saved a great deal of himself for his audience. Sometimes he would, as he put it in *Just a Minute*, 'let it all hang out'. This is probably why he enjoyed the show so much. He could talk and play-act to the studio audience to his heart's content.

He had been a very disciplined actor in his time, giving memorable portrayals of, for instance, the Dauphin in Bernard Shaw's *St Joan*. In later life he preferred to be in a show that was less structured, where he could be spontaneous and ad-lib if necessary. I am sure that is why he loved the atmosphere of the *Carry On* films, where he was also working with his friends. He enjoyed radio because it gave him an opportunity to display all his voices and characters. In *Round the Horn* and *Beyond Our Ken*, he was able to be vulgar and very basic – he has been quoted as saying, 'I like smutty old jokes. Honest vulgarity is the central tradition of English humour, and uninhibitedness the essence of comedy.'

Kenneth's very last professional job was a recording of *Just a Minute*. He had been booked to do two more recordings, but phoned at the last minute to say that he could not take part. Knowing him as I did, I realised there must be something seriously wrong. I wrote to him saying how sorry I was to hear he was unwell and how much we had missed him in the last session. Being the punctilious letter-writer that he was, he sent me a note in reply. He had suffered from a stomach complaint for some time and had already told me they were 'trying something new'. If that failed, it could be the 'surgeon's knife', which he dreaded. I am sure that something so personally intrusive as an operation deeply disturbed him. It seems he died unexpectedly before this operation he feared so much could take place. He had always said to me that he was not worried about the passing years, or troubled by the thought of death. He once said that he thought sixty-five to seventy was a good time to go. 'Why hang about?' he said. Sadly, he did not 'hang about', falling well short of the age he thought acceptable.

A comedian who has not gained the recognition he deserves is Peter Jones. We have worked together a great deal, not least on *Just a Minute*, where his witty interjections and sometimes caustic remarks have frequently produced the biggest laughs in the show.

Some of the shows in which we have been involved have not been without their problems. The first was a tour of *Doctor at Sea*, adapted by Ted Willis from the Richard Gordon novel and launched on 8 May 1961 at the New Theatre, Bromley. The play was directed by the then resident producer, David Poulson, who was presumably used to mounting productions on a weekly basis, because by the time we reached the second week of rehearsals, he seemed to have nothing further to add. Peter and I were not only developing comedy business ourselves, we were also creating moves for the rest of the cast.

Certain scenes needed more work, but after a run-through, David Poulson did not say one word or give us a single note; he just asked us to go through the play again. After another run-through with no comments from the figure sitting alone in the stalls, Peter, who is normally very gentle, could take no more and shouted across the footlights, 'For God's sake say something, even if it's only goodbye.'

The tour which followed was reasonably successful, but memorable for the final week at the Theatre Royal, Nottingham. Peter had developed mumps and his neck glands were swollen to such a size that he was almost unrecognisable. There being no under-studies, he was persuaded to soldier on to the end of the week. As if this was not bad enough, I then caught gastric flu, and could not keep anything down. The flu reached its peak on the Friday night, and we were both soldiering on. A bucket was placed beside each exit on the set, and more than once I had to rush off in the middle of a scene, throw up while the other actors ad-libbed, and then stagger back to carry on with the performance. I will always remember the forebearance of Patricia Garwood, who played my character's girlfriend and had to act with two performers who looked nothing like their normal selves, one of whom must also have smelt most unpleasant from his frequent trips offstage to the waiting buckets.

Peter played the lead role in a tour of *Boeing-Boeing* in Australia – the part that I subsequently played in the West End. In early 1965 he had just returned from this tour to star with me in a comedy thriller series on BBC television, *Night Train to Surbiton*, in which two unsuspecting businessmen become innocently involved, while travelling on their commuter train, with murder, spies and all kinds of skulduggery. The series was written by John Chapman and the pilot show had been directed by David Croft. Unfortunately, he was not available to direct the series, which I am sure he would have turned into a very successful spoof spy story. The producer who was put in charge was Bryan Sears, who seemed to have no sense of comedy and certainly no feel for this particular storyline. He seemed more concerned that the actors always arrived at rehearsal on time and knew their lines, rather than be able to develop the comedy inherent in John Chapman's script.

Peter had wisely given up trying to work with Bryan and make the show funnier. At one point he said to me, 'Stop struggling, Nicholas. He's talking a different language, and in this medium producers can damage you professionally. Keep your nose clean and just try to survive.' I wish I had listened to him.

In one scene, I was about to make an entrance through a door and had a gun in my hand, which the character I was playing was not experienced at using. There was a camera on my side of the door, and I was doing some comedy business with the gun before entering, thinking this camera was filming it. Suddenly, over the studio tannoy, Bryan's voice was heard: 'Nicholas, this is your entrance. Where are you?' I opened the door, walked on to the main part of the set, and said, 'Bryan, I was doing some business with the gun behind the door before my entrance.' There was silence, so I continued, 'I thought you were shooting on camera 2 behind the door, but if you've cut to camera 3 on the other side of the door, I'll drop the business and make my entrance.' There was a further silence, which seemed ominously long. Then the voice came back over the tannoy, 'You get on with the lovely acting, and we'll make the pretty pictures.' From then on I took Peter's advice. I ceased to try to be inventive, and just hoped I would survive to be asked to work for BBC Television again.

It was a long time before I was asked to do any comedy for them again, and when I did it was because Peter asked for me. He had written a show for the 'Comedy Playhouse' series called *The Rescue*, which featured me as a successful businessman who rescues someone from committing suicide and takes him back to his house, only to discover that he is an ex-employee. This character, played by Peter, turns his whole life upside-down. I was really playing the straight man to Peter's character and the whole idea had great possibilities. The show was successful in the 'Comedy Playhouse' slot, but was never taken up for a full series, in spite of the excellent direction of John Howard-Davies. Once again, I think the powers that be had not recognised the great comic potential Peter displays in all his work, which is often underplayed. While he has had many major successes and would be the last person to say he was at all unhappy, he is the kind of comedian the British do not turn into big stars.

Someone who was not in show business, whom I got to know very well and who demonstrated on many occasions when we met socially that he could have been a successful professional entertainer, was Jeremy Thorpe. We first met in 1957, when Denise and I were having a summer holiday at Calvi in Corsica. We were staying in an ancient bishop's palace in the old town of Calvi, then owned and run as a night club by Count Tcherikoff, who had been one of Prince Yusupov's faithful followers, and had escaped with him from Russia before the tsarist regime was toppled in the Revolution. The count, or Tao as everyone called him, sat in the bar most of the day while his wife ran the hotel. They only accepted as guests friends, or those introduced by friends, as we had been. The conditions were fairly primitive: there was no running water and no drains in this part of the town, and the residents resorted to the simple expedient of throwing their slops and other waste out of their windows onto the cobbled streets below. It felt a bit like primitive camping, but not under canvas.

The only other guest at the hotel while we were there was a young Jeremy Thorpe, who at the time was not even an MP. He was nursing a seat in a north Devon constituency, which he hoped to win for the Liberals at the next general election. He was interested to discover my commitment to the Liberal cause and we talked politics a good deal. Jeremy, however, could talk about any subject, and had a fund of stories which he often illustrated with brilliant characterisations of the people involved. He was also an exceptionally clever mimic. Later, when he had become an MP, he would do a number of impersonations of leading politicians of the day, the best of which, to my mind, were of Michael Foot, Harold Macmillan, Rab Butler and the great Liberal leader Archie Sinclair.

I later made a personal appearance for Jeremy in his constituency, which was the first of several such appearances made to support candidates at by-elections and general elections. I was particularly disappointed when Des Wilson, for whom I spoke, failed to win the Brighton seat in a by-election, as he would have made an excellent MP. I was delighted, however, when Clement Freud won the Ely seat, overturning a previous Tory majority. I spoke for him in every election in which he stood.

My involvement with the Liberal Party resulted in them asking me to take part in a party political broadcast on the radio during one election campaign, and I suppose it was this that prompted the local Liberal Party in Yeovil, in 1976, to ask if I would consider being adopted as the prospective parliamentary candidate for their constituency. I was flattered by the invitation and told them that I would be happy to consider it. Denise and I travelled to Yeovil, where we met the party officials and were taken on a tour of the constituency. During a long and serious discussion, I told them my reservations about accepting. Being a successful MP was a full-time commitment, especially if you wanted to be a good constituency MP. I would have to consider giving up most of my professional work, particularly any idea of working again as an actor. They were very persuasive, and said that they could live with the demands of my other work. I pointed out that I did not think others, particularly the Party itself, could live with the demands if I accepted a part in a play and there was a three-line whip in the House. I could not ask to be excused the last scene or the curtain call in order to hurry down to the Palace of Westminster to vote.

I thought very deeply about the offer all the way back to London and knew I had to decide between possibly becoming a politician or staying in a profession that, whatever its ups and downs, I loved and, most of the time, found rewarding. The entertainment profession won. With great reluctance I decided not to stand as an MP – in a constituency that had a strong Liberal following and a fine local party to work for me in an election campaign.

Some time after this, Paddy Ashdown was adopted as the Liberal candidate. I am sure the good people of Yeovil now feel that I did them a favour in turning down the offer.

17
· · · · · · · ·

Sailing in a Different Direction

T the beginning of 1971 I was going through one of those 'quieter' periods when, out of the blue, I received a phone call from Peter Joy, a senior producer at Anglia Television, who wanted to know whether I would be interested in fronting a quiz show that they were planning to pilot. My only previous, and brief, experience of this sort of work had been in the 1950s, in a local quiz show at Westward Television, which I had left because of the ITV strike. Keen to accept the challenge and do something different, I agreed to meet Peter for an initial discussion. I did not realise at the time that I was about to become the straight man to the general public.

At Anglia's London office, Peter showed me a video of a programme called *Sale of the Century*, which was already doing very well on American television. I watched as a very laid-back American compère asked some rather banal questions and three over-excited contestants, continually applauding themselves, won fabulous prizes for answering correctly. I told Peter that if Anglia Television wanted someone to perform in the style of the American host I had just seen, I did not think I was right for the job. He assured me that he was very happy for me to front the show in my own way, and thought I was the ideal person to make this very American-style quiz show acceptable to the British public.

Peter and I worked well together and he was happy to consider any suggestions I had that might help the show. As an actor, I was very aware that any show needs to be paced, so I suggested that perhaps the show should start quite gently, with some fairly simple questions to put the contestants at their ease, then move to slightly more difficult ones before increasing the pace – and excitement – to end with the most 'expensive' questions. I also suggested that the contestants be carefully auditioned beforehand, not just to make sure that they would not dry up in front of the cameras, but also to be certain that they could answer general knowledge questions to a good standard, which would make the show more interesting. Both of these ideas were adopted. When the show became successful Bill Perry, who succeeded Peter Joy, travelled up and down the country auditioning anyone who had written asking to be in the show. He said that he was lucky to find five people in a hundred who had enough knowledge even to be considered as a contestant. It seems that either most people think they have more knowledge than they do, or they regard the 'high reward' quiz as a kind of 'give-away' show, with winners awarded prizes from luck or guesswork. This is true of some shows, but Anglia Television never intended that *Sale of the Century* should fall into that category. In fact, it was one of the fairest of all television game shows, as the contestants had to win their prizes solely on merit.

Initially, *Sale of the Century* was to be transmitted only in the Anglia Television region. What I did not know, when I went to Anglia's headquarters in Norwich to make the pilot, was that Thames Television – a major company – had previously made a pilot with Wilfred Pickles as host. It had, apparently, failed quite dismally. Had I known, I might not have been so keen to accept the engagement.

The musical director at Anglia was Peter Fenn, who was asked to play the electric organ, which, it was decided, would be the instrument used at different times in the show for the link music and to punctuate various moments. Peter was also commissioned to write a signature tune for the show, which he orchestrated, and this tune was played at the start and the end of the programme. He called the tune 'Joyful Pete' as a gesture to Peter Joy. I am sure he never imagined that it would come to have such a long run, and that I would frequently be greeted by people humming it to me.

Prior to the pilot, Peter had sent me a bundle of questions which had been supplied by the American creators of the game, and asked me to choose the ones I preferred. I told him there were very few that I liked. It was important that they should be interesting enough to hold viewers' attention and those we had been given were all extremely boring and American-oriented. As a result, I ended up writing most of the questions myself, which I thoroughly enjoyed.

Anglia Television was a small company serving a large geographical area, and produced some of the highest-quality shows on independent television, including *Survival* and peak-hour drama productions. No small company at the time had ever had a light entertainment or game show on the network; this was the preserve of the four major companies – Thames, LWT, Granada and ATV (later Central) – later to become five when Yorkshire Television was formed. The only large studio at Anglia was really too small for the complicated set that had been designed for the pilot and all the goods that had to be displayed, and so much rehearsal time was taken up trying to solve the technical problems that we were never able to have a complete run-through. If ever a pilot programme seemed doomed to failure, this was it. The game's creator, Al Howard, who had flown in from America, was so convinced that it was going to be a disaster that he rang Heathrow to see if he could fly home that night rather than watch his show being destroyed before his eyes. There were, however, no flights available. He told me later that they piloted the original show in America for three consecutive days in the studio with different audiences, following a week of rehearsals. We were trying to do it in one afternoon and evening, in a studio that was too small for the purpose.

Al, however, was unaware of the skill of British technicians, and the ability and professionalism of Peter Joy. The pilot went surprisingly well and, although I felt as if I was making it up as I went along, the audience obviously loved it. When it was over, I stepped forward to thank them, as I always do. Peter's voice came over the sound system, 'Thank you, everyone, you did a good job. It's in the can, in time, and it's a wrap.' All rather laid-back and very British. This was too much for Al Howard. He rushed out of the control room and into the studio, spraining his ankle on the stairs in his haste, and shouted, 'Hold the audience, hold the audience.' Hobbling up to me and introducing himself to the audience, he then proceeded to tell them how marvellous he thought I was and what an incredible job I had done under difficult circumstances. I was rather embarrassed: no one had ever heaped such praise on me before. He was equally complimentary about Peter. It was, however, so un-British. The audience seemed confused, if impressed, and clapped politely, while the studio crew ignored the whole thing and simply carried on dismantling the set.

Sale of the Century was an immediate success when it was launched in the autumn of 1971, and other independent companies began to take an interest. There was, luckily, a vacancy on the ITV network for a good new quiz show. (In an attempt to maintain the overall quality of independent television, the IBA had ruled that there could only be two high-reward game shows on the network in any one week, and three in any one region. There was no restriction on other game shows, provided big prizes were not involved.) London Weekend Television were the first major company to take *Sale*; by early 1972 a quarter of the network were taking it; but it was not until early 1973 that it was fully networked, and then it became so popular that it ran for nearly a year without a break, which is exceptional for a quiz show. I knew it was popular, and that it first went to number one in the ratings in 1974, but I discovered even more from Paul Gambaccini and Rod Taylor's recent book *Television's Greatest Hits*. In 1976 it was in the top ten for thirty-six weeks and reached number one on Friday 23 January, with viewing figures of 19.5 million. In 1977 it spent thirty-two weeks in the top ten and reached number one on 18 November with viewing figures of 20.6 million. In 1978 the run was shorter, but when it reached number one on 22 December, the viewing figure – 21.2 million – was the highest of any show that year. Thereafter, the programme planners moved the show to different days and times according to the strength of opposition from the BBC. As a result, the programme was regularly in the ratings, but did not have the same consistently high viewing figures that it had had when transmitted at the popular time of 7.30 p.m. on Friday nights.

When the show became fully networked, John Jacobs, then senior producer of Drama at Anglia, joined us as executive producer. Peter Joy continued to direct, and it was a very happy team. They were worried, however, when they discovered that I was writing most of the questions, because it was against IBA rules. Another rule was that the questions should be kept in a sealed envelope and only opened by the host once the show had started. This was designed to eliminate any favouritism or the possibility of cheating and, while understandable, made it difficult to pace the shows. In addition, it was hard for me to deliver the questions with confidence when I was seeing them for the first time at the recording. It was also helpful to be able to discuss the questions with the producer and adjudicator beforehand to decide what range of answers I could accept if the contestants' responses were not entirely accurate. Anglia negotiated with the IBA, who relented over the sealed envelopes. I hoped I would be asked to write the questions as official compiler, but was told that a local man, John Erskine, had been employed. It was agreed, however, that I could help him, for which I would receive an extra fee, but no credit. John and I made a good team. Over the years we must have devised more than 30,000 questions – I used about ninety-five a show, sometimes it was more than one hundred, which is surprising because, after the introduction, the Instant Sales and the Sale of the Century at the end, there were only nine or ten minutes left for questions. John was later replaced by David Self, a writer and broadcaster who had worked a great deal at Anglia and Bill Perry, who was by then producing the show, decided that I should no longer be involved with the questions. This was a great disappointment, but it seems that, in this country, if you have made a reputation doing one thing, it is difficult for people to accept that you can do anything else.

There was a very pleasant working atmosphere at Anglia, par-ticularly during the early years of *Sale*, which was due in part to the attitude of the senior executives. The ones with whom I worked most closely were John Jacobs, Canon Peter Freeman and, of course, Peter Joy. John was an inspired director who could empathise with actors. He went out of his way to see that we worked in as relaxed and harmonious a way as possible given the demands of the show.

Canon Peter Freeman was Anglia's head of religious broadcasting and much loved by everyone at the studios. Full of energy, he produced five late-night items a week for the region, as well as looking after his parish outside Norwich. He also acted as an adjudicator for the show and I got to know him quite well as a result of our regular meetings. His counsel on any subject was always wise and no problem of whatever kind was ever too small.

There were many occasions when members of the staff at Anglia would seek him out for advice or comfort.

Peter Joy was different in many ways from John Jacobs and Peter Freeman. Like them, he was sympathetic to performers, and always saw that anyone who worked for him was well looked after. He could, however, be impatient with, and shout at, technicians who did not measure up to his high standards. This never bothered me: I knew it was just Peter doing his job. There is also a difference between a director who does not know his job and who shouts or bullies to cover his inadequacies, and a director who knows exactly what he is doing and unfortunately has a short fuse. I remember an occasion when one of the studio crew said to me, 'Doesn't it worry you when Peter starts shouting?' I replied, 'I get more worried when he's not shouting. Then I think there's really something wrong, or perhaps wrong with Peter.' I could understand, however, how the crew felt, and it is not the best way to direct, or to get the best out of your team. Eventually, the technicians made representations to management, who tried to persuade Peter to change his ways. He was so upset that he resigned. The show lost a great talent, and I missed him sorely.

Very few funny or embarrassing situations occur behind the scenes in a quiz show. You are under such pressure to see that everything runs smoothly so that the participants do not become inhibited by technical slip-ups, that you try very hard to avoid mistakes. The funny moments come from unexpected answers to questions. On one occasion, I asked an easy £1 question, 'According to proverb, what should you not do if you live in a glass house?' A contestant pressed her buzzer and replied, 'Take a bath.' It received a huge laugh, and she blushed. I thought it was better than the correct answer of throwing stones, and said I was sorry that I could not give her the money for inventiveness.

There are occasions when you feel you have to protect a contestant. If they give a foolish answer, they feel they made themselves look stupid before millions of people and you run the risk of them becoming completely inhibited, which can spoil the show. There was one occasion when a contestant's involvement was almost lost before we even started. It was my policy to meet the three people taking part each week and chat to them all together so that we could get to know each other. They would then, I hoped, be confident with me on the show. I used to stress that I was working for them, and wanted them all to succeed, emphasising that they should not be inhibited if I appeared to be abrupt with them in the closing stages, since the quicker I accepted their replies, the more questions I could deliver and, win or lose, the better their chances of making more money.

On this particular occasion, the three contestants were an attractive young woman, a quiet, self-effacing middle-aged man, and a very friendly, voluble cockney character. I spoke to the woman first, and discovered a little about her. I then turned to the Londoner and said, 'On the card I have here, it says you're a pawnbroker . . .' Before I could go any further, he jumped in to explain rapidly that, while he did that kind of work, his main source of income came from working off barrows in the market, where most of his money was earned in cash. 'Mostly back-of-the-hand stuff, you understand, Nicholas. What the eye don't see, the heart don't grieve over, if you get my meaning, Nicholas. I couldn't put that down as my living for obvious reasons, so I thought pawnbroker covered a multitude of sins, without raising any suspicions . . .' He carried on loquaciously for a time, then said, 'Oh, look at me, I'm talking too much.' Turning abruptly to the other man, who had been listening quietly, he said, 'And what do you do for a living?' This contestant replied drily, 'I'm an income tax inspector.' I had never before seen anyone actually turn green. Needless to say, he did not do very well in the show.

A different kind of embarrassment, this time over prizes, occurred after the show had been running for some time. The IBA had strict rules about the value of prizes that could be offered in a quiz or game show: the top prize could not be worth more than £1,000. The top prize on offer each week in *Sale* was usually a car and when the show first began there were about twenty small cars on the road at under £1,000. Within six or seven years, there were only three cars on the market under this figure, and they were all foreign makes. The IBA refused to change the rules in line with the cost of living, and the programme was taken to task by the press for being unpatriotic. One week, to try to ring the changes, we had on offer one of the new Lada cars, which were just coming on to the market. During the rehearsal to time the sale section at the end of the show, I arrived at the car, extolled its virtues, then went to open the door. It came off its hinges. I think jokes about Ladas, now common, started then.

Anglia used the bad press we had received to reason with the IBA and the Authority relented. As the price of a small British car increased over the years, further adjustments were made. By the time *Sale* finished in 1983, the rules had changed again. It was possible to offer an individual prize of up to £1,750 and a major prize of up to £3,000 to cover the price of a new car, but not every week, and all this was conditional on the total money given away in a four-week period not exceeding £17,500.

Once *Sale* was networked and its popularity increased, small changes were made. The hostesses were replaced at frequent intervals, which always resulted in good publicity in the papers as all the girls were most attractive (they were chosen by the producer and senior executives for that very reason). In 1973 it was decided to replace Peter Marshal with John Benson, who became the unseen voice that introduced the programme and described the prizes on offer. His smooth, velvet voice was ideal for the show and he stayed until the end of the run. It was he who suggested the programme's opening words, which became its trademark: 'From Norwich, it's the quiz of the week.'

In 1974, Peter Joy resigned and Bill Perry took over. He was skilled and capable, but lacked Peter's flair and inventiveness. From the start he let it be known that he would be making certain changes, the most significant of which, as far as I was concerned, was that he wanted to cut out any talk or ad-libs to the contestants and concentrate on getting through as many questions as possible. He said he recognised my ability to deliver questions quickly and he wanted to exploit this to create more excitement. While I could see that this would be good for the show, I explained that he would be turning me into a kind of automaton. I had to be allowed the occasional comment. He came back with, 'All right, but if you ad-lib, it must only be one line, and if it's not funny, don't say it.' What a straitjacket in which to work.

He also decided that, although the show was recorded, it was to be performed like a live show, with no stops or retakes. There were two breaks in the recording, at the halfway mark and before the final sale of the century, when any errors could be discussed and explained. I realised that it was important to keep the show moving at all costs, but now felt under extreme pressure to be fluent and make the correct decisions all the time.

I was in an impossible situation. I knew Bill's idea was fine for the style of show, but his constraints made it difficult for me to appear natural and easy. Since the public and the press are used to seeing quiz shows with no fluffs, as they have been edited out, if I stumbled on occasions and joked my way out of it, I was accused of being unprofessional. If I was one-hundred-per-cent fluent, I was accused of being smooth, impersonal, autocratic, even school-masterish.

Another pressure came from the fact that I never had the back-up of an autocue, which is fairly standard for presenters nowadays. Working in repertory and with Arthur Haynes had helped to train my memory, but in the quiz I was faced with a different task. I had to absorb very rapidly a vast amount of facts and figures about goods, their function and price, and deliver this in a precise time, having been given the details on a card only an hour previously. At the same time, I had to commit to memory the names, occupations, home towns, family details and other pieces of information about the three contestants so that I would be fluent when introducing them some four or five hours later. I did have a crib card for this if required, but no presenter wishes to be seen reading out information when it is his job to speak directly to the viewers. I had so little time to absorb all this information because, within an hour of arriving at the studio, I was rehearsing the walk through of the Sale of the Century itself, the last sequence in the show. It had to be word-perfect and exactly two minutes long after only two rehearsals. After that, I had to familiarise myself with the questions, marking them up so that I could deliver them quickly, partially memorised. I then met the contestants for a dummy run before a discussion with the adjudicator and producer about the margin of error we could allow in the answers to the questions.

As a result of having to memorise so much so quickly, I discovered something intriguing about memory. It seems that facts can be memorised very quickly but, as soon as they're no longer required, can be 'unremembered' with equal speed. I am often amazed how I can recall quite fluently a poem, joke or part of a comedy routine that I have not used for years, but something in my conscious or unconscious has 'wiped' information that I did not think I would need to have recourse to again. This can lead to embarrassment. On one occasion, I was at Liverpool Street Station when a man I did not recognise came up in a most friendly and informal manner and started to chat. He said he assumed I was going to Norwich and, as he was going the same way, suggested he might join me. I talked pleasantly with him, hoping for some clue as to who he was. After about half an hour on the train, he said suddenly, 'You don't recognise me, do you?' I admitted that, while his face was familiar, I could not place where we had met. He said, 'I was the winner on your show a few weeks ago.' I was mortified. There was nothing I could say. His face had been erased from my memory along with the facts and figures. No apology or explanation would have been adequate.

The success of *Sale of the Century* was exciting, and because it took up a relatively small proportion of my working life, I was able to pursue other interests. I built up my production company; I also wrote my one-man show on the life and work of Edward Lear. I treated *Sale* as another job. I enjoyed it, but it was not a way of life. I was therefore unprepared for the effect it would have both on my personal life and my professional standing. Up until *Sale* began, I had been accepted as an actor and comedy entertainer, as well as a straight man. Now it was suddenly as if any talent I had in these areas had disintegrated overnight.

The press had previously been very kind to me, particularly during my early years. Now their attitude suddenly changed, and they began to be critical and aggressive in a way I had not experienced before. If you appear in a theatrical production in any medium, you will be criticised for the quality of your performance, or even ignored if it is not thought worthy of attention. It seemed to me that if you fronted a television game show, you were no longer judged on whether you were doing a good or bad job as compère; you were criticised for the way you looked, or smiled, or even spoke. Any technique you were employing to help make the show a success was totally ignored.

Every newspaper, from *The Times* to the tabloids, had a go at the show – and me – in different ways. Each time it happened, the show's ratings went up, which I am sure is not what the press intended at all. I gradually learned to live with the comments and criticism, but it did come as a shock when the show business columnist of the *Sun* went as far as to run a campaign to have me taken off television. She said that the time had come to get rid of 'the great switch-off' personalities on television, and her particular 'switch off' was Nicholas Parsons. She encouraged all her readers to join together and try to have me removed from our screens. In fact, she did me a tremendous favour. The more she criticised me, the more the viewing figures went up.

While I learned to live with this kind of treatment, I became very upset when my family was affected. The first time I realised this was happening was when Justin was in his early teens. The school he attended, King Alfred, encouraged parents to become involved in its activities and for a number of years I had attended as many functions as I could and undertaken some very enjoyable tasks, such as talking to the sixth form about careers in the entertainment profession. The school was about to hold its next open day and I told Justin that I would be able to come. He did not seem as pleased as usual, and after some hesitation said he did not think that he would be going himself. I asked him whether he was allowed to excuse himself from such an important event. From his oblique excuses, I sensed that something was wrong. After some discussion, I asked him frankly whether he was worried about me coming to the open day because of the things that were being written in the press. He admitted that he was; he also said that the children at school had been teasing him about the facetious and unkind comments being printed about me and the show. I said that he must go to the open day himself, but that, if he preferred, I would not attend. In addition to feeling sad that I was not going to join him, I was very upset that the things a newspaper printed about me could so cruelly hurt an innocent party.

One of the most unexpected outcomes of my success in *Sale of the Century* was that comedy shows started to use my name as the butt for some of their jokes. The Goodies consistently poked fun at me, but then they had no straight man in their team, so perhaps they needed a foil for some of their jokes. Nearly every pantomime at the time contained a joke about me, as did many radio and television shows. I never minded when fellow artists made a joke at my expense, because it was always done to raise a laugh, and when it was funny I would laugh as much as anyone. Derogatory remarks in print, however, even when meant to be amusing, do not succeed. They lack the comedian's delivery, so they fall flat, or are simply embarrassing.

There was one line written about me that I will never forget, if only for a quite different reason. It was a piece of graffiti along a hoarding near a railway bridge in the Harrow area which read, 'Nicholas Parsons is the neo-opiate of the masses'. It was quite an achievement to paint it so large and so high, and it was many years before it was removed. And when it was, the author returned and repainted it. Someone must have felt passionately about the show. And why did the local council leave it up so long? Perhaps they never understood it; or perhaps they did, and approved.

Comments and reactions were not limited to the press, or to hoardings; they also came from members of the public. On one occasion I was returning to my car having been working in Broadcasting House. I reached the car, got in and started the engine, and then there was a tap on the window. The man outside indicated that he wanted me to wind it down, which I did. He then spoke to me with that complete informality that some people have when they recognise somebody who, appearing frequently on their television screens, is as familiar as any other piece of their furniture. A rough character with a cockney accent, he greeted me as if we had known each other for ages: 'Hello, Nicholas, I'm glad I've caught you. There's something I've been wanting to ask you.' I explained that I was in rather a hurry and did not really have time to chat, to which he replied, 'Now hang about, Nicholas, hang about. I'm one of your public, now, aren't I?' I realised he was not going to be put off, so I asked him what he wanted. 'It's about that show of yours,' he said, and then paused. I nodded, and he went on, 'I can't stand it.' 'Is that what you've stopped to tell me,' I asked. 'No, fair do's, fair do's, the wife – she's potty about it; but then all her family are like that. What I want to know is this. Can you take criticism?' I realised something unusual might be coming, so smiled and told him that I hoped I could. He continued, 'Well, I've watched your show . . .' I interrupted, 'I thought you said you couldn't stand it.' He came straight back, 'That's true, but I didn't say I don't watch it. Now, what I want to know is this. I see you standing there, looking all smart and suavey, with all the clobber and everything.

You have all the questions in your hand, and you're flipping them out – boom, boom, boom, and giving out all the answers; it's all flowing like; and you just keep going like that all the time.' 'Yes,' I said, 'but what exactly is worrying you?' He said, 'Well, sometimes I just wish you'd stop and do something.' There was a pause, and then I asked him what he wanted me to do. 'I don't know,' he replied. 'Why don't you fart?' He left me speechless. The natural come-back might have been, 'Well, I don't think it would come over all that well on television.' Instead, I said something to the effect that it was not the sort of thing I normally did in public, and would probably find it difficult to do on television, even to please him. He seemed quite happy with my reply, having obviously got something off his chest that had been bothering him for some time. Thinking about our conversation later, I decided that he did watch the show, but found the slickness of the delivery too much for his taste; he wanted me to prove that I was really just like the fellow next door.

Instant recognition is flattering, but sometimes things can go rather too far, such as when you are at home relaxing. Briar Cottage had no boundary fences between it and Hampstead Heath, and a public footpath skirted its small garden. As the heath sloped up from the footpath, people could sit on the bank and peer in through our first-floor windows. If they walked round the footpath, they could see right into our ground-floor rooms. Most of the week it was very quiet, but on Sundays there were a lot of people walking on the heath and we would sometimes see them sitting on the bank, trying to gaze through our windows. On one occasion, a man arrived complete with binoculars, and followed our every movement in the house. On another, three rough but friendly lads were sitting on the bank, watching me in the garden. I tried to ignore their persistent stares until I realised that they were not only watching me, but discussing my whole personality.

I had experienced this type of situation before on the London Underground, when two women sitting opposite me started a very frank discussion about me and the way I looked, as if I was not there. I felt rather like an animal in the zoo, and would not have been surprised if they had started prodding me to see how I would react. The three characters on the heath, however, were slightly different. After one of them had pointed out to his friends who I was and what I did on television, he shouted over, 'Nich'las, I've brought me friends along. I told 'em you lived 'ere. We've just been down the pub. I've brought 'em up 'ere to show 'em yer 'ouse and yer little bit of garden. We're fans of yours. Me mates didn't believe you were the sort of fellow that ever got 'is 'ands mucky.' He then turned to his friends and began to discuss me in the third person, before turning back and shouting, 'What you doing now Nich'las? Shovelling the old manure round yer rose trees, are you? Does wonders for 'em, so I'm told.' It is very difficult to concentrate under these conditions; you become very self-conscious. They then invited me to join them for a drink at the Bull and Bush, the pub opposite. I thanked them but declined, explaining that their conversation had put me behind with my gardening. These are the kind of fans whom you can enjoy, but they make it difficult to go about your life easily when you are as exposed to them as we were in Briar Cottage. In fact, it was principally because of this lack of privacy that we eventually decided to sell our home and live elsewhere.

We put the cottage on the market towards the end of 1979. There was a lull in my professional activities because of a strike of ITV technicians, and the next series of *Sale of the Century* was postponed. Since I had turned down other work to be available for the series, I found myself unexpectedly free. Denise had often talked of living in the country, but I had resolutely wished to remain in London while Suzy and Justin were young. Now, however, they had left school and I decided that we could start to look for a home within commuting distance of London. We found a beautiful period house in the village of Swallowfield, Berkshire, which was not too far from the M4 or main line stations. Not being good at business, however, we put Briar Cottage on the market at the wrong time, and also foolishly took out a huge bridging loan. The bank rate unexpectedly rose to a ridiculous figure and we were put under considerable financial strain as we could not sell the cottage. By this time, Denise felt we were doing the wrong thing and that it was probably too late in our married life to consider a major move. I persuaded her that we should persevere, and managed to let our London home. All this put a huge strain on our marriage, and when we eventually moved to the country, Denise found she did not enjoy it. I, on the other hand, found the country so peaceful that I never wanted to return to live in London. To add to the personal strain, my mother unexpectedly died, and my father became increasingly debilitated with Parkinson's disease. All the travelling, both professionally and for personal reasons, meant that I was seeing less of Denise. She began to feel more isolated: in addition to my unavoidable absences, most of her friends were in London, Suzy had her own flat, and Justin was at college. It has often been said that the trauma of moving after a long period in the same home can put a severe strain on a marriage and, with all the other factors, it proved to be true with us. It was Denise who suggested that we should separate. I agreed, because I recognised that, in many ways, we had grown apart. The separation inevitably led to a final break-up. We have always remained friends. We certainly never broke up in acrimony; you simply cannot just throw away all you have experienced together as your children grew up.

Our divorce came a number of years after the separation. I had managed to keep the news of our break-up from the press; when the actual divorce went through, however, the newspapers naturally latched on to it. Only one newspaper made a double-page spread of the situation, the *News of the World*, who printed columns of intimate and mostly fictitious details of our private life. The sad thing about such coverage is the harm it unintentionally does to the people involved. Denise was convinced that I had been paid for the article, the content of which, while pleasantly written, was in no way accurate. I could not convince her that I had not given permission for it, or said the things that were quoted, which did cause a great deal of aggravation between us. I think the article also embarrassed Suzy and Justin, neither of whom have ever sought publicity, especially of such a personal kind.

18
. . . .

Raising Money the Hard Way

OVER the years, I have been involved with a number of charities, most of which concern children, and I feel it is a privilege to be able to help. I was on an NSPCC committee in Hampstead for many years, which raised a great deal of money and helped found what was then called the 'battered baby unit' (they are now given the more sympathetic title 'sheltered home'). The money we raised helped to set up a home at Denver Hall in Harringay, north London, which was officially opened by the Society's patron, Princess Margaret, on 14 October 1974. It is good to know that there are now a number of these units throughout the country.

One of the first charities I became involved with was the Lord's Taverners, set up in 1950 by a group of actors who, as cricket enthusiasts, wanted to put something back into the game that gave them so much pleasure. Their aspirations were quite modest to begin with: they made a few thousand pounds from one or two cricket matches. In many ways they pioneered the idea of charity cricket, with a team of show business personalities and former professional cricketers playing against an opposition organised by the sponsor of the particular game. I first turned out to play for them in 1956, and it has never ceased to excite me, walking out to field in a team containing some of the great cricketers, now retired, whom I admired in my youth. As a member now of both the Council and the Cricket Committee, I have seen the charity grow from one which raised between £2,000 and £3,000 in its first years to over £1,500,000 by 1990. The money goes to help under-privileged and handicapped children, to 'give them a sporting chance', to quote our slogan. We now arrange many more activities besides cricket matches and the Annual Ball, and have branches throughout the country, as well as the Lady Taverners and the Young Lord's Taverners. We have also travelled widely, to places such as Hong Kong, the Caribbean and Africa, playing cricket and golf and providing other entertainment.

In June 1978 I took a team to Corfu, one of the few places in Europe outside Britain where this very English game is played – a relic of the British occupation of Corfu, dating back to the nine-teenth century. The Corfiots play the game with extraordinary dedication and application; but they have few pitches. The one we played on, in the centre of Corfu town, is more often used as a car park.

I thought it might be a good idea to make a film about the cricketing activities of the Taverners, including the Corfu trip, to promote the charity. In order to do that, however, I had to find a sponsor, and to attract one, I had to make sure the film was going to be interesting enough to be taken for cinema distribution. This was achieved, most of the money was raised, and the Rank Organisation distributed the finished film worldwide. I called the film *Mad Dogs and Cricketers* and, because it was promoting the Lord's Taverners, all the stars gave their services free. For the Corfu sequence – the major part of the film – I had a magnificent cast, which included John Cleese, Willie Rushton, John Alderton, Brian Rix, Ed Stewart, Bill Simpson, Roy Kinnear and Peter Gordeno, as well as the professional cricketers Ken Barrington, John Price and Jack Robertson. The feat of organisation was only possible because of help in the planning from a good friend, Brian Langford, who was then working in the travel business. The budget went on the film crew, led by a superb freelance cameraman, Ernest Vincze. In fact, I ran out of money. I used some of my own capital; I was also helped by a donation of £2,000 from David Evans, a generous member of the Taverners' Council.

The Corfiots treated us royally, and there was only one slight misunderstanding: they thought they were welcoming and playing against a top MCC team sent out from Lord's, the home of cricket. I had given all the non-cricketers fictitious teams for which they were supposed to have played, based on their best-known television or theatrical credits, and these were printed in the programme for the match. Any British tourist who watched the game would not only have recognised the celebrities, but also the fictitious clubs to which they were supposedly affiliated. Not so the Corfiots. Ken Barrington was correctly down as having played for England and Surrey, John Price and Jack Robertson for England and Middlesex. Alongside John Cleese I had put 'Python Irregulars' and 'The Towering Faulties'. Brian Rix turned out for the 'Whitehall Farcers'; Willie Rushton's club was 'The Tele- Eccentrics'. The two clubs I represented were 'The Old Centurians' and 'The Ancient Order of Straight Men'. Every player had two teams against his name and the local Corfu paper, in promoting the match, mentioned all of them as if they were clubs almost as famous as Lord's itself.

The day of the cricket match arrived. All cars were cleared from the extremely hard boundary area and a tannoy system had been installed. During the planning stages I had asked if it might be possible to have the local band playing at some point. I assumed that they would perform during the tea break. Since the mayor of Corfu, who was looking after all the arrangements, was so fired by my enthusiasm, and since he thought I was bringing an England team with me, he had organised a complete parade to open the proceedings. We not only had the local band, colourfully dressed in their uniforms, but also the Boy Scouts and Girl Guides, followed by a contingent from every cricket team in the Corfu league, all in pristine whites. Marching on to the pitch in time to the music, the Lord's Taverners team brought up the rear of the procession. There were civic dignitaries present from Corfu and Athens; there were speeches and presentations, and then the national anthems of both countries. It was a delightful and at times moving occasion, and an original way to begin a cricket match.

I had asked Ken Barrington to captain the Lord's Taverners' team, which he did with great style and authority. He also understood how we play our charity cricket. By tradition we go through the formality of tossing a coin, but irrespective of which side wins, it is arranged that the Lord's Taverners bowl first so that all the celebrities can be seen on the field from the beginning. More important, this means we can stage-manage the game so that as many runs as possible are made in the allotted time, thereby making the match as entertaining as we can for the spectators. If, for instance, the opposition is weak and begin to lose wickets, our professional bowlers are taken off and the less able ones amongst the celebrities come on. The captain of the opposition is also requested to do the same – if his team start to take a lot of quick wickets when we are batting, then his weaker bowlers and even non-bowlers are put on.

This was explained to the captain of the Corfu team, Yannis Arvanitakis, who was extremely puzzled, especially by the request for his team to bat first regardless of who won the toss. We tried to explain that this was how our charity cricket matches were played, and he responded in his broken English, 'I do not understand. What has charity got to do with cricket?' I realised the significance of this remark when his team later took the field and his players threw themselves about on the hard ground with an abandon that was in complete contrast to the relaxed attitude of the Lord's Taverners. Part of the outfield was made of concrete, and there was an occasion when one of their fielders threw himself full length along it to stop a ball speeding to the boundary. He finished up with his trousers ripped and blood running down the side of his leg. Instead of leaving the field for first aid, he seemed to treat this as all part of the noble game of cricket as they understood it in Corfu.

The game was extraordinarily close. With only two balls to go, the Lord's Taverners needed five runs to win. Ken Barrington was in to bat. He hit the penultimate ball magnificently for four. Everyone in the crowd and in the teams felt the tension as the last ball was bowled. Ken steered it somewhere between mid-wicket and mid-on, and he and John Price ran two for good measure. They came off the field exhausted and elated. Both British and Corfiot spectators had witnessed a magnificent game, decided on the last ball and the last stroke of the match. The Taverners team, along with many British members of the crowd, surged on to the pitch to greet their two batting heroes – John Price had scored a century – and carried them shoulder high to the edge of the playing area. The Corfiot team applauded. They had not won, but they had played magnificently and everyone felt they had witnessed one of the most exciting games ever played on the ground in front of Corfu's famous Esplanade.

In a charity cricket match I would always rather bat against a professional bowler than a keen club cricketer. The latter, who probably plays in front of a handful of spectators at club events, is often extremely keen to get you out, and then presumably boast later to his friends about all the celebrity 'scalps' he has taken. An experienced professional bowler is going to be much more easy-going. He knows that if he puts his mind to it, he could probably bowl you four balls out of six. He also has the skill to place the ball fairly gently outside the off-stump, so that if you have any ability at all, you can score runs off him.

I had the perfect example of this in a charity match in 1990. The sponsors were Gestetner and their managing director, who was an Australian and also captaining, had reinforced his side by inviting a friend of his, Dennis Lilley, to turn out for them.

As captain I put myself on to bowl quite late in the innings. In my first over Dennis Lilley was still batting. I am capable of bowling one or perhaps two good balls a season. One of these went to Dennis Lilley, and whether it was surprise on his part or sudden mental blackout, I will never know. I bowled him middle stump. With the audience applause resounding in my ears, it would have been marvellous to retire gracefully from the sport at that moment, especially in view of what happened next.

Dennis Lilley was followed to the crease by the captain of the Gestetner team, the man who had underwritten £5,000 to the charity. The next ball I bowled turned out to be the other good ball I bowl in a season, and I claimed his wicket as well. I had done the unforgivable: I had dismissed not only their captain but the man responsible for the sponsorship, first ball for a duck. I turned to the umpire and suggested he should shout that it was a bumped ball and call the batsman back, but he was not an umpire conversant with the ground rules of a charity cricket match, and informed me that the batsman was out. My elation turned to embarrassment; I wished to retire from the sport at that moment for a quite different reason.

Later, when I went out to bat, Dennis Lilley was bowling. The crowd thought they would see a few sparks fly. I was a little anxious myself, but in the tradition of true sportsmanship and fair play that exists among professional cricketers, he bowled me a gentle one, which I surprisingly struck for four. I even took another boundary off him, and then he decided that I had had enough fun at his expense and sent a ball down that bowled me all ends up. Two fours off Dennis Lilley, however, became another reason why I wished to retire gracefully after this particular match.

My association with cricket and the Lord's Taverners played a significant part in what was one of the most memorable events in my professional life, when in June 1977 I was chosen to be the 'subject' of *This is Your Life*. (The term is used by the production team at all times during their planning, for fear the real name slips out accidentally in their research and the secrecy is destroyed.) The priority is that the 'subject' remain unsuspecting, and such emphasis is placed on secrecy that the subject's friends are only invited to take part two weeks before the recording.

The producers make such efforts to eliminate the possibility of the subject becoming suspicious during the 'pick-up' that they almost trip over themselves in their conscientiousness. This certainly happened with me. My press agent, Margo Lovell, had arranged for me to give an interview to *Woman* magazine for an article they were putting together about cricket teas. I had to have some photographs taken for this at the Oval. About a week before this was due to happen, I was told that it was not going to be me alone as originally planned, but that a number of other well-known names in the entertainment and cricket world were also going to be at the Oval to be photographed for the article. The fact that they were all personal friends did not make me in the least suspicious.

Thames Television had decided to send a crew to film the others talking in my absence about my love of cricket and involvement with the Lord's Taverners, after the magazine's photographer had finished. I heard afterwards that Margo Lovell had suggested that the Oval would be an ideal venue for the pick-up but Thames vetoed the idea since I might see the television recording van and become suspicious. So it was decided that the pick-up should take place at the White House hotel and Anne Knight, from my agent's office, agreed to be involved. She told me on the phone that an American impresario was interested in talking to me about a job on television in the States. She said that she would accompany me to the meeting.

This is where things started to go slightly wrong for Thames. I placed so much importance on the outcome of this meeting with the American producer that I rang Margo and asked her to get me out of the photo session at the Oval. The lines between her and the production team of *This is Your Life* must have been buzzing. When she came back on the phone and said that this was going to be difficult, I pointed out that they had a lot of people for the photograph, so they would not miss me. It was very important that I was not late for the appointment at the White House hotel. The phone lines buzzed again, and the producer of *This is Your Life* thought up another ploy. Margo was soon back on the phone to me saying that Thames had decided to cover the photo session and would actually interview me for a sports programme, talking about cricket. I was still worried, however, that I would not make my appointment with the American. Again, the lines buzzed. Again, Margo was back on the phone to me: 'Thames Television,' she assured me, 'are so keen for you to do this interview that they'll supply a car to take you from home to the Oval, wait there and be available to take you to your appointment at the hotel, and will guarantee that you're not late.' The situation had been salvaged, but all the plans nearly foundered again.

On the day of the Oval interviews and my meeting with the American, it so happened that a researcher from BBC Television came to my house to discuss my appearance in a series they were producing and was still asking questions when the car from Thames Television arrived to take me to the Oval. I asked the driver to wait while I finished the interview. He seemed rather agitated and the longer I kept him waiting, the more anxious he became. I thought this a little unusual – of course he was in on the plot – but I still was not suspicious. When we did finally leave, he drove me at breakneck speed from north London, south of the river to the Oval. On arrival, I quickly changed into my cricket clothes as requested and joined the others, who were already in their whites, standing around a large table magnificently laid out with the most sumptuous cricket tea I had ever seen. The photographs were taken. The magazine was delighted, then the producer of the television film unit arranged for me to be 'interviewed' by a Thames sports commentator. In no time the cameras were rolling ... but all the technicians were acting, and nothing was being recorded. As soon as it was over they suggested I should hurry upstairs and change so as not to be late for my next appointment. This I did, but once again the whole secret was nearly blown.

After I went to change, they began the genuine filming of

comments from others about me. In packing up my cricket things, I discovered that I had left my sweater in the room where the filming was taking place. On my way downstairs to the waiting car, I walked into this room to collect it. As I went in, there was an instant silence in which you could almost have heard a bail drop. They had been in the middle of filming and someone had just recorded a remark about me. Everyone assumed that I had heard it. Not having heard anything, I thought I had walked in while the camera was running and that I had ruined the take. I was extremely embarrassed, so I mimed to everyone that I had forgotten something, tiptoed across the room, picked up my sweater and tiptoed out, waving my goodbyes. The secret was still intact. I hurried out to the waiting car and we set out for the hotel.

Anne Knight greeted me as soon as I arrived and suggested that we might go to the bar for a drink. This was to be the spot where the actual pick-up was to take place. Anne was going to call for the barman, and Eamon Andrews was going to pop up from behind the bar with his famous red book. As we walked in, I noticed two of the girls who had appeared with me on *Sale of the Century*, who should have been out of sight. They were, of course, to be part of the programme. When people who are naturally honest tell lies to keep a secret, they feel very guilty, and think they have given themselves away. If you are on the receiving end you do not suspect anything, so any situation, however odd, seems normal. As I had not seen either of the girls for a while, I said to Anne that we should go over and say hello. Anne, who is by nature very gentle, then did something utterly uncharactcristic, which at the time I did not understand. She grabbed me aggressively by the arm and said, 'Oh, no you're not. You're going to have a drink with *me*,' and forcibly propelled me to the bar. Before I had time to think, Eamon had appeared and all was made clear. It was one of the most exciting and memorable evenings of my life. In what other circumstances could you have such a marvellous surprise party, with so many relatives and friends all brought together at someone else's expense!

Another memorable, but quite different, event arose from my association with the charity Action Research for the Crippled Child. In 1977 they ran a fundraising scheme in which they encouraged people to try to break records of various kinds. If you succeeded, they arranged for you to be listed in the *Guinness Book of*

Records. The charity sent me details of the scheme and from the ideas included, I thought that a speech record might be something I could do. I discovered, however, that Gyles Brandreth was already committed to trying to do the same – he was going to speak for as long as he could to a small dinner party in a certain London hotel. Anyone was invited to sit in on the event, having first made a donation to the charity.

I went and listened. Gyles spoke very entertainingly for three and a half hours, and subsequently appeared in the *Guinness Book of Records* as having given the longest after-dinner speech. The event organisers asked me that evening whether I had decided on a record that I wanted to attempt. I replied that talking and entertaining was the one skill at which I was experienced, but that record had already been broken. They said immediately that they would be perfectly happy to organise another dinner at which I could try to beat Gyles's record. I accepted the challenge and a few months later they organised a dinner at a college of further education in Berkshire, where the guests at the small gathering were staff from the college. There were two adjudicators, whose responsibility was to see that the 'rules of engagement' were strictly adhered to: the speaker had to be consistently entertaining or interesting, or he would be ruled out of order. My two adjudicators were that fine master of ceremonies Bryn Williams and a member of the college staff. Denise nobly joined me at the dinner, even though she knew she was probably going to hear material she had heard many times before. There was a huge clock in the background, which showed everyone, including myself, how long I had been speaking.

After three and a half hours, a big cheer went up. I worked through all the material I had ever used in previous speeches, in cabaret work and as a stand-up comedian. I soon discovered that this audience was unlike the average audience to whom one might be playing for laughs, where the surest way to success is to be as succinct as possible. This audience was willing me to succeed not only in entertaining them, but in keeping going as long as I could. Any opportunity to elaborate or embroider on material I was using, therefore, was not only seized upon by me, but was not at all irritating or frustrating to them.

After seven hours I had worked my way through most of the material I had prepared; I was also exhausted. Furthermore, the audience, although they had been able to get up and move about when they wanted, were obviously anxious to go home. I finally sat down, worn out but happy that I had raised some money for the charity, and broken the record. My name was now in the *Guinness Book of Records*.

In early January 1978, the charity phoned and asked if I would like to try to beat the record. I said immediately that I would not, as the last attempt had nearly killed me. They went on to explain that Gyles Brandreth, being of a competitive nature, was disappointed at having the record taken from him so quickly and was keen to have a go at winning it back. The charity had the idea that Gyles and I should compete for a new record at separate dinners, set up in adjoining rooms at a big London hotel, and they felt that, with the right publicity, the event could generate strong media coverage. I asked them how much money they hoped to raise. They replied that their target was £10,000. I immediately agreed to take part.

The event was scheduled to take place on Monday, 13 February, at the Hyde Park Hotel in Knightsbridge. The whole proceedings were to be covered by Capital Radio, who broke into their programmes throughout the evening to report progress and broadcast snatches from one or other of the speeches. The newspapers were briefed, and the public were encouraged to drop in to the hotel at any time, make a donation to the charity and sit in on either or both of the speeches.

A few days before the event, the organisers rang to say that, as we were probably going to be speaking beyond the existing record of seven hours, Gyles was worried about calls of nature and wanted to be prepared, as the rules of the contest prohibited us from leaving our rostrum or pausing for any reason. I thought it was unnecessary, but the charity insisted, as they did not want any embarrassment or unfortunate accidents. They said that they had been in touch with John Bell & Croydon, a very superior chemists in Wigmore Street, who were prepared to fit me with what they described as an 'astronaut bag'. It all seemed a bit much, but they were very insistent, so I duly called on the chemist.

I was greeted by a very old-fashioned type of shop assistant in a black jacket and striped trousers to whom I explained my mission, muttering something about 'astronaut bag . . .' He did not bat an eyelid. As he turned, he said, 'Would you care to walk this way, sir?' All I could think of was an alternative version of the music-hall reply, 'If I walked that way, I wouldn't need the astronaut bag.' He led me to a cubicle and, drawing back the curtains, asked me to step inside and get undressed. Someone would then come and measure me. I was now very puzzled and a little unsettled. In a few minutes he returned with a cardboard box, passed it round the curtain and asked me to try the contents on for size. I felt as if I was being treated like someone with a terrible affliction and tried to explain that there was nothing physically wrong with me; I was merely attempting to break a speech record. He looked at me with complete disdain. I asked him what he had given me and he replied, 'It is our standard urinal bag, sir, for those of above average stature.' If he sensed my embarrassment, he certainly did not show it. He merely pursed his lips again and said, 'They are quite simple to fit. The instructions are contained within the box. Would you like our Mr Percy to bring his tape measure and see if you have the right size to accommodate a man of your build?' I declined his offer. I did not want to meet Mr Percy, or his tape measure.

When I got home I discovered how to attach the contraption to me. It felt very uncomfortable and I sensed that it probably was not going to be necessary. I discovered later that this was true; when your adrenalin is pumping, the waterworks seem to dry up.

As it happened, the story of the astronaut bag turned out to be a great bonus for the speech. I was able to relate how I had acquired it, the experience of visiting the chemist, and then embroidered on details of how it was fitted. During the speech the bag slipped, so I was able then to go into graphic details of what had happened. Later on, it fell off completely and finished up on the floor. I described this in detail, which was valuable extra padding for the speech.

Once more, I worked my way through all the speech material I had ever used – all my cabaret material, stand-up comedy routines, even some revue numbers. All this was interspersed with theatrical anecdotes and other humorous experiences from my professional life. As the night wore on and dawn began to break, most of the audience had retired to bed, except for the few stoical characters who had volunteered to attend the dinner in the first place – something I am sure most of them were now regretting. A doctor had been in attendance during the event for emergencies, and apparently he was now worried that Gyles and I were going to continue until one or other dropped, and this would be bad publicity for the charity. It was decided to bring the marathon to an end. I was passed a note to inform me that in thirty minutes' time, I would have been speaking for eleven hours, and it had been decided by the adjudicators that, if Gyles and I were both still speaking then, they were going to finish the contest and, literally at the eleventh hour, declare it to be an honourable draw.

Both of us kept going for the thirty minutes, and then stopped. We woke up those at the dinner table who had fallen asleep and, in what I can only describe as a zombie-like state, I gathered my papers, woke Denise, found the car and somehow drove home. I was far too exhausted to appreciate that I had actually broken my own record, and it was a week before I felt fully recovered.

Our record remained in the *Guinness Book of Records* for some time, until Gyles decided that he did not enjoy sharing, and set out to beat it. Since then, I understand a Welsh preacher has set a longer record, but I am sure he did not have our rules about being consistently entertaining and amusing. After that, the record was credited to someone who has spoken for longer, but every fifty minutes he had a rest for ten minutes, which seems quite a different sort of record. Perhaps our original record should be reinstated alongside it as the longest uninterrupted humorous speeches ever made.

19

· · · · · · · · ·

Back to Comedy

1983 was a difficult year of transition. The last series of *Sale of the Century* had been recorded and, in that sense, an important period in my life had come to an end. The programmes were still popular when transmitted and we went out on a high note, the demise of the series resulting from the IBA ruling that there should be no more than two high-reward quizzes on the network in any one week. The programme planners had other quizzes they wanted to introduce and it was time for *Sale* to make way for something new. Professionally, I was not disappointed: if it had continued much longer I ran the risk of being so identified with it that I might not have been offered other interesting work elsewhere. It is amazing how strong an impression the quiz made during the 1970s and early 1980s, particularly amongst those who were growing up then. In spite of the adverse press comments, it is still remembered with great affection and I have discovered that some of the following I have built with young adults today is based on happy memories they have of the show. If I had known that at the time, perhaps I should have persuaded my agent to find a similar show for me, to capitalise on the following I had built. At the time, however, I was not looking for another quiz show. I had enjoyed the success of *Sale*, but I was an actor whose life had been in comedy. The only comedy I was achieving from the quiz was the humorous send-ups of me that fellow professionals resorted to in their own shows.

Throughout the fourteen-year run of *Sale*, I built up my production company; I also continued to work in the theatre. In fact, more of my life was spent in comedy in the theatre and on radio than in playing it very straight in *Sale of the Century*. The irony is that, after all the hard work that goes into a theatre production with performances eight times a week, fewer people will have seen you perform by the end of the run than in one appearance in a television show. We work in the theatre because we love it, and that is where you learn your craft; but it is television that makes you a household name.

Of my theatre work during this period, one tour, in 1982, stands out in my mind. The play was *Stage Struck*, by Simon Gray, in which Alan Bates had starred in the West End. I played the lead and Dermot Walsh, who produced and organised the tour, played one of the other leading roles along with his very pretty wife, the late Elizabeth Scott. The play is a clever psychological drama, and it gave me a chance to perform a serious role again. I also had a death scene – something I had never played before.

There was a blank week in the tour and Dermot said that the only date he could obtain was at the little Rosehill Theatre in Whitehaven. He said that the theatre was so tiny I would not make any money from my percentage on the returns, but it had a lovely atmosphere and audiences tended to dress up to go to performances there. I was happy to go, and to visit Cumbria again.

Dermot's description of Rosehill was correct. It is charming but so small that it was difficult to fit the set within the proscenium arch, and the front row of the audience seemed almost to be sitting on the stage with us. The play went well, but business was not good, and none of the smartly dressed people Dermot had described appeared. He was very embarrassed. Since he had last worked there, the theatre had changed hands and was obviously struggling. To provide an audience for the mid-week matinée, the management gave the theatre over to an old people's home, who brought in two bus-loads of excited elderly folk. They seemed to enjoy it immensely, and presumably because they were used to watching television in groups at home, where they might comment to one another on the action or the actors, they behaved in just the same way during the play. As the theatre was so small, we could hear every word. 'Ooh, look at her, she's a saucy one.' 'He's nice, isn't he?' 'Doesn't he look sad?' 'I like his pinny.' 'I think she's up to no good.' 'Wouldn't trust him.' 'Why's he saying that?' 'Look, he's got a gun.' 'I don't think he'll use it.'

We reached the end of the play, and my death scene. I am shot, stagger, fall and deliver my last speech, which was received in silence. Then, as I had done for a number of weeks, I sank slowly to the floor, with blood oozing from my wound, and died. As I gasped my last breath, a woman with a slight Cumbrian accent said with great feeling, 'He doesn't have much luck, does he?' Her timing was perfect. No one on stage could keep a straight face, and the corpse literally 'corpsed'. I was just glad that I had no more words to speak.

Another significant tour came in 1983, after the last recordings of *Sale* had taken place. The play was *Keeping Down with the Jones'es* by John Chapman and Jeremy Lloyd. It was well cast, had some marvellous moments, but never fully succeeded with the audience, as the premise seemed to worry them. It was set in a nuclear fallout shelter. An eccentric, played by myself, builds the shelter in his garden and decides to spend his family holiday there to find out what it would be like if he ever had to use it for real. Before the holiday starts things go wrong, and the family are trapped there, along with the milkman and odd-job man. It had all the classic ingredients of traditional farce, but some of the audience were not amused. They felt they could not laugh about something so horrendous. No bombs, however, had been dropped. A group of ill-assorted people were simply trapped in a confined space – a usual setting for any successful farce. The play never came to London as we had hoped. My fortunes were ebbing.

Just prior to the play's opening, Denise and I had separated. Briar Cottage, which had been our home for over twenty years, was finally sold; everything was divided up, and I was going to move into the flat that I had inherited following my father's death. Separation is distressing for everyone involved and I think, in retrospect, it is more difficult in some ways when it is amicable. The friendship and consideration remain; it is the emotional relationship that has broken down. Those who break up in acrimony have someone to criticise, someone on whom they can vent their emotional pain. Denise took off for a holiday to stay abroad with her sister. I had to keep working. The stress of the previous year was difficult to handle, and it was hard to rehearse when I was so preoccupied. I was not telling anyone what was happening to Denise and myself, as neither of us wanted the press to intrude into our private lives. Suzy and Justin were wonderful, recognising our distress and trying to make things as easy as possible.

I had usually always refused pantomime offers when my children were young. Arthur Haynes had asked me more than once to join him, but Christmas at home was very important to me during Suzy and Justin's childhood. Pantomime is demanding work, with two shows every day and, at some theatres, three performances on a Saturday. Some pantomimes now have shows on a Sunday as well, with only Christmas day off during the peak period.

The only time I relented was when I was asked to play the Baron in *Cinderella* at Oxford, a pantomime that starred Roy Castle as an excellent Buttons. Denise, Suzy and Justin joined me over the Christmas period and it was possible to commute from London the rest of the time. I can only assume that I was cast as the Baron because of my reputation as a straight man. To me, however, it is not a conventional straight-man role: most often, as written, he is a boring stooge to the other characters. The only time I enjoyed playing the role was many years later in Mansfield. On this occasion, Peter Simon played Buttons, and we had some great scenes together. Peter, who presents children's programmes on television, has that rare gift of being able to talk easily with children, even make jokes at their expense, without ever patronising them. He also has a youthful charm that adults love.

I think one of the reasons I regularly do pantomime now is that I miss the fun I had with my own children when they were small, and it is a pleasure and compensation to have contact with so many children during the Christmas season. Now that I have grandchildren, however, I may begin to refuse pantomime again, so that I can occasionally spend Christmas in Guernsey with Suzy, her husband Jamie and their children, Annabel and Tom.

I began to accept pantomime engagements in 1982, when I played the Wicked Sheriff in *Robin Hood* at the Ashcroft Theatre in Croydon. Richard Briers was the Nurse, the Dame role in this pantomime, and I do not think he was very happy. He was the first Dame I have seen who did not wear false bosoms and make himself matronly. Consequently, he looked like a repressed spinster. He gave a good performance – he could not give a bad one – but I do not think he has ever been tempted into the world of panto again.

I was not sure how to play a pantomime 'baddie' because I had never done it before. I soon discovered a technique: I was outrageous, insulting the audience whenever I could, so that they enjoyed hating me. If you play the villain in a pantomime in the same way as you might in a drama, as genuinely evil, it destroys the fun.

The following year, I was invited to star in the pantomime at the Empire Theatre, Sunderland. When you are top of the bill in a pantomime, you are usually consulted as to which part you want to play, and some of the script is then written around you. I said that I would like to play the Dame, which surprised everyone, including my agent. The pantomime was *Jack and the Beanstalk*, and the Dame character is Jack's mother. Geoffrey Hughes, who was starring alongside me, was playing Simple Simon. He was lovely to work with, and it was one of the happiest pantomime companies, and a highly successful season.

One of the requests I made when accepting the engagement was that I be allowed to talk to the children at the end, inviting five or six of them on to the stage. It is unusual for the Dame to do this, but then I was not the conventional Dame. Instead of being an unattractive, rather vulgar and, above all, forbidding creature in the traditional style, I was saucy and over-the-top, with glamorous make-up and a flamboyant wig.

The fun in talking to the children comes in trying to elicit some spontaneous reactions or remarks. The problem in Sunderland was that a lot of them had broad Wearside accents and I was not always sure what they were saying. On another occasion, I could understand what the child was saying, it was just that he did not say very much.

'Where's your home?' I asked.

'It's oot there.'

'I know, but where out there?'

'It's a long way away.'

'Has your home got a name?'

'Oh aye.'

'Well, can you tell me?'

'No. Me mam told me not to talk to strangers.'

I was invited to repeat my efforts at playing Dame the following year at the Orchard Theatre, Dartford, a magnificent new civic theatre completed only two years previously. It was *Dick Whittington*, with Barbara Windsor playing the name part. The script had been written and the show produced by Charles Vance. In my opening scene, he had put in the script, 'The Dame enters on roller-skates', which I thought was a great idea. I had seen *Starlight Express*, the roller-skating musical, and made enquiries from them as to where the best skates could be bought and who could give me a couple of lessons. The then skating instructor from *Starlight*, Eamon Geoghan, gave me some basic instruction, and suggested a simple routine.

The Orchard Theatre is modern and well designed. The auditorium is not much lower than the stage and has a ramp either side, so it was possible to make an entrance and skate right into the centre of the audience. Fortunately, the side aisles and the gap in the seating half-way back was a smooth, uncarpeted surface ideal for my purpose. I used to sweep on, circle the stage, zoom down into the auditorium, shoot across the middle between the seated customers and then back onto the stage, do a couple of figures of eight, then glide off into the wings, smiling triumphantly at the audience with my shopping basket raised high. There would then be the most almighty crash, from which we hoped everyone would assume I had suffered some terrible mishap. I would then immediately sweep on again upstage, as if nothing had happened.

It is not easy skating in a long dress and carrying a shopping basket, and there is quite an art in skating on stage, because it is raked. If you stand still, looking at the audience, you automatically freewheel into the orchestra pit. When circling the stage, I found I had to accelerate going up to compensate for the incline, and ease back on the return, as the momentum gathered going down the slope could take me over the footlights to land unceremoniously among the orchestra.

Charles Vance, who produced and directed the pantomime, is one of those slightly larger-than-life characters with a warm heart and exuberant personality. He has a reputation for being very careful about money. After the show opened, I said, 'I assume you'll be paying for the skates, Charles? D'you want the bill?' He replied that the purchase was my responsibility. I pointed out that he had even written the skates into the script. 'Oh, I just intended you should be dragged on wearing any old pair we could scrounge.' 'But Charles, aren't you pleased with the success of the skating?' 'Of course, dear boy, of course. It's wonderful. I love it. It's one of the hits of the show. You are now my skating Dame.' 'Well, will you contribute towards the cost? They weren't cheap.' 'Dear boy, you have made a small investment, and had a huge success from it. You should be thanking me for putting the idea in the script in the first place.' I thought that if I continued the conversation, I might end up paying *him* something. If he had not convinced me, he had certainly convinced himself. His argument may have been implausible, but as it turned out, he was correct: I had made an investment, as I was to discover a few years later.

I was able to skate in two more pantomimes. The first was the following year at the Ashcroft Theatre, Croydon, where I again played the Dame in a different production of *Dick Whittington*. The principal boy was played with great aplomb by Helen Shapiro. The other pantomime was a few years later, when I was the Dame in *Babes in the Wood* at the Churchill Theatre, Bromley.

The two most memorable things about this pantomime were firstly that the top billing was taken by a rat – Roland Rat – played expertly by David Claridge. It was a little bizarre on occasions accepting that the two robbers were both animals, Roland Rat and his friend the Gerbil. Pantomime, however, as performed in this country, is such a broad form of entertainment where all kinds of anomalies occur that the audience at the Churchill Theatre soon accepted the incongruity of two members of the rat family the same size as humans, and speaking the same language.

The other unusual thing concerning this pantomime was something of which I became aware a few months later. I was offered a part in a *Dr Who* story. It was to be the last series of *Dr Who*, which was to be made up of three separate stories, each running to four episodes. The one in which I appeared was called 'The Curse of Fenric'. It was a brilliantly written script by Ian Briggs, which could have made an excellent screen play. The regulars, Sylvester McCoy and Sophie Aldred, were great fun to work with and were so conversant with all the non sequiturs in the plot and all the time-warp references, so beloved of the fans of the show, that they took them in their stride. It was sometimes very confusing to a newcomer, until I realised it was best not to try to unravel the mysteries of the plot, but to play each scene as sincerely as possible and let the director and producer put it all together.

I was playing a vicar, as I have done on a number of occasions in the past. I was a very sincere and devout cleric by the name of Wainwright who had unravelled some Viking hieroglyphics in the crypt of his church, the dreaded 'Curse of Fenric'. He was deeply troubled that the information might become public knowledge, and Dr Who was anxious to have his help in staving off some national disaster. When the translation does escape into the village, the curse takes effect and slowly the villagers are turned into haemovres. Eventually, the good vicar is overwhelmed by the curse himself, and trampled to death in the mud by the haemovre creatures. It was classic *Dr Who* material, and voted one of the most popular stories in all the series by the Dr Who Fan Club.

One day I asked the director, Nicholas Mallet, why he had cast me in such a straight and dramatic role. I assumed he had seen me in a serious play somewhere. Apparently, he had seen me playing the Dame in the Bromley pantomime, and he said, 'The empathy you showed when talking with the children at the end was the quality I wanted for the vicar.' I was impressed by this leap of imagination, and reassured that there were creative directors around who did not follow the usual type-casting.

The filming of 'The Curse of Fenric' was all done on location. My chief memories are of working in an army training camp in Crowborough, Sussex, where the final scenes were shot, out of sequence. It was April and bitterly cold, and the snow that had been missing all winter suddenly arrived. It soon melted, and the place was a quagmire. The film crew and technicians were wrapped in warm overcoats and balaclavas. The poor vicar, the good Doctor and his assistant were in thin summer clothes. I was literally blue with cold. At one time my teeth were actually chattering during a take, and they had to break the filming to thaw us out over a primus stove in an army hut. The rain, snow and slushy ground gave considerable atmosphere to the scene, and when I was overcome by the haemovres and trampled to death in the mud, I did not have to fake anything: I was in genuine distress as I lay in the squelchy mire.

The shooting that was enjoyable came a week or two after the army camp experience. There was now warm spring sunshine and we were in Hawkhurst, Kent, using a beautiful old church as the rectory in the story. On location, there is a mobile wardrobe van, where you change. There were no dressing rooms, so I was moving about the village quite a lot in costume. On one occasion I was standing beside the lych gate to the church when a lady came up and said, 'Oh, vicar, I'm so pleased to have caught you. Can I come and talk to you about a christening?' I replied that she could, but that I doubted very much whether I could help. She looked at me for a moment, and then recognition dawned. 'Oh, I'm so sorry. You're not ... I mean you are ... Oh dear ... I recognise you ... You're Nicholson Parkinson ... I mean ... the century man ... Oh, I do feel a fool.' I quickly reassured her that she was not foolish, and she had flattered me by mistaking me for the genuine article. I could take her to the real vicar, who was inside the church, and who had been very kind and lent me some of his vestments to wear.

In 1986 Harold Fielding decided to revive *Charlie Girl*, the musical that had been so successful for him in the 1960s. It had starred Anna Neagle then and, in spite of the most appalling reviews – enough to finish any new production – survived and continued at the Adelphi Theatre for a record run. Its success was principally due to the popularity of its star, who seemed to hold a very special place in the affections of the British public. Harold, who loves to give the public glamorous, exciting shows, had persuaded the legendary Cyd Charisse to play the lead in the revival. To top the bill he engaged Paul Nicholas, whose looks and talent had won him a huge following. Dora Bryan was playing the other leading lady, and Mark Wynter the young American who falls for Charlie Girl, only to lose her to the hero of the piece.

Charlie Girl is a kind of Cinderella story in which Cinders marries Buttons rather than the Prince. It is very romantic, rather sentimental, with some good song-and-dance routines. There is a character called Mr Wainwright – a name that has figured more than once in my professional life – who comes to tell the hero he has won a fortune on the pools, and stays to become a temporary butler in the household. Derek Nimmo had played the part to great acclaim in the original and I was flattered when Harold Fielding interviewed me for the revival and offered me the role. I was also able to get some of my own back on Derek, who is a year or two younger than I am, for his jokes about my age in *Just a Minute*: I could say that I was now playing a role in which he was type-cast over twenty years ago.

The show had all the ingredients for a popular success. The director, Stewart Trotter, did a fine job in the preliminary rehearsals, but the technical requirements when you move into the theatre and have to blend music, dance, lighting, sound and the intricacies of the set, can be overwhelming. Before the dress rehearsal, things were becoming fraught, tempers were getting short, arbitrary cuts were being made. I was particularly worried, as I had suggested that in the ballroom scene, where my character, now posing as an eccentric butler, comes on to serve champagne to the waltzing couples, it might be fun if I appeared on roller-skates and wove my way between the dancers, balancing the tray of drinks. Stewart took up the idea, but due to lack of time, it was never rehearsed. When I pleaded with him for a chance to practise the routine, he said it was impossible, and he would try to insert it after the dress rehearsal. I knew this was a gentle way of saying he was going to cut it. Nothing goes in after the final dress rehearsal; it is usually the opposite.

I then did something I have never done before, and it was rather cheeky. I said to the leader of the orchestra, Ian MacMillan, in the break just before the ballroom scene, 'I'm doing the skating at the next run-through. It's all fixed. Will you keep playing so the dancers can continue? I'll skate on and move among them.' He looked at me sceptically. I added, 'All right. Will you do this for me? I'll take full responsibility.' He smiled and squeezed my arm. 'No trouble,' he said, 'and best of luck.'

When the ballroom scene arrived, I was nervous. I knew I was disobeying instructions. Then I thought, 'What the hell. They can't sack me.' The cue came and Ian kept the orchestra playing, the boys and girls kept dancing and I swept on, balancing a tray of drinks, chanting 'Champagne, champagne anyone?' As I did so, I managed to circle the stunned dancers. Fortunately, there were no collisions. One or two were rooted to the spot in amazement. I completed the intricate manoeuvres, handing out champagne as I did, and as a final flourish took the last glass for myself. So delighted at having achieved it all without mishap, I relaxed and immediately fell over.

Harold was the first to speak. 'That was great. Why haven't we seen it before?' I said that there simply had not been time.

I performed the routine throughout the run, usually without mishap. The only serious trip-up happened when a dancer's necklace fell to the floor as I circled her. It caught in my wheels and I went down with a tremendous smack, my tray and glasses scattering everywhere. Paul Nicholas, who was waiting in the wings, rushed on and helped me to my feet. He was most concerned, as I looked rather stunned. The audience, meanwhile, were roaring with laughter. It sometimes seems that the more painful the indignity you suffer, the funnier the audience find it.

I came to know Paul quite well during the run. He is very warm and easy to work with, and has a lovely sense of humour. I felt an empathy when working with him that I had only experienced before with Arthur Haynes. His thoughts come out fresh at every performance, so the inflections are not the same every night. This keeps you on your toes and you respond in the same manner, so there is always a sparkle in the performance.

Cyd Charisse is someone whom I had adored in many classic Hollywood musicals. She was charming, reserved, almost shy, and dedicated to her dancing, which she practised assiduously to keep supple. She played an English aristocrat who was trying to keep the debt-ridden family home together. Dora Bryan played her visiting American friend. It was rather incongruous to have the very English Dora trying to speak with an American accent, and the very American Cyd Charisse trying an Anglicised one.

Acting with Cyd was not always easy because, being a film actress first and foremost, she was not accustomed to projecting her voice for a large theatre. Nowadays in a musical, everyone has an individual neck microphone which is valuable when singing, and necessary for those with untrained voices. I had never worked in a modern musical before, and assumed my microphone was only to help project my very weak attempts at singing. In the dialogue scenes I instinctively projected for the large auditorium. The director gave me a note at the early dress rehearsal that my performance was rather forced. I was worried, until I discovered that the microphone would never be switched off. No wonder I was sounding unnatural. All I had to do was use some projection to give colour to the voice, and leave the rest to the technicians.

Cyd performed a modern ballet routine to a jazz tune in the second half of the show with an outstanding black dancer, John Paul Henry. He had great charisma; he was also a fine choreographer. Due to the limited dressing-room space at the Victoria Palace, he and I shared a tiny room throughout our eight-month run. Doing quick changes in such a confined space would have tried the patience of the best of friends, but we never had a cross word or a tense moment. I commented on the number of attractive young women who visited him; he returned the compliment by saying he thought one of the most attractive women to visit our room was coming to see me.

This was Annie, whom I had first met when I went to the Duke of Westminster's home to chair a cricket quiz for charity. We were now seeing each other regularly. Annie has no connections with show business, but accepts the stresses that often occur in the profession with great calm and tolerance.

The revival of *Charlie Girl* opened to rather indifferent reviews, but Harold Fielding was not worried. His shows had survived a poor press before. He believed that if you gave the public what they wanted, they would come to the theatre, and he had certainly tried to do that in this production, with an attractive cast, a stunning set and a simple, romantic story with a lot of humour. Times had changed, however, over two decades. The London public were more cynical and demanding, and less willing to accept a show that relied a great deal on charm. At first, business was good and those who saw the production enjoyed it. After the Christmas period, the bookings dropped. Cyd Charisse had to return to America, and the show was too expensive to maintain when not playing to capacity, so our stay at the Victoria Palace finished in January 1987.

Starring in a West End show is enjoyable, but nowadays if you are off the television screens for too long, the public begin to think you have disappeared, or died. I had been off the small screen for some time, and no enquiries were coming in. I also had the impression that my agent's office had lost a certain interest. Richard Stone was doing less, and slowly handing over the running of his agency to his talented team. Anne Knight was seconded to look after my affairs when I was busy with *Sale of the Century*, but she had sadly died of cancer a few years previously and I felt that there was no one in the organisation who was seriously concerned with seeking work for me. I thought the time had come to have a serious talk with Richard about my future.

I did not often go to Richard's office, and perhaps he sensed why I had come to see him and wished to pre-empt any embarrassment. As soon as I walked in, he greeted me with, 'Nickie' – he was about the only person in show business who called me that – 'if you want to leave the agency, I quite understand.' I was used to Richard's directness and honesty, and respected him for it, but this completely floored me. I said, 'Well, actually, Richard, I've come to talk about staying.' His remark did make me feel that he had little confidence in my prospects, which was worrying. Then I wondered whether it was the team who were now running the organisation who were not confident of finding me good work, and he was speaking for them, not himself. I decided to take Vivienne Clore, the agent in the office directly concerned with light entertainment on television, out to lunch to talk the matter over. As we sat down at Orso's, and before we had even ordered, she said very pleasantly, 'Nicholas, if you want to leave us, we quite understand.' I was staggered and told her, 'I've brought you out to lunch, Vivienne, to discuss staying with the office.'

It was a depressing situation, and very incongruous. Here we were, having a pleasant lunch, talking in a relaxed way, yet I had the impression I was being told as gently as possible that I was over the hill. I tried one more time: 'I know you have some of the most talented young performers in the profession on your books now; one or two you have discovered yourself. They'll demand a lot of your attention. I like to think I've quite a few good years left in me that are worth exploiting.' She smiled and said, 'I'm sure you're right,' but I did not feel her heart was in it.

Very reluctantly, I left the organisation I had been with for over thirty years. For all Richard's professional idiosyncrasies, I was extremely fond of him. A good agent not only becomes a friend and confidant; he or she is present at nearly all your most important occasions and shares the emotional highs and lows with you. A special bond is formed, which when successful is rather like a marriage. When the partnership breaks, you feel a great sadness.

When I was in *Charlie Girl*, Paul Nicholas had told me about his excellent agent Jan Kennedy, who worked with Billy Marsh at London Management, and suggested I talked to her while I was working successfully in the West End. Paul is very shrewd. I should have taken his advice. I felt at the time that it was not professionally correct to leave an agent when you were successfully in work, and profiting from one of their introductions. I now know better. The time to change an agent is when you are busy. A track record seems to mean nothing. When *Charlie Girl* finished its run at the Victoria Palace, I contacted Jan Kennedy and we got along very well. I believed her when she said that it was impossible to take on any more clients and do justice to them all, but she asked me to keep in touch, as things might change in her office. What she could not tell me was that Billy Marsh was about to leave London Management and set up on his own.

There now followed one of the most difficult and depressing periods of my professional life. I contacted a number of top agents at different times and the reaction was always the same. At first they were interested and wanted to talk more, and then, within a week, came a letter with some excuse: on reflection, they had decided they did not have the staff, or the time, or whatever, to represent someone with my particular talents.

Some time previously I had bought a small cottage in the Cotswolds near Stow-on-the-Wold. I sold the big flat where I had been living in Hampstead, and bought a small studio flat in the Belsize Park area, so I had somewhere to stay when working regularly in the theatre. I was seriously wondering whether I should sell one or the other. Annie moved into my cottage in 1987 and was very supportive, as were Suzy and Justin.

Suzy, who often visited and stayed at the cottage, and who also got along well with Annie's daughter Nikki, made a very practical suggestion. She pointed out that if I sold my property in this country, I could move to Menorca, an island that I loved, buy a house there, have some money over to invest, enjoy a comfortable lifestyle in a place where I already had friends, and could make a living landscaping gardens – something I enjoyed – while following my interest in water sports. I was very touched that she was so concerned and was genuinely tempted. I knew, however, that after a year or less, I would get restless and itch to get back to show business. Also, I was not going to be defeated because a number of agents thought there was no work for me. Throughout my life, agents and employers have never seemed to recognise that I had any talent or potential until I had proved it to them. I just thought I would have to go out and prove it to them again. I also made a promise that, if I had not proved it within a year, I would take Suzy's advice.

20

·······

Rediscovered

I DECIDED that I would not approach any more top agents and found someone who had just started, Joan Brown, who had previously been a casting director. I hoped she would have time to pursue ideas for me. I think I bored her to death with suggestions of what she should try to do. I do not think she secured me any actual work; I myself managed to persuade LBC to let me do a weekly late-night quiz for them on Saturdays. I think I was paid about £70 a show, and I wrote all the questions, sometimes preparing nearly a hundred a week. There was talk of *Just a Minute* not returning. I devised new television formats and tried to sell them; I also finished another short film, *The Best of British*, a send-up of the British way of life, into which I put some of my own money. It was distributed by Rank, and was about the last comedy short ever shown in the cinema. I do not think I ever saw my money back.

I also spent time working on my one-man show, *How Pleasant To Know Mr Lear*, based on the life and work of the great nonsense poet. I have always been fascinated by nonsense, whether it is the often meaningless professional gobbledy-gook of civil servants, or the creative writing of poets such as Lear, which is full of significance and insight. Lear called his nonsense verse fantastical rhymes without reason. They are much more than that, and it is a joy to perform them.

I had written and first performed this solo show in 1984, trying it out in small theatres in Cumbria; I now spent time polishing and improving it. My first major engagement with it was at the Cheltenham Festival of Literature and Art, and I have subsequently presented it at various theatres and festivals around the country including, in 1990, the Edinburgh Festival. It is also scheduled to be recorded for BBC radio.

I was determined to prove that this low period in my career in 1987 was only temporary and that those agents who had rejected me had made inaccurate assessments. During the spring and summer I worked extremely hard on all kinds of projects, and consequently earned very little. On a number of occasions I pursued programme ideas with tremendous energy, only to see them come to nothing. I have always held to the biblical expression about casting your bread upon the waters; right now, most of mine seemed to be coming back soggy. Then, in late summer, I received a phone call from Dave Morley, a producer who had worked in radio and seen me presenting *Just a Minute* at the studio recordings. He was now at London Weekend Television, working as producer of a new, youth-oriented show to be called *Night Network*. Jill Sinclair was executive producer. Transmitted in the small hours following Friday and Saturday nights, between 1 and 4 a.m. and in the early hours following Sunday night, between 1 and 3 a.m., it was to include pop videos, interviews with singers and groups, and revivals of the Gerry Anderson cult puppet series *Captain Scarlett*. There was also to be a quiz show, 'The All New Alphabet Game', which they said they needed someone with experience to front since there was neither time nor money for retakes. The overall budget was very modest; all the other presenters were young and comparatively unknown, and the show itself was recorded in the smallest studio imaginable.

Dave and I met in the very elegant tea room at the Waldorf Hotel, a strange setting for a discussion about an innovative, up-to-the-minute, pop-oriented television show. We immediately hit it off. His opening remark was, 'Nicholas, how would you like to do a television series for radio money?' I said, 'I'd rather do a radio series for television money.' He then told me what the salary actually was and I realised that he was not joking. He explained that it was an insult fee, but their budget was genuinely very low, and they had a large cast and eight hours of screen time to fill at a time of day when there was little revenue coming in from advertising. He outlined the format of the quiz and we discussed the ways in which we could make it different and zany. I saw the potential in the idea and we decided to turn the whole thing into a pastiche of a conventional quiz with celebrity guests. The money became secondary. If it worked, it would be fun. It is only in retrospect that I see it as the unexpected beginning of my climb back.

Night Network began in early September 1987. There was a great deal of pre-publicity: I was photographed in my nightshirt, and also with a number of young presenters, who included Craig Charles and Emma Freud, and much was made of the weekly item in which Emma was to interview someone while in bed with them. Rowland Rivron did an interview each week from his nuclear bunker, which, when you have a guest with as brilliant a sense of the absurd as Mel Brooks, produced an interview that was a classic of its kind.

'The All New Alphabet Game' was promoted in the advance publicity as a 'new, hip, spoof quiz'. Dave Morley worked extraordinarily hard on it, and it did require more of his time and energy than a lot of the remaining eight hours of programming. Once the show was running and we had discovered the offbeat kind of questions that were fun and made the quiz work well, he would telephone two days before the recording and sometimes spend up to three hours with me going through all the questions that the creators of the game had devised, to see where we could improve them, or even substitute better ones. It was not our responsibility, but we were both anxious to make each recording as strong as possible. It paid off: the quiz developed a cult following, and we heard that viewers who went to bed at a civilised hour were taping it to watch at a more comfortable time.

David Hillier was the director responsible for the look of *Night Network* on screen. Such were the restrictions of the budget, he had only one full day in which to record six hours of programmes for the Friday and Saturday transmissions (Sunday was mostly film) With a schedule that did not permit retakes, or even breaks in the recording, I was under instructions that, if there were mistakes of any kind – technical, verbal or otherwise – I had to ad-lib my way out and keep going. That was not particularly difficult for someone reared in live television, but I did not expect to have to contend with practical jokes from some of the production team. I would introduce the quiz as if we were in a huge studio, playing to a vast and excited audience, at which point the director cued in a sound tape which was the audience reaction. Sometimes it was a recording from a packed Albert Hall, sometimes a few desultory claps, sometimes inane laughter, sometimes normal applause cut off abruptly. One one occasion it was silence. I had to react to them all. One of the most difficult was when, after I had made my usual reference to our vast and excited audience, everyone heard a lot of dogs barking and howling. I responded with the only remark possible, 'For those who are confused, this programme is being performed before an audience at Crufts Dog Show.'

We had some marvellous guests throughout the show. Alice Cooper appeared on the very first programme, produced a snake and handed it to me. I hate snakes, and had never touched one before. I asked him, or her as she is known professionally, to put it away or, better still, to eat it. She pretended to do so, which looked disgusting, then palmed it away. Katie Boyle brought her small dog with her. I think it became affected by the heat in the small studio, because after the recording, it attacked me. Perhaps it blamed me for the fact that Katie did not win.

During the summer I had been told that Harold Fielding had decided to revive *Charlie Girl* for a three-month season at the Opera House in Manchester from the end of September, followed by three months at the Hippodrome in Birmingham from the beginning of 1988. My status clearly was not felt to be as high as before, since I was offered £100 a week less to appear in the show than I had been in the West End. I was happy to accept the job, however, and *Night Network* were prepared to pay my train fares to come down overnight from Manchester to record the quiz.

The cast for *Charlie Girl* in Manchester was different from that in London. Bonnie Langford was engaged to star alongside Paul Nicholas, playing the name part, and Doreen Wells, the former prima ballerina with the Royal Ballet, who had understudied Cyd Charisse in London, was guest star.

The opening night in Manchester went extremely well and, in spite of average reviews, we played to capacity for the whole three months. It was certainly a more lively production than at the Victoria Palace, and there were more laughs. Dora Bryan, in particular, found places where she could build on the comedy, at one point demonstrating her amazing suppleness by doing incredible tricks with her legs while attempting yoga positions.

Harold's faith in the show had been proved right. After the first performance he gave a supper party at a restaurant and, by chance, I sat at the same table as Paul Nicholas. His agent Jan Kennedy came and joined us. She was charming and complimentary, and asked if I yet had anyone to represent me. It transpired that Billy Marsh, with whom she worked, was no longer attached to London Management. They had now formed Billy Marsh Associates and had room on their books for more artists. I believe that if you are in good work, everyone is interested; if you are going through a fallow period, no one wants to know. I went back to the hotel that night and composed a letter to Joan Brown, explaining why I was leaving. She had not actually secured me any work, so there was no embarrassment. In fact, I think she was probably relieved. I joined Billy Marsh Associates, where I am represented by Susan Shaper, and it has been a very happy relationship ever since.

Charlie Girl also went very well in Birmingham, playing to capacity again for three months. When we came to the end of the run, Harold made a special journey to visit us, and took the whole cast out to supper to say goodbye and thank you. I have worked for many managements in my time, and few bother to make a personal gesture when a show reaches its end. Harold, however, is a true man of the theatre, and it is in such personal ways that he shows his sensitivity towards performers.

'The All New Alphabet Game' had stayed on air until Christmas, and then it was decided to 'rest' it. It never returned, probably because it was realised that now *Night Network* was established, it did not need an item that demanded such a disproportionate amount of precious planning and recording time. Also, in spite of the success that Jill Sinclair and Dave Morley had achieved, London Weekend Television were not increasing their budget, so it was becoming embarrassing to ask those taking part in the quiz to work for such small amounts.

The programme had surprising consequences for me: I became popular with a new audience from a younger generation. This was probably due to the fact that I had become associated with their culture, and also because I appeared to be sending up the image I had on *Sale of the Century*. I was, in fact, just enjoying myself. Then the Renault commercial was released and it, too, gave the impression that I was sending myself up, whereas I was merely trying to do a professional job. About the same time, the film *Mr Jolly Lives Next Door* was shown on television, was successful, and was subsequently released for cinema distribution. In it, I had the mickey taken out of me unmercifully by two very popular young comedians who first came to prominence in *The Young Ones*, Adrian Edmondson and Rik Mayall.

Mr Jolly was a fun film to make and I adored the utterly anarchic humour of Rik and Ade, who had written the script with Rowland Rivron. When I was asked by The Comic Strip, the production company, to read the script and give them my reactions, I had the feeling that they were not sure I would accept when I discovered the way I was to be mocked in the story. When I phoned to say I thought it was all very funny, they seemed quite surprised, but very happy that I wanted to do it.

The film was superbly directed by Stephen Frears and had a very talented cast. Peter Cook played Mr Jolly, a hit man who cuts up bodies while singing along to jolly tunes. He had an office next door to two alcoholic incompetents, Rik and Ade, who run a disastrous agency called Dreamytime Escorts. Even Dawn French and Jennifer Saunders, who were then just becoming well known for their comedy work, played small supporting roles. Rowland Rivron played some sinister character and the deranged Mr Lovebucket was played by Peter Richardson who, as a result of a catalogue of misunderstandings, pays Rik and Ade £3,000 to 'take out' Nicholas Parsons. They naturally misinterpret the murderous implications of the request and blow the money on drink. On their way to Broadcasting House, they knock a harmless couple off the road, who have won a prize of 'an evening with Nicholas Parsons'. Armed with this couple's ticket, Rik and Ade arrive to meet me. I think they are surprising winners, but feel obliged to fulfil the conditions of the competition and take them to the Dorchester. From there on, chaos and anarchy reign as these two horrendous characters latch on to me and slowly begin to wreck my life, my home and my sanity. The Dorchester Hotel refused permission for filming to take place on their premises, so the production company hired a banqueting suite at the Café Royal, who did not seem to mind that in the film they were referred to as the Dorchester.

Rik and Ade were very easy to work with and, like a lot of comedians, took their comedy very seriously. Everything is meticulously worked out and, where possible, thoroughly rehearsed. Some of their comedy is so broad, however, that it can only be planned technically in the hope that it will fall into place in front of the cameras.

At the end of the scene in the Dorchester, where Rik and Ade have thoroughly embarrassed me with their vulgar behaviour, they decide we must all go back to my place. They get up from the table, turning it over in the process and scattering the contents in all directions, and make an outrageously drunken exit. The first take went well. Then Stephen Frears said he needed a shot from a different angle of them staggering between the tables towards the door. The people sitting at the tables were all extras, members of Equity, and middle-aged and elderly – the sort of clientele the Dorchester would attract. One or two were looking a little apprehensive. They had never worked with anyone quite like Rik and Ade before. As one elderly extra said, 'It was never like this when I acted with dear Leslie Howard. I just don't know what they're going to do next.' 'Exactly,' said his companion. 'I never thought I'd be in a film where someone actually farted to get a laugh.' 'And then set fire to it,' added his friend.

The next take of the two rogues staggering between tables and dragging me towards the exit went reasonably well. One more table was upturned as we went, a lady had her hat knocked off, and one or two were accidentally buffeted a little. Stephen decided to go for another take. Everything was put back in its place, but I noticed that one or two of the extras were not sitting in the same seats, which strictly they should have been to keep continuity. I tactfully said to one woman close to me, 'Weren't you sitting on the other side of the table in the last take?' 'Yes,' she replied, 'but I'm not going to get near those two maniacs again. I might lose more than my hat next time.' 'Look what's happened to my hat,' said another. 'And it's my best one, which I keep for posh scenes.' We did another take and the fear on the faces of some of the diners, who were close to the two stars as they staggered by, was very real. It was not all acting.

I was playing myself in the film, or at least an extension of myself, and I like to think that it was my shock and horror at what these two characters were doing which helped to make the scenes believable and the vulgarities acceptable. In other words, I was back playing the role that had brought me most success – the straight man. At times it reminded me of working with Arthur Haynes, though the situations in this film on the whole were broader, and my apparent suffering at the hands of my two tormentors was more acute.

For the scene in my home, the film company had hired a private house just outside London. Being paid to let a film company have full use of your house, and being able to mix with celebrities, sounds an easy and very pleasant way to make some extra money. Unless the people concerned are used to having a film crew move in with all their cameras, lights and cables, they can be in for quite a shock. When, in addition, the scenes to be filmed concern two outrageous characters who systematically drink their way through a man's alcohol supplies and slowly wreck his home, the effect on the actual owners of the property can be traumatic. On this occasion, the family and some friends had gathered in the house, presumably hoping for a happy day watching some gentle filming, and talking with the principal actors. It was chaos throughout the whole of the elegant ground floor, which had been commandeered by the film crew. The family and their friends retreated to the first floor and more than once the wife winced and put her hand to her cheek as she heard a loud bang or crash from below. The film company might agree to pay for any repairs or breakages, but it is your personal possessions that are suffering. During filming I saw one small coffee table crushed, a cabinet dented, wine spilled, a settee damaged, and a mirror knocked off a wall.

The success of *Mr Jolly* was quite amazing. After the cinema release, it came out on video; it even spawned Mr Jolly fan clubs. One club wrote and asked if I would like to attend one of their evenings. I gathered they watched the video through twice, then re-enacted the whole story, playing all the parts. This was followed by a meal, and then they all watched the video again. It sounded a rather bizarre way to spend an evening, but it was good to have such devoted followers. I declined the invitation, adding that I did not think I would be much use in the performance part as they probably knew the words better than I did.

*　　*　　*

In the summer of 1988 I received a letter from a young student, Andrew Burnett, who asked if I would consider standing for the position of Rector of St Andrews University.

There are four ancient universities in Scotland: Glasgow, Edinburgh, Aberdeen and, the oldest, St Andrews, which was founded in 1413, not long after Oxford and Cambridge. In all four the Rector, an honorary position, is elected by the students and has the responsibility of chairing the meetings of the Court, the university's governing body. I was delighted and flattered to be asked, and when Andrew discovered my Scottish connections, he and his team were even more keen.

The election, which takes place every three years, is a very serious affair. Groups of students put forward the candidate of their choice, and when I stood, there was some formidable opposition. Glenda Jackson had been proposed by a left-wing group, Auberon Waugh by a right-wing one. I was standing as a non-political candidate in the sense that, while I had political opinions, I considered the appointment, if I was successful, a non-political position. There was also opposition from a popular candidate who ran an art gallery in Edinburgh, Richard de Marco, who had been putting himself around and, in the party-political sense, 'nursing the seat'. Another group proposed a popular presenter from Radio Scotland, Neville Garden. There was also, as in all elections, the joke candidate, Attila the Stockbroker, a rock poet who insulted everybody and created a lot of fun, but received very few votes.

The team who were promoting me, led by Andrew, did an excellent job. Andrew persuaded me to ask a number of my friends in the media to endorse my election bid with a humorous or witty comment, which he then incorporated into a poster. There were quotes from Willie Rushton, Rik Mayall, Barry Norman, Jonathan Ross, Angela Rippon, Robert Powell, Barry Cryer, Bill Tidy, Tim Brooke-Taylor and John Benson. Andrew asked me to visit St Andrews four days before the elections in early November. He took me to all the halls of residence, to the bars, restaurants, discos – anywhere the students gathered. He even got me to put on my tracksuit and join in the weekly 'swingnastics' keep-fit class. I visited the union many times, and was generally seen to be around.

The most important part of the campaign is what is called the 'heckling meeting', where each candidate is given ten minutes to explain to a packed student audience in the union theatre why he is standing, what his policy and attitudes are, and what he thinks he can do for the students, his constituents, if elected. He then takes fifteen minutes of questions from the audience. This can be make-or-break time, as opposition teams have come prepared with some loaded questions. One of the first I received was from an ardent feminist who accused me of being a condescending sexist, as I had been heard to use forms of endearment, such as 'my dear', to strangers of the opposite sex. I respect the feminist movement and had no wish to alienate anyone. I pointed out that affectionate terms were used naturally in our society when addressing strangers and that the actual words used varied throughout the country, adding that I worked in a profession that was informal and egalitarian and if I met someone to whom I was drawn, I liked to convey how I felt. I then said, 'If it makes you happy, I won't use any form of endearment when addressing you.' This fortunately received a laugh and, I believe, even a smile from the questioner.

I had serious questions about Clause 28, the controversial government proposal to ban 'the promotion of homosexuality' in schools; I had flippant questions, outrageous and political ones. I was serious, I made them laugh, and we had fun. The election was run on a proportional representation basis. At the first count, I had about forty-nine per cent of the votes, after subsequent counts, it was over fifty per cent.

I had won an election. I was now Rector of a respected and ancient university, following in the footsteps of some exceptional men of letters and distinguished people from all walks of life. I took my team out for a celebration meal and then, when I returned to the hotel, sat on the bed and said to myself, 'What on earth have you done?' I did not know whether to be elated at my success, or depressed at the thought of the responsibility I had taken on.

In the first year of my rectorship, I visited St Andrews no fewer than eleven times. Besides the regular Court meetings, there was a special event celebrating the 450th anniversary of the founding of St Mary's – the youngest college in the university. There was also my Rectorial Address, delivered in April, in which I took the subject of language, with emphasis on the spoken word. It was one of the few things I felt confident enough to speak on to an audience of academics and students. There were the graduation ceremonies in July, in which the Rector is only a figurehead. There was also the responsibility of keeping abreast with what was happening in the world of education. I was helped here by receiving all relevant newspaper cuttings from the University Secretary's office. On my visits I kept in touch with my 'constituents', the students, by visiting the union and talking with them. I was also kept informed of student opinion by my Assessor, a student elected by popular vote who sits on the Council and is technically the contact between the Rector and the students. I was lucky in my first year to have a very helpful young man, Barry Hughes, and in my third and final year I had a first-class Assessor in Pete Brown, who had been my original proposer. He had a feel for public relations, and even arranged 'surgeries' for me, and a 'Meet Your Rector' evening.

The most challenging responsibility was chairing the Court meetings, particularly during the first year, where you arrive to join a group made up of academics running a successful educational establishment, lay members from the local community and respected people from other walks of life. You have to learn on your feet, discovering all the problems, both academic and fiscal, with which the Court is battling, while absorbing the names and background interests of those debating policy. I was fortunate to be guided in my first year by an excellent Secretary to the university, Martin Lowe, and I was able to build a good relationship with the university's Principal, Professor Struther Arnott, who guides the university with wisdom and skill during a difficult period when education is suffering severely from short-sighted political policies.

Over the three years, I undertook the responsibilities of the position as conscientiously as I could, and I hope I contributed something. When my rectorship came to a close, it made me very proud that the university conferred on me an honorary degree of Doctor of Laws – whenever the university write to me now, they always address me as Dr Parsons. I sometimes wonder what my parents might have thought if they knew. I know they would have been pleased, and probably surprised.

In February 1989 I undertook one of the most gruelling professional commitments of my life. The previous year, I had been engaged by Sandy Ross of Scottish Television to host a comedy game show, then called *Rhyme or Reason*, in which five young comedy performers tried to supply the last three lines of a limerick, having been given the first two by me, and two contestants tried to win money by guessing what the last word would be. The pilot was successful and STV had secured a contract to supply sixty-five programmes for the newly formed BSB satellite channel, who wanted to transmit them five days a week over a thirteen-week period. The show's title changed to *Laughlines* and the panellists were reduced to four. The director was Paul O'Dell. It was agreed to record the sixty-five shows over three and a half weeks at the Gateway Studios in Edinburgh, doing two programmes in the morning and two in the afternoon. The panellists, with rare exceptions, were all from the new alternative comedy scene. It would be unfair to single out only one or two, but as an example of the talent that appeared, I will mention only those in the pilot programme, who helped to sell the show and who also appeared in subsequent recordings: Sandi Toksvig, Jenny Eclair, Nick Revell, Tony Hawkes and Mickey Hutton.

I knew the only way to handle the demands of these sixty-five shows was to be very disciplined. We had only one hour for lunch, but I always shut my eyes for thirty minutes and usually slept for twenty. Every night I returned to the hotel and had an evening meal with the writer Howard Imber, and we worked on some humorous introduction for each guest the next day. This resulted in a friendship with Howard, who was very kind when I set out to write this book, and helped me to get started.

The recordings of *Laughlines* were tremendous fun, and the programmes were very popular when transmitted. When BSB was launched, *Laughlines* was one of the shows they promoted vigorously, and it was immediately repeated after its first three-month run. It sadly disappeared, however, when BSB and Sky merged.

While *Laughlines* was being shown in the summer of 1990, and Annie and I were trying to improve the home in the Cotswolds into which we had moved the previous February, a most unexpected enquiry was made as to my availability. David Mirvish Productions were presenting the Stephen Sondheim musical *Into the Woods* at the Phoenix Theatre in London and asked if I would be interested in playing the part of The Narrator. The director was Richard Jones, about whom I had heard glowing reports, particularly of his outstanding work in opera. Julia McKenzie, Imelda Staunton and

Patsy Rowlands had already been cast as the show was opening in September and it was now almost July. My agent sent me the script and asked if I would meet Richard Jones the following Wednesday. This was the last thing I wanted to do as I was going to St Andrews on the Sunday night for a Court meeting early on the Monday morning and had other meetings in the afternoon. As the graduation ceremonies were taking place on the Thursday and Friday, for once I planned to stay over and perhaps, at last, play some golf on the Old Course. Instead, I took a train to London on the Tuesday, read the script, had the meeting on the Wednesday, and endured the six-hour train journey back to Leuchars, the nearest station to St Andrews.

I was very impressed with the book and lyrics of *Into the Woods*, a brilliant musical pastiche of all the fairy stories, emphasising their dark and even sinister side. I was not, however, impressed with the role of The Narrator. He seemed a very dull and colourless character who appeared at frequent intervals, stood at the side of the stage and merely commented on the action. At one point he joins in a musical number, which I thought I would find difficult, knowing my limited ability as a singer and aware of Sondheim's brilliant musical creativity. Besides, I was not sure I wanted to be tied up in a London production for a long time when my career seemed to have taken off again on television. I did not want to accept the part. This is probably the best mood in which to go into an interview; it is also interesting that it has often been the engagements I did not particularly want that have been my most successful.

I met Richard Jones and the more we talked, the more I became aware of his powerful imagination and exceptional insight into the intricate writing of Stephen Sondheim. By the time we had finished, I was happy to accept the engagement, confident I was going to be in an exciting production, and that my character was going to be a significant part of a complex whole.

The rehearsals began soon after the meeting, and I was amazed to discover that we had eight weeks scheduled for them. To someone who was used to having a touring production of a play rehearsed and running in three weeks, and a pantomime in ten days, this seemed a real luxury. Once I discovered the meticulous way Richard rehearsed, I realised that we would need every minute. Each tiny movement and nuance in every characterisation was assessed and planned. I had never worked in such a detailed way before, and found it fascinating.

Stephen Sondheim came to an early rehearsal and, after a read-through in his presence, we listened while he talked about the work and the way he saw the characters and their relationships. Outwardly easy-going and gentle, he is the kind of genius who, if you met him in the street, you might imagine was holding down some humdrum nine-to-five job. He invited questions from the cast about their characters, the lyrics and the text, written by James Lapine. He then left us alone with our director, and did not return until we began the technical rehearsals in the set with all the mechanical props, two weeks before we opened.

I had endless solo rehearsals with the assistant musical director on the brief number I had to sing. I realised very soon why we needed so much rehearsal time. Nearly all my dialogue – sometimes only single sentences – had to be fitted exactly into certain bars of music. It is one thing to deliver dialogue in character, but when it has to come in and out on a note of music and still sound natural, it becomes more difficult. Fortunately, we had an excellent musical director, Peter Stanger, and until I was completely conversant with the show and recognised the note or beat, he was wonderful at nodding me in on cue.

I lost a week's rehearsal as it had been agreed in advance that I could travel to Edinburgh to present my Edward Lear show at the Festival. On my return, it was explained to me what would happen in the dramatic moment mid-way through the second half of the show, when The Narrator is drawn into the drama centre stage, offered to the unseen giant to placate her, and then thrown to his death. Richard Jones had decided that my body should actually be seen being hurled back onto the stage. A dummy was to be created with exactly my proportions, dressed in the same clothes, and with a complete reproduction of my head and features. I was asked to visit the factory where *Spitting Image* had all their puppets made. To create a complete likeness, they needed a mould of my head and face. My hair was held down with a stocking, and then plaster of Paris was heaped all over my head, down to the neck. I was told that it would be uncomfortable, that I would not be able to see anything and, once my ears were covered, would not be able to hear anything either. I had to keep my mouth shut. To make sure I could breathe, they put a straw up each of my nostrils, around which they then packed more plaster. If I wanted to communicate with them, I had to gesticulate, and if I felt I was suffocating, I was to clap my hands and they would immediately break off the cast. I had not been warned in advance what was involved and found it all very uncomfortable. I must have looked strange, too, sitting upright in a chair, my head completely covered in white plaster, with two long straws protruding from my nostrils through the mould. I tried to relax, but was suddenly seized by a mild panic. How long was I to stay like this? No one had told me. It might be half an hour. They might have gone off for coffee. I started to gesticulate, and tried desperately to mime that I wanted to know how long I had to suffer this isolation. I got the message through eventually, and was told about ten minutes. It was still difficult to relax, and it was not an experience I would like to go through again in a hurry.

My body with complete facial reproduction was apparently one of the most expensive items in the show, but Richard's brilliant idea was more than justified. When the body was thrown from a great height to hit centre stage with a thud, there was always an audible gasp from the audience.

The technical rehearsals are always tiring and tedious. There were so many mechanical props built into this show – cows, carriages and other items moving across stage on special runners – which all happen on a given musical cue, that there was endless hanging around while all the technical problems were resolved. By the time we reached the full dress rehearsal, the adrenalin had sunk so low you wondered whether you were capable of a performance. Slowly, however, all the work of the early rehearsals returned, and the show really began to take shape.

The precision of the notes I received from Richard was extraordinary. I made a simple gesture with my hand at one dress rehearsal that I had not done before. Richard asked me to cut the movement, saying that he was impressed with the way I could convey stillness and did not want me to spoil it with any gesture. It was a nice compliment, but what struck me was the fact that he had noticed the gesture at all.

After one technical rehearsal, Richard told me, 'I've decided that when you walk on and begin singing, and introduce the first half finale, you should have a garland of daisies round your head. I have ordered them.' There was no logic to it; it was simply fun. I never questioned it, but just enjoyed the humour. It was little touches like that which highlighted his brilliance.

The musical opened to universally good reviews, and some critics gave rave notices. We were packed until January 1991, when the fighting in the Gulf started, and theatre business in the whole of the West End was affected. David Mirvish had invested over £2 million of his own money in the show and needed capacity business for a long time to recoup his outlay. How long could he carry a loss? And would the visitors return after the war? He waited, then decided to finish the show in March and we were all given three weeks' notice of the termination of our contracts. Almost the next day, the Gulf War ended and the public slowly started to return to the theatre. Unfortunately, it was too late for him to change his mind; the theatre had been let.

There comes a time in your professional life when someone gives you the epithet of 'Golden Oldie'. You hope it is a compliment. It certainly was in November 1989, when I was booked by the American office of P & O to be a guest on one of their cruise ships, *Royal Princess*. They were featuring a special attraction on board while the ship cruised from Barcelona through the Strait of Gibraltar to San Juan in Costa Rica. It was called 'Salute to the Golden Years of Television'. As most of the passengers were American, they had booked popular stars of 1960s' American television, including Steve Allen and Jonathan Winters. They wanted one British name from the same era. They were offered a shortlist and chose me. I was surprised, as there were names on the list who I thought were better known.

It was not the first time I had entertained on a cruise ship. A few years before, I had been on the *Canberra*, one of the *Royal Princess*'s sister ships. On that occasion, it was to help raise money for the Lord's Taverners. This time it was more prestigious. *The Royal Princess* is a magnificent liner and heaven on the sea for gourmands. Annie and I were given the most luxurious cabin, and flown in and out first-class. We were given an extra few days' holiday in Orlando, so that we could visit Disneyworld and Epcot. I performed my Edward Lear show, and it was the Americans rather than the British among the passengers who reacted most enthusiastically. Perhaps it is familiarity, or perhaps the British are naturally laid-back about their national geniuses and take them for granted.

During the cruise, I was also interviewed. This, too, was well received and gave me the idea for another one-person show, based on my professional experiences. Entitled *An Evening with Nicholas Parsons*, I have since performed it at a number of venues around the country, including the Edinburgh Festival in 1991. In it, amongst the anecdotes and stories, I talk, as I have written here, of the continual labelling I have received which has, on occasions, been a drawback. I also illustrate how something has always turned up to allow me to change direction.

I am frequently asked to appear on television and radio; I perform my solo shows regularly, give after-dinner speeches and compere corporate events. I still run my production company and work on new ideas. One of these, a comedy game show called *Celebrity Gossip*, which I have written with Danny Kishon, has been sold to BBC radio for production in 1994. I still have the mickey taken out of me, particularly on *Just a Minute*, and it seems the younger generation are taking over in this respect where older friends and colleagues have left off. I was completely taken for a ride when Noel Edmonds, dressed as a policeman, conned me in the 'Gotcha Oscar' section of his *House Party*. I am still prepared to try practically anything once; I have even done a parachute jump in tandem for the Yorkshire Television *Stargazers* series made by Geoff Wilson. It was only when I arrived at the airport at Weston-on-the-Green in Oxfordshire to be filmed making the jump that I discovered I was to do a free-fall descent first, strapped to the instructor, from 30,000 feet. You drop at over 120 mph until your parachute opens as you near the ground. I enjoyed the parachuting, but the free fall was unnerving. What made it worse was that I had to try to look at the cameras attached to two other parachutists and smile for the film. After it was over, Geoff told me he had not wanted to worry me in advance, but apparently the man who had done it for the first time the previous week, who was considerably younger than myself, had broken his ankle on landing.

I often wonder what my mother's reaction would be, if she were alive now. Would she still be surprised? Would she be impressed?

Would she still be thinking that I should have gone into a more sensible and secure profession? As small children we set out to please and impress our parents. If we are not given the encouragement we seek, consciously or unconsciously some of us go on striving for that recognition, seldom realising what is driving us. I do not feel driven now, but am aware that I am forever seeking new goals. At one level, I think this must be connected with the desire to please and impress. In her later life, I think my mother did feel that she had failed to give me the encouragement I needed, and not long before her death actually said that she felt she had not been entirely fair to me, which must have been extremely difficult for someone of her nature to say. Once I became an actor, she was loyal and supportive, though she could be sharply critical on occasion. She came to see me when I was working in rep in Bromley, and also to any West End show in which I appeared. She did frequently try to persuade me to concentrate on being a serious or dramatic actor, where she thought my talent lay. She could not understand my wish to be involved with comedy. Perhaps she thought it was more frivolous and less demanding, whereas it is quite the reverse.

My father was quite different from my mother. He was not a theatregoer and did not see much of my stage work. I know he listened to me on the radio and, in later life after he had retired, he probably tuned in when I was on television. He never said much about it, but I just felt that once I was established he was pleased, and perhaps even proud of what I had done. I had touching confirmation of this right at the end of his life. He had been taken temporarily into the Masonic Hospital, Hammersmith, where my sister and I would visit him daily – our brother was too far away to come frequently. Except for one brief lapse, his mind was clear and lucid, he had not lost his sense of humour, and we had some interesting conversations. One Thursday, I discovered that Patricia could not visit him that night. I had a feeling that I must see him. When I arrived, he was sitting beside his bed, fully dressed, trying to eat his supper. He was so weak that I had to feed him, and his voice was down to a whisper. He complained of excessive tiredness, and then began to make endless requests of the things he wanted me to do, most of which were unnecessary. I told him not to worry; I would take care of everything. He seemed reassured, and then said for no reason, 'Jack Warner's in this hospital.' The comedian had been one of my father's favourite performers during the war. I was amazed, and asked him how he knew. He replied that someone had come into his room and asked if he was Jack Warner. I said, 'What did you reply, Dad, "Mind my bike"?', which was a catch-phrase Jack Warner used in the wartime Garrison Theatre radio shows. My father shook with laughter, and it was wonderful to see him, frail as he was, enjoying a joke. He then said suddenly, '*Sale of the Century*'s on the television.' I replied that I thought he was mistaken, as the transmission time had been changed. I switched on the set in his room to discover he was correct; he had remembered. I asked him if he wanted to watch the show. He nodded, and I turned up the sound. He seemed to have fallen asleep, so I thought I would let him doze. The programme finished, and I turned off the set. He suddenly said, 'I've always thought you were particularly good the way you handle that quick speed-up at the end.' So my father had regularly watched the show, and been impressed. Now, very late in life, he was paying me a lovely compliment.

Those words of praise were almost the last my father spoke to me. A nurse came in and said it was time to put him back to bed. I left the room to speak with the Sister. He seemed so weak, I wondered whether I should stay. She said that patients in his condition sometimes lingered for days. I went back to his room. He was asleep. I kissed him gently on the forehead and crept out. He never woke up. What a peaceful way to die.

As you grow older, you begin to think about death, but it has never been a subject I have been afraid to talk about. I would like to go as my father did, peacefully. Before then, I look forward to enjoying a great deal more laughter with my family and friends. I hope to go on creating laughter, whether it be on my own or as a humorous straight man. Nothing replaces the sound of laughter, the best therapy in the world.

Index

Index

Index